THE MUSIC OF
CHRISTIAN HYMNODY

THE MUSIC OF
CHRISTIAN HYMNODY

*A Study of the
development of the hymn tune since the
Reformation, with special reference to
English Protestantism.*

by

ERIK ROUTLEY

*Mackennal Lecturer in Church History
Mansfield College, Oxford*

INDEPENDENT PRESS LIMITED
MEMORIAL HALL · LONDON · E.C.4

First Published 1957

Printed and Bound in Great Britain by
NOVELLO AND COMPANY LIMITED, LONDON W.1

To
KENNETH LLOYD PARRY

CONTENTS

PREFACE

IT was recently written by an authority for whom I have the highest respect that nothing could so damage a book's chances of success, nothing is so surely calculated to put its reader off, than the announcement that it is based on a thesis.

I must take my chance of that. This book is an abridgement of a thesis which was in early 1952 presented through the Board of the Faculty of Theology at Oxford. Since it is permissible to inflict upon examiners works of much greater length that it is practicable to offer to the public (let alone a publisher), I have had to shorten the work for its present purpose to about two-fifths of its original compass. Furthermore, and this is really vexatious, it has been necessary to reduce the number of examples from eight hundred to just over two hundred. The abridgement of the text has meant omitting a good deal of church history; that will have to be read elsewhere. It has also meant omitting some observations on the hymnody of the younger churches; the reader who wants to study this subject may well begin by laying hold on *Cantate Domino*[1] (all three editions if possible), and on *Hymns of Universal Praise*,[2] the Hymn book of the Churches of Christ in China. Thirdly, it has meant the recasting of the work so that it presents the hymnody of other traditions than that of English Protestantism less as a subject of study in their own right than as subsidiary to the study of English hymnody; references have been more closely confined than they were in the original work to tunes which have come into English Protestant use from these other traditions. The work will therefore present a rather insular aspect; and I should like to disclaim any pretension to the view that this is the proper perspective in which to examine tunes of other traditions.

The omission of three quarters of the original examples makes necessary a rather complicated system of references. It would have been intolerable to demand of the reader that he should have at his hand copies of all the hymn books at present in use. I have so designed this book, therefore, that the general reader will be able to follow the story quite clearly if he has by him, in addition to the examples, a copy of the 1933 edition of the *English Hymnal* (which is also incorporated in the *Hymnal for Scotland*, 1951). Conversely, I have referred in this work to very nearly all the tunes in that hymn book. Subsidiary references—almost always corroborative of references in *E.H.*, but

---

[1] World Student Christian Fellowship, 13 Rue Calvin, Geneva, 1928, 1938 and 1951.
[2] Shanghai, 1948.

occasionally bearing on points which *E.H.* does not cover—are made to *Hymns Ancient and Modern* and to *Congregational Praise* (1951). A conversion-index at the end is designed to help those who have by them some other standard modern hymn book.

Concerning abbreviations—*E.H.* always stands for the 1933 edition of the *English Hymnal*, *C.P.* for *Congregational Praise*, and *S.P.* for *Songs of Praise* (enlarged edition, 1932). References from *Hymns Ancient and Modern* (called in the text "*A.M.*") accommodate both the Standard and Revised editions. Where a tune appears in both at the same number, it is referred to thus: *A.M.* 165; where it appears in both at different numbers, thus: *A.M.* 180/198, the number in the earlier edition standing first; where it appears in one but not in the other, reference is made thus: *A.M.(S)* 223 or *A.M(R)* 223. All other hymn books are referred to in full, or by initials which the immediate context makes plain.

My authorities for this work must now be briefly but gratefully cited. They fall into four classes. First, there are the hymn books themselves. The modern sources best to be relied on for historical reference are these: *The Yattendon Hymnal*, edited by Robert Bridges and H. E. Wooldridge (Clarendon Press, 1899); the *Oxford Hymn Book* (Clarendon Press, 1908); *Songs of Syon*, edited by G. R. Woodward (Schott, 2nd edition, 1910), and, of course, the *English Hymnal* (1933). For America, the *Hymnal (1940)* (Church Pension Fund, New York, 1943) is by far the best source.

Secondly, there are what I compendiously call in footnotes "The Companions". These are Cowan and Love. *The Music of the Church Hymnary* (Frowde, Edinburgh, 1901), Frere, *Historical Edition of Hymns A & M* (Clowes, 1909), Moffatt and Millar Patrick, *Handbook to the Church Hymnary* (O.U.P. 1929 with Supplement of 1935), Dearmer and Jacobs, *Songs of Praise Discussed* (O.U.P. 1933), and K. L. Parry (ed.) *Companion to Congregational Praise* (1953). The American *Hymnal* (1940) already referred to has its own Companion *The Hymnal (1940), Companion* (1949). These represent a symposium of research which has provided a great deal of material for the present work. The four modern English Companions are referred to by the initials *H.A.M.*, *H.C.H.*, *S.P.D.* and *C.C.P.*

Thirdly, there are primary sources, which are mentioned as the text proceeds, and the two great anthologies, Zahn's Catalogue of Evangelical Lutheran melodies (1888–93) and Bäumker's annotated catalogue of Catholic melodies (1883–1911, 4 volumes). The only connected study of the present subject is that part of Frere's classic

Introduction to *H.A.M.* which deals with music. This Introduction is "required reading" for any who take a serious interest in hymnody.

Fourthly, and perhaps most important, I must mention the personal help I have received from friends who have in various ways made contributions to this work. The Rev. Dr Maurice Frost, of Deddington, near Oxford, the best living authority on sources, has generously allowed me access to his magnificent library of hymnology, and to the proofs of his definitive work, *English and Scottish Psalm Tunes*, 1525–1677 (S.P.C.K. and Oxford University Press, 1953). He has also given me much personal help and encouragement for which I must here record my gratitude. The Reverend K. L. Parry, of Bristol, Editor of *Congregational Praise*, by his skilful chairmanship and by much kindly personal help, did much to initiate me into the business of hymn book editing and the tracing of sources. The late Reverend Millar Patrick (1868–1951), by his books and by much courteous correspondence gave me help on Scottish matters which was vital to this work, and this is the place to pay tribute to the memory of the greatest Scottish hymnologist of his generation. Finally, although it would be ungracious to make them in any way responsible for the infelicities of this work, my Supervisor, Dr Andrews, of New College, and my Examiners, Dr Adam Fox, Archdeacon of Westminster, and Dr Thomas Armstrong, then of Christ Church, all three of whom made, at their appointed times, most valuable and penetrating criticisms which I have done my best to incorporate, deserve my thanks.

E.R.
Oxford, 1954.

1

PROLOGUE

THIS is the story of something very familiar. It is not so much like the story of art or architecture or poetry as like the story of interior-decoration, of domestic architecture, of furniture-making, or of popular ballads. Hymn tunes are the folk songs of the Christian faith. They are familiar in the way that chairs and tables and suburban houses and Morris cars and music-hall jokes are familiar. This fact has several consequences which determine the shape of the story. Here is one consequence: that we are dealing not with music as a whole but with music disciplined by a certain restricted form, music domesticated, if you will, but not music debased. Here is another: that just as a chair or a table or a suburban house may be serviceable although it be aesthetically offensive, so a hymn tune may be serviceable, and in constant use, though it be musically defective. Moreover, enlightened spirits have said that our chairs and tables and houses ought not to be aesthetically offensive, and painstaking sociologists have shown by what sinister processes the common people have been brought to tolerate the second-rate but serviceable where, in better spiritual climates, in better economic conditions, with better awareness of things, they would not have tolerated them; and by the same token it will be part of our purpose to expose and to analyse the second-rate in hymnody. It is widely accepted now that a depressed standard in chairs and houses and jokes bespeaks a depressed civilisation. It will be our contention that a depressed standard of hymnody betokens a depressed spiritual state; and this we shall demonstrate from history.

But there is a third and practical consequence of the peculiar nature of our study. This is that we may without impropriety begin it elsewhere than at its historical beginning. When the subject of a study is remote or abstract, nothing is to be gained by the process we shall now follow. But when living examples, organic parts of the study, lie within arm's reach, it is well to take one such part, no matter where it lies in relation to the whole story, examine it, and undertake to show by what means it evolved from the more primitive stages. Let us therefore take one of our most familiar and finest hymn tunes,

HANOVER (*E.H.* 466), and extract from it those qualities which represent separate strands of development. This will show us what we may expect of the story we shall afterwards unfold.

This tune was first published in 1708. Since that date it has enjoyed unbroken popularity; it may now fairly be regarded as a typical English hymn tune of the best kind. Its power and appeal are derived from the interaction of certain disciplines. These we must separate and define.

1. MELODY. This is a highly-organised melody, commanding in its opening phrase, rising to a climax or key-stone at the end of the third phase, conclusive and epigrammatic in its final phrase. It is a popular tune and also a well-wearing one. This is the listener's and singer's impression. The development of melody will, then, be one of the subjects we shall need to examine.

2. HARMONY. It is only in its harmony that the tune as printed in *E.H.* is not original. But as printed there, its harmony is strictly diatonic, its modulations direct, its bass in excellent counterpoint with the melody. The development of four-part harmony, its uses and abuses, and its intimate association with counterpoint, will be another line of investigation.

3. RHYTHM. The tune is in simple four-bar units of triple rhythm. In this respect it is of the modern, rather than the ancient school. The rhythm is subject to the four-bar unit and the metre of the words. The progress from free rhythm to metrical rhythm, and in later times the new return to free rhythm, will be a third line of investigation.

4. METRE. The metre which forms the framework of the melody and rhythm is symmetrical. English metres are normally symmetrical, foreign metres less so. We shall see how the hymn tune in England was uniquely subjected to the discipline of the symmetrical metre, and what effect this had on its present form.

To these four categories we might add a fifth; the discipline imposed on the tune by the sense of the words to which it is set. This we shall find to be an intricate subject, and we shall find also that the application of this discipline is entirely inconsistent in history; at times it is carefully applied, at other times it is ignored.

These then are the disciplines which, acting upon the music from their different directions, produce as a resultant this highly successful and popular tune. As we now tell the story from its historical beginning, we shall see how the variation of force in the direction of one of the disciplines at the expense of others produces tunes of different shapes and styles. We shall also be able to distinguish between those occasions upon which deliberate or traditional variation produces strong tunes, and those upon which arbitrary and disorganised variation produces weak ones. The order in which the disciplines will present themselves will be this: Melody, rhythm, metre, and (last by a long way) harmony.

2

THE LUTHERAN CHORALE

THE place of Luther's hymns in the history of the Reformation has been well described by a historian of fifty years ago. A. F. Pollard, in the *Cambridge Modern History* (1903)[1] wrote:

> It was not these questions of ecclesiastical government or ritual which evoked enthusiasm for the Lutheran cause. Its strength lay in its appeal to the conscience, in its emancipation of the individual from the restrictions of an ancient but somewhat oppressive system, in its declaration that the means of salvation were open to all, and that neither priest nor Pope could take them away . . . To this moral elation Luther's hymns contributed as much as his translation of the New Testament.

"Emancipation" . . . "Moral elation"—that is where the Reformation touched the common man, and the hymns of Luther, with their tunes, were the common man's response to this mood. Luther was, of course, an artist; he had the artist's temperament, leaning to emphasis, high colour, and rhetorical power rather than the just and balancing mind of the philosophical theologian. It is impossible to be sure which of the early Lutheran tunes are of Luther's own composition; such a conclusion, in any case, would matter less than the obvious characteristics which we can observe in the early Lutheran tunes considered in a body. And their clearest quality, to be seen in their urgent rhythm and wayward but persuasive melody, is just that enthusiasm most naturally to be associated with a movement which (whatever its theological tenets and controversies) impressed the common man as a movement of emancipation and elation.

The musical antecedents of the chorale

The inheritance upon which Luther and his friends built their treasure of chorales was bequeathed to them from two distinct testators. One of these was the plainsong office hymn and sequence of the medieval church; the other was the popular melodies which, in the later Middle Ages, were to be heard from the Minnesinger and Meistersinger, and which overflowed into the popular music of certain heretical or schismatic sects in Europe.

Plainsong. The earliest organised hymnody of the church (if we discount those hymns or parts of hymns which some believe to be embedded in the New Testament, and that shadowy and primitive

---

[1] *Cambridge Modern History* (1903), Vol. II, p. 201.

body of praise which is hinted at in the φῶς ἱλαρόν[1]) was the Ambrosian system of Office Hymns. These hymns began, it is supposed, as congregational replies to the more or less ribald songs sung by the Arians during the Arian controversy of the fourth century. Born, thus, in high controversy, they laid the foundation of a settled liturgical hymnody which became the backbone of Western public praise in the Middle Ages. These hymns were, of course, associated with the Offices of the church, not with the Eucharist. They were uniformly in octosyllables, and they are called Ambrosian because it was under the inspiration of Ambrose, Bishop of Milan (d. 397) that they were composed and collected. Of all this, and of the subsequent liturgical developments under Gregory I (Pope, 590–604), the story can be read in the textbooks of hymnody.[2]

In the same sources it may be read of the development of Sequences, first in prose and then in verse.[3] The music of the Office hymns may be found well set out in the *English Hymnal*, which preserves a complete cycle of these, with their traditional tunes (usually according to the medieval English uses).[4] English translations, adapted to the original plainsong tunes, of the chief Sequences may be found at *E.H.* 10, 22, 130, 155, 172 and 351.

If the sources we here mention be consulted, the remarkable and romantic story of plainsong will begin to unfold itself. This is not part of our present study, and it will be enough to say here that that is a story of tension between the development of plainsong from simple syllabic chants to melodies of great imaginative complexity and that public opinion, expressed in ecclesiastical edicts and in the writings of churchmen, which sought to impose restraint upon it. The flowering of Byzantine chant in the seventh and eighth centuries is authoritatively dealt with in Dr Egon Wellesz's book, *Byzantine Music and Hymnography* (to which we have just referred), and a reading of that work will show how great was the force exerted on the Western church of the Middle Ages by the free imagination of the Eastern church[5]. And if the reader will glance at two successive plainsong settings in the English Hymnal—No. 738 in the 1906 edition and No. 737 in either the 1906 or 1933 editions—he will see, in No. 738, something of

---

[1] " O gladsome light ", translated at E.H. 269; more freely translated at A.M. 18.

[2] For information about the hymnody of the early church, see the relevant chapters in C. S. Phillips, *Hymnody Past and Present* (S.P.C.K., 1937), Millar Patrick, *The Story of the Church's Song* (Church of Scotland Publications, 2nd edition, 1947), and Egon Wellesz, *Byzantine Music and Hymnography* (Oxford, 1947).

[3] See especially, W. H. Frere, Introduction to *Hymns A & M*, Historical edition (1909), section VIII, pp. xxviii ff.

[4] These should be studied with Dr J. H. Arnold's excellent pamphlet, *The Approach to Plainsong through the Office Hymn* (Oxford, 1936).

[5] See also G. B. Chambers, *Folksong - Plainsong*, (Merlin Press, 1956)

the extravagance to which later plainsong became addicted, and in no. 737 (*Crux Fidelis*) the sublime beauty of plainsong when under discipline it reached its highest imaginative pressure.[1]

Plainsong, then, was one stream which Lutheran hymnody was able to draw on for its inspiration. The other was the popular song of secular musicians and of religious enthusiasts; there is no clear dividing line between a secular and religious style here, so they may be taken together.

On the one hand, there were the songs of Troubadours and Trouvères, and of their Teutonic counterparts, Minnesinger and Meistersinger. Gustav Reese, in his authoritative book, *Music in the Middle Ages* (Dent, 1942)[2], shows how their popular music derived its forms from those of the litanies, sequences and hymns of the church. It was these singers of epic and lyric who developed the strophic form, the simple tune, the refrain and the chorus. Through all the long catalogue of musical forms affected by the Troubadours—*chansons de geste, routrouanges, rondeaux, virolais, ballades, lais*, and the rest— we find the common quality of a simple tune and various devices of repetition, all designed to make the song memorable and pleasing to its hearers.

The Minnesinger, and later the Meistersinger of Germany[3] adapted the same technique to their own language, and their songs differed only in so far as they had to accommodate the stress-metres of German poetry and not the syllabic metres of the Romanesque tradition. From the introduction of the technique into Germany from the marriage of Frederick Barbarossa with Beatrix of Burgundy, in 1156, to the death of Heinrich von Meissen, in 1318, the Minnesinger formed a well-respected musical tradition in Germany; the Meistersinger, although allowing the folk-song tradition to give way somewhat to that of virtuosity, added little to the techniques coined by the Minnesinger.

One point of form in this folk music of Europe may as well be noted at once as bearing immediately upon our study. It was their custom to form their songs on the pattern of a phrase repeated and followed by an answering phrase, the repeated initial phrases being known as *Stollen*, the answering phrase as the *Abgesang*. The *Abgesang* might be fairly long, or quite short. It frequently contained at the end some echo of the material used in the *Stollen*. The result is always both memorable and also pleasantly unsymmetrical. This is,

---

[1] For a study of ecclesiastical pressures upon musical development the reader may care to glance at my own book, *The Church and Music* (Duckworth, 1950).
[2] op. cit., pp. 219 ff.
[3] Gustav Reese, op. cit., pp. 231 ff.

of course, the common pattern in early Lutheran chorales. It will be found to survive even in the modernised forms of EIN' FESTE BURG and NUN FREUT' EUCH which can be read in *E.H.* at Nos. 362 and 4.

Along with these secular popular songs we must refer to the spiritual songs of certain enthusiastic sects of the later Middle Ages. Monsignor Ronald Knox's recent book, *Enthusiasm* (Oxford, 1950), contains many references to these which should be consulted; in one place[1] he rehearses with some gusto the names of thirty-five such sects, ending his list with the words "and many others". From one of these sects, the Flagellants of northern Italy (who flourished about 1260) there came a tradition of *Laudi Spirituali*, popular hymns sung by these enthusiasts at public demonstrations; hymns cast in the mould of the secular song of the time. One of these tunes has survived in ALTA TRINITA BEATA (*E.H.* 184), although what we read there is a reconstruction by Dr Burney which probably leaves the original a good way behind. A similar tradition of popular hymnody appeared a century later among a German sect of flagellants who became conspicuous for a time after the Black Death (1348–9). Some of these *Geisslerlieder* (Songs of the *Geissler*, or Flagellants) bear a close resemblance to the later chorale form.[2]

It is therefore to be believed that this strange underworld of enthusiasm did much to spread a tradition of popular religious song, corresponding to the revival-songs of more modern times, which made the common people familiar with a strophic, simple melodic hymn-form.

Contemporary experience of revival music makes it easy to believe that the popular nature of these songs found a warm welcome in the minds of those who found the music, not to say the dogma, of the Catholic church irksome in discipline and austere in form.

Finally, let it be recalled that between church music and secular music there was two-way traffic. We may quote in conclusion a note from Chappell's *Popular Music of Olden Time* (*c.* 1850):

> If any of these ancient church melodies should be found to resemble secular music, it is, in all probability, because they were originally secular tunes, for we can trace the clerical practice of writing hymns to airs sung by minstrels in every century from the time of William the Conqueror to the Reformation and the system has continued to the very present time not only in England but also abroad.

From this we may gather that although hymns formed no part of the liturgy of the Mass, and Office hymns and Sequences were officially

---

[1] *Enthusiasm* (1950), p. 71 f.
[2] Reese, op. cit., p. 239.

strictly limited in their use, the tradition of the strophic hymn as a vehicle of popular praise was well established in the Middle Ages.[1] What happened at the Reformation was that this liturgical cinderella was raised to an unlooked-for eminence.

---

[1] ORIENTIS PARTIBUS (E.H. 129), is a celebrated melody from an extra-liturgical source. CHRIST IST ERSTANDEN (E.H. 134), derived from the Easter Sequence (E.H. 130), or possibly preceding it, is another.

3

THE LUTHERAN CHORALE II, 1524–1615

THESE are the characteristics which we find most commonly in Lutheran chorales of the earliest period:

1. A rhythm so marked and so urgent as to make harmony, or even a minimal accompaniment, virtually unnecessary for a successful performance.

2. A waywardness and informality of melody which contrast sharply with the poised and restrained Genevan style from which the English style is mainly derived.

3. A wide compass—often more than a tenth—in the melody.

4. A tendency, especially in the earliest tunes, to melismatic decoration, especially at the closing cadence.

5. A strongly conservative attitude towards the new tonality which begins to replace the modes in the sixteenth century.

6. A wide and inspiriting variety of metres, unlike any that are found in England before Charles Wesley began to popularise German metres in our language.

7. A tendency to adhere to the principle of "proper tunes", a tune being written for a hymn and thereafter always identified by the opening words of that hymn; this principle is so widely observed that it isnot until the eighteenth century that any serious confusion between different tunes for the same hymn arises.

The examples which we have chosen to illustrate this period of Lutheran hymnody (Exx. 1–26), together with some references to the *English Hymnal*, will bring these generalisations to life.

Exx. 1 and 2 illustrate the derivation of chorales from plainsong. Ex. 1 is a fairly faithful transcription of a primitive and renowned plainsong tune, CHRISTE QUI LUX ES ET DIES. It was thus transcribed for use with a German translation of that hymn, and is therefore in Long Metre. It does not manifest any of the character- istics of the chorale; the almost syllabic plainsong tune (see *E.H. Appendix*, No. 1) makes a chorale that is able to stand on its own feet without adopting the special diction of the new popular hymnody.

Ex. 2 shows the same principle differently applied. Here we have part of a plainsong Gloria, more florid and highly developed. The chorale derived from it is a sturdy tune in triple time, breaking away abruptly from the plainsong style in adopting a uniform three-beat unit throughout. We shall see in a moment that a uniform three-beat unit is no more characteristic of the chorale than were the steady crotchets of Ex. 1. ALLEIN' GOTT, as set down at Ex. 2, may be compared with the post-Bach version at *E.H.* 103. Ex. 2 is the form in which it is still sung in Lutheran circles to the traditional and invariable congregational act of praise that stands in the Communion service where the Nicene Creed stands in the Anglican order. But although the rhythm is regular and the compass of the melody, again plainsong-like, is restricted, its metre and melodic form show the 'Meistersinger' form to which we referred in the previous section. Its resolute F-major tonality and its regular rhythm are marks of a popular, rather than a church style.

When we come to Ex. 3, EIN NEUES LIED, we see at once the difference between chorales deriving from plainsong and chorales which we may presume to have appeared for the first time after the Reformation. This comes from one of the earliest Reformation chorale-books, Walther's *Encheiridion* of 1524. Here we observe at once the manner in which everything is subjected to rhythmical urgency in the typical Lutheran tune. Note (1) the short up-beat at the beginning of each line, (2) the syncopated cadences at the end of the sixth and eighth phrases,[1] and (3) the added urgency of the five crotchets in the last phrase. Over against these marks of melodic urgency, set (a) the repeated notes which form so large a part of the tune, and (b) the absence of that smooth melodic architecture with which we are familiar in the English style of tune, and of which we had an example in Ex. 2.

Parallel examples will be found in the tunes ES IST DAS HEIL (originally, ACH GOTT VON HIMMEL), *E.H.* 478[2] and NUN FREUT EUCH, *E.H.* 148,[3] both of which are in the very popular metre of Ex. 2. *E.H.* 478 is an ancient tune which appears in both Lutheran and Roman Catholic sources, and is probably derived from a late plainsong tune of the middle ages; *E.H.* 148 may be an original Lutheran tune. Another well-known tune from the *Encheiridion* is AUS TIEFER NOTH, the original tune for Luther's version of Psalm 130. It is in the Phrygian mode throughout, and though it begins with a note of double length, all its lines after the first begin

---

[1] A repeated unit of two phrases will always be counted as four phrases.

[2] To read this tune in its original version, make the following alterations in *E.H.* (i) Begin each line with note of half value, (ii) omit all crotchet passing-notes, (iii) phrase 5 *nn.* 2–3 in dotted rhythm, note 3 flattened, note 5, B for D: phrase 6 *nn.* 2–3 in dotted rhythm, last 4 *nn.* E-G-B-G: phrase 7 *n.* 7 F for D.

[3] Alter thus from *E.H.* melody: (i) begin each line with note of half value, (ii) omit passing note in phrase 2, (iii) phrase 5 *n.* 4, C for A: phrase 6 *n.* 1, high F natural for D: phrase 7 *n.* 5, C for A.

with a note of half-length. Its opening phrase is a primitive example of tone-painting—B-E-B-C for 'Out of the deep'.[1]

Ex. 4, WIR GLAUBEN ALL', from Walther's other 1524 book, *Geistlicher Gesangbuchlein*, is an admirable example of the complexity of metre and rhythm which makes Lutheran chorales so essentially dramatic. Here we have ten phrases of eight syllables, some of which are trochaic and some iambic; there is also a long ligature near the end to be sung to one syllable.[2]

Ex. 5 is the famous EIN' FESTE BURG, which, in its original version, admirable shows the ambiguous rhythm of the chorale. Here we have a time-signature denoting duple rhythm, but a considerable measure of triple rhythm throughout the tune. The melodic virtues of the tune become clear when it is recalled how effective it is in its Bach version (*E.H.* 362), from which all the rhythmic interest has been removed; but in the original version it epitomises the elation and urgency of the Reformation in its early days.

Ex. 6 is interesting because it shows a typical melismatic cadence in phrase 2, expanded and developed at the end of the tune. In EIN' FESTE BURG we have the 'Minnesinger' echo of phrases 1–2 in the last phrase; here we have a similar echo by development rather than by verbal repetition. The 1662 version and Bach's version will serve as illustrations of later styles when we come to them. It will be noticed how comparatively tame this tune sounds when its florid cadences are removed at *A.M.*(*R*) 625.[3]

Exx. 7 and 8 introduce a subsidiary source which enriched the hymnody of Lutheranism, the tune-books of the Bohemian Brethren. The Bohemian Brethren, or Moravians, were a small company who kept alive the principles for which John Hus laid down his life in 1415.[4] Luther disliked their theology, but admired their music; this admiration was kindled by the work of Michael Weisse (*c.* 1484–1534), who edited in 1531 a song-book to replace a 1504 book. Many of Weisse's tunes and adaptations became classics in Lutheran hymnody. Exx. 7 and 8 show that their style was quieter, more akin to plainsong, than the style of the classic Lutheran tune. Both these tunes were set

---

[1] See *H.A.M.* (1909), hymn 133, page 189, or Zahn 4437 for the original form of this tune. It is preserved, but in a de-modalised version, at *C.P.* 381.

[2] G. B. Chambers, in his recent book *Folksong-Plainsong*, offers a theory of the origin of long melismas in plainsong which can certainly be applied to the frequent elaborations of final phrases in the early chorales. The reader should compare what is written there with Exx. 4, 6, 11, 13, 23, 24 (a) and (b), 83 and 87. The Genevan style has nothing to correspond with this.

[3] VATER UNSER (*E.H.* 462), from V. Schumann's *Gesangbuch* (1539), is in rhythm, metre and melodic form a singular exception to the early Lutheran technique. It went, like O MENSCH BEWEIN' (see below, p. 27) straight to Geneva, and from these into the earliest English psalters. From that time it has had continuous popularity both in Germany and in England.

[4] See, for an account of the history of the Moravians in the sixteenth century, *Cambridge Mediaeval History*, vol. II, pp. 635 ff., and for comments on them, R. A. Knox, *Enthusiasm*, p. 392 f.

by J. S. Bach, the former in the Orgelbüchlein (No. 3), and the latter in the *St John Passion* (Ex.8b). Other tunes of Weisse may be seen in their original versions at *E.H.* 314 (FREUEN WIR UNS) and 652 (MICHAEL). He also preserved in the 1531 book a plainsong-tune[1] from Abélard's hymn book prepared in about 1125 for the Convent of the Paraclete. This has almost unrecognisably survived in English hymnody as the S.M. tune, GILDAS (*C.P.* 64). Ex. 7 is, of course, the original of RAVENSHAW (*E.H.* 436).[2]

Ex. 9, WIR LOBEN DICH, is a very highly developed melody, full of rhythmic subtlety. Observe how, although the metre of the hymn happens to be a strictly symmetrical pattern, the tune stretches here and compresses there in order to set up a tension between rhythm and metre in a manner which the Lutherans loved, and which is, in the days of English psalm tunes, virtually unknown.

Ex. 10, the original of *E.H.* 284, HERZLICH THUT MICH ERFREUEN, is as clear an example as we can find of rhythmical ambiguity. You would think that it was chiefly in triple time—but its time-signature indicates common time. The tune comes, almost certainly, from a secular source.

In Ex. 11 (CHRIST DER DU BIST DER HELLE TAG) we have a melody of comparatively simple and austere outline which explodes in its final phrase in a shower of rhythmical sparks, leaving a single syllable of text to support ten notes varying in value from the minim to the semiquaver.[3] We shall find, at a later stage, that this is nothing to what the seventeenth century musicians could achieve in florid melody; but here it is still a survival of the addiction of medieval plainsong to ornamentation on the final syllable of 'Alleluia' on festive occasions.

Exx. 12 and 13 give further examples of chorales derived from secular melodies; their special interest is that the secular melodies are in each case not very much older than the chorales. Ex. 12, WAS MEIN GOTT WILL, immortalised by J. S. Bach in his *St Matthew Passion*, appeared as a secular ballad in 1530 and as a chorale, in characteristic chorale-style, in 1572. Ex. 13, known in England as INNSBRUCK, and likewise preserved in the *St Matthew Passion*, was first published as 'Innsbruck, ich muss dich lassen' in 1527, and first appeared with a hymn derived from the words of the ballad, 'O Welt, ich muss dich lassen', in 1598.

Two important composers of the mid-sixteenth century are Nicolaus Hermann (*c.* 1485–1561) and Nicolas Selnecker (1532–92).

---

[1] See, for the story of this tune, *Companion to Congregational Praise*, at hymn 64.
[2] See *E.H.* 5½, 121, 202 and 604, for tunes from later editions of this collection.
[3] A demure recension of this tune will be found at *A.M.* (1904) 604.

Hermann, Cantor of Joachimsthal, has left two tunes that have become well known outside Lutheranism. One is KOMMT HER, IHR LIEBEN SCHWESTERLEIN (1554), which is now known in England as NICOLAUS (*S.P.* 481); as Hermann wrote it, it is a very simple tune, the first of the very few German tunes in ballad metre (C.M.), and its last line, with its repeat, ran thus:

(Zahn 198)

Its metre and form suggest that it was borrowed from a secular source. The other famous tune, ERSCHIENEN IST DER HERR-LISCH TAG, which may be read in almost its original version at *C.P.* 146[1] (where it is called HERMANN), has a melodic continuity and rhythmic regularity which again suggest a source, or at least an inspiration, in the secular ballads of the time, and it is, in fact, derived from a song beginning 'Quand Jean Renaud de guerre vint'.

Selnecker, one of J. S. Bach's predecessors as Cantor at the Thomaskirche, in Leipzig, left a large collection of new tunes, dated 1587. The most accessible of these is NUN LAST UNS GOTT DEM HERREN (*E.H.* 126). Another is at Ex. 14, ICH GLAUB' AN GOTT. Many of his melodies are of this restrained, rather unenterprising kind. In Selnecker we have the beginnings of a reaction against the exuberance of the classical chorale in favour of a less picturesque idiom. Ex. 14 sounds more like an English hymn tune of the baser sort than anything we have yet encountered. In Zahn's catalogue there is a series of fourteen of Selnecker's tunes in this metre of four eights (Nos. 407–420). All of them show this singular lack of Lutheran urgency.[2]

Ex. 15 is the famous tune, WIR CHRISTENLEUT, used by Bach in his *Christmas Oratorio*. The reader may compare this rhythmical version with Bach's redaction in that work, also to be found at *S.P.* 638. Here is a tune of very narrow melodic compass, relying on melodic repetition and urgent rhythm for its effect. Removing its rhythmic urge, Bach, it will be seen, has to rely on every other device at his command to make this tune powerful and majestic. In its original form it is lighter in movement, but, sung in unison, not at all less powerful.

---

[1] From *C.P.* 146 alter thus: phrase 2, bar 3, for D-B-C, read D—C-B-C, dotted minim, two crotchets tied, minim: phrase 3, bar 2, for A—F, read A-G-E, dotted minim-crotchet-minim, or See Zahn, 1743.

[2] *E.H. Appendix 46*, O JESU CHRIST, comes from a contemporary source (Reinigius). Its last line is in irregular rhythm ♩ ♩ ♩ ♩ ♩ ♩ ♩ ♩ ‖·

Exx. 16 and 17 are the two celebrated chorales of Philip Nicolai (1556–1608), pastor of Unna in Westphalia. WIE SCHÖN LEUCH-TET bears a close resemblance to the carol RESONET IN LAUDIBUS (compare in *S.P.* Nos. 90 and 700); we may assume here (although at a later stage we shall draw attention to the dangers of tracing these resemblances and building too much on them) that Nicolai adapted RESONET IN LAUDIBUS, which appears in *Piae Cantiones* (1582), and must have an earlier European source, for the hymn which he had written. No such suggestion need be urged concerning WACHET AUF (Ex. 17), which is universally held to be Nicolai's own work. Both tunes have the typical rhythm of the chorale. The second even more than the first shows how heavily, and to what good purpose, the chorale-style leans upon the cumulative effect of a series of rhetorical phrases, rather than upon melodic continuity, for its effect. WIE SCHÖN LEUCHTET, we may say, achieves its compelling force in spite of an obvious sag in inspiration just before its final phrase. WACHET AUF is purposeful throughout—but in its original version a modern Englishman would consider its boundlessly energetic second phrase a trifle unvocal. In this he would follow J. S. Bach himself—compare Ex. 17 with *E.H.* 12, and observe how Bach has rounded-off this phrase in order to make it easier for singers who have not the primitive exaltation of the Reformation (in the year 1597 brought back to life by the peculiar sufferings of the congregation at Unna) to carry them through.

The Example raises another matter with which we may deal here for the first time—that of harmony. We give this melody in the version published in 1609 by Praetorius (whom we shall meet again in a moment) for two reasons. One is to give an early example of a harmonised chorale—but Ex. 18 is, as a matter of fact, better for this purpose. The other and more pressing reason for giving this harmonised example is the object-lesson it gives us in modality and its effect on melodic construction.

The secret of that melodic continuity which we shall encounter in the Genevan style is, of course, modulation. The reason for the relative discontinuity of the German chorale in its first century is that the composers and singers of the chorale were not as sensitive to the harmonic implications of melody as were the composers and singers of the countries where polyphony was at its height. They did not think of their melodies as implying basses and chords. They gave us the nearest thing we have ever seen outside plainsong to pure, unsupported melody. Therefore, modality, which thrives in a purely melodic style but immediately fades into tonality when polyphony appears,[1] flourishes in the chorales. The contention at this particular point is that Praetorius heard the first three phrases of WACHET AUF not in D-major (or F, as he wrote it), but in the Ionian mode. A modulation there is, indeed, in the first cadence; but a composer who was influenced, as the Germans of Bach's time were, and as the Frenchmen of the sixteenth century were beginning to be, by tonal and contrapuntal conventions, could not have brought his bass back to the tonic at the second cadence. The extremely primitive sound of that cadence tells us all we need to know about the persistent modal convention in the time of the early chorales. Whatever Bach may have made of them, or Mendelssohn (and their harmonic scheme in this chorale should be carefully studied against that of Praetorius), their melodies are modal, even if the prevailing mode is the Ionian, and the minor-third modes are seldom seen without a touch of *musica ficta* to make them sound like minor keys.

Modality persists, then, in the church style long after it has given way to tonal conventions in the secular style because the church style depends on unison singing more than does the secular style. And it persists in Germany long after it has given way in Switzerland and France and England because, despite the Calvinists' insistence on unison singing, the musical climate in those countries was impregnated with that polyphony which, as any text book of harmony will tell, is the foundation of the tonal style.

To proceed—we have in Ex. 18, which comes from Praetorius, an admirable example of the quasi-polyphonic style of harmony which begins to appear about this time (1599–1609). Although congregational singing is in unison, it is natural that a cultivated musician should seek, for private amusement or for the delectation of a small and cultivated group, to ornament and embellish the familiar tunes with harmony, counterpoint, and descant.[2] Ex. 18 is a good straightforward example; but there are a few cases in which this practice produced very remarkable results. For one thing, there are the exquisite settings of chorales by Johann Eccard (1553–1611), too lengthy for quotation here, but preserved in Zahn's catalogue. The reader is referred to Nos. 2489–90 and 8301–2 in that work. In the former of these examples he will find a melody by J. von Burck (1578) set as a tenor part to a new melody by Eccard, in the treble, the other two parts providing florid ornamentation. Again, the great chorale

---

[1] On the breaking-up of the modes, see R. O. Morris, *Contrapuntal Technique* (O.U.P., 1932), p. 65.

[2] For another and more celebrated setting of Praetorius see ES IST EIN' ROS' (*E.H.* 19), and for a tune of his composition, ACH GOTT VON HIMMELREICHE (*E.H.* 179).

which ends the *St John Passion* of Bach, HERZLICH LIEB HAB ICH, takes for its melody a descant written by P. Reinigius (1587) to an earlier tune (see Zahn 8326). Another famous tune, ACH BLIEB BEI UNS or CALVISIUS (of which Bach's version is at *E.H.* 510) originates in the alto part of a four-part setting by Calvisius (1594) of an older tune (see Zahn 439).

This, then, is the impact which the practice of harmony, or rather of counterpoint and polyphony, begins to make upon the chorale. To reinforce the point we are here making, we may refer to Ex. 19, which shows the first harmonised appearance of HERZLICH THUT MICH VERLANGEN, known to us as the PASSION CHORALE (cf. *E.H.* 102). Here, in the example, is the tune arranged and harmonised in five parts by Hassler (1601) for a secular song. It is uncompromisingly, indeed, rather dully, set in D major. It first appears in hymn books in 1613, and thereafter is one of the most popular of chorales. It retains, of course, the ambiguous rhythm; but it is always clearly in the Phrygian mode, and where it is harmonised, it is always harmonised with clear reference to that mode. Bach himself, to whom modality was virtually a foreign language (though when necessary he spoke it fluently enough) respects the modality of this tune on certain occasions. Modality for the church, tonality for the people—that is the rule; and we shall see how an exalted church style accompanied the genuinely prophetic days of the Lutheran church, while a degenerate church style accompanied its fugitive and decadent days.

A few examples remain for comment. Ex. 20, from Gesius (1601 cf. *E.H.* 417), is a typically robust modal chorale. Another Gesius tune, smoothed out into modern rhythm, will be found at *E.H.* 345 (DANK SEI GOTT IN DER HOHE); read it in the characteristic rhythm of the chorale (we have by now sufficient practice in this rhythm) and you have the original.

Melchior Vulpius (*c*1560–1616) is one of the more celebrated in England of the German cantors of this period, inasmuch as there are three of four of his melodies that are well known here. The most familiar are GELOBT SEI GOTT (*C.P.* 149; but *A.M.*(*R*) 603 is the original rhythm) and CHRISTUS DER IST MEIN LEBEN (*E.H.* 360).[1] Another accessible example of his style is DER TAG BRICHT AN (*E.H.* 101),[2] and we give two more at Exx. 21–2. Of these five tunes only JESU, KREUZ, LEIDEN UND TOD, Ex. 22 (cf. *E.H.* 187) employs the irregular rhythm of the old chorale style. This is, as

---

[1] To read the original version, substitute for the last line the familiar psalm-tune stock phrase which forms the last phrase of *E.H.* 30 or 428, in equal notes. In phrase 3, *nn.* 2–5 read B-B-C-D- for B-C-D-C. Present version from *Praxis Pietatis*, 1662.

[2] Alter from *E.H.*: phrase 1, *nn.* 7–8 in dotted rhythm; phrase 2, *nn.* 4–5 in dotted rhythm; phrase 3, *nn.* 6–7 not of double value.

its name implies, associated with a very solemn devotional hymn, and in it, therefore, the distinctive 'church style' is accentuated. DER TAG BRICHT AN (*E.H.* 101), almost as solemn, is only a little less removed from the chorale style. GELOBT SEI GOTT and CHRISTUS DER IST MEIN LEBEN are much lighter, and their interest is entirely melodic.[1] Ex. 21 combines a high degree of rhythmical interest with a well-organised and continuous melody. It is probably Vulpius's most sophisticated tune, and in it we observe clearly the movement towards the continuous tonal melody and away from the modality and disjointed rhetoric of the earliest tunes. If, then, the reader will compare this tune with EIN' FESTE BURG, composed three generations before, he will catch a glimpse of the road along which we are travelling. From ecstatic and disjointed melody to shapely and organised melody; from rhythmic tension to metrical convention; from modality to tonality—that is the general direction of travel. The modifying agent throughout is counterpoint and harmony. We shall observe a little later on that by 1609 the influence of the Genevan style was already being felt in the Lutheran congregations, and we shall see, when we return to the chorale, how this style was triumphantly conflated with the Lutheran in the work of the greatest single genius in Lutheran hymnody, Johann Crüger.

ADDITIONAL NOTES. (A) *Piae Cantiones*, 1582, (B) Points of Contact between German and English styles.

A. Piae Cantiones (1582)

This collection of Protestant hymns and carols from Nyland, in Finland, may well be dealt with at this point because its contents admirably illustrate the popular style of sacred music from which the chorale-style derived. Its full title, translated from the Latin, runs as follows: *Sacred Songs of Church and Cloister of the clergy of past ages, in common use in the Renowned Realm of Sweden; newly and accurately revised and corrected by the labour of the same most reverend and honourable member of the Church of God and of the School of Abo in Finland,THEODORIC PETER of Nyland, now committed to print,* 1582.

It claims, therefore, to be a definitive collection, and it is an archaistic and scholarly one. The 'new and accurate revision' may be regarded as applying to the tunes. The words of the ancient carols are drastically amended in order to remove those evidences of Catholic piety which would offend the sturdy Protestants of Scandinavia. Indeed, in its general approach to words and music it reminds us of

---

[1] *E.H.* 67, DAS NEUGEBORNE KINDELEIN, not by Vulpius, is from his book, and shows the style of melody which he often favoured.

our own *Songs of Praise*. For one example alone, it is thought offensive to sing of 'Jesus, Son of Mary'; and adequate substitute is thought to be 'Jesus, Son of Lucrece'—an allusive and academic paraphase which, by its reference to Lucretius, the author of the Latin philosophical poem *De Rerum Natura*, we may interpret as 'Jesus, goal of the world's wisdom'. This substitution of a classical and humanist mythology for the religious folk-lore of medieval catholicism provides a piquant parallel to the theological sensitiveness of *Songs of Praise*.

All this is well expounded by the late G. R. Woodward in his edition of *Piae Cantiones*,[1] to which the reader should refer. Our concern, however, is with the music, some of which has survived in English common use.

Every time an urchin seeks to earn a copper by singing 'Good King Wenceslas' outside a street-door in Balham or Bradford, we are celebrating *Piae Cantiones;* for he is singing the melody of TEMPUS ADEST FLORIDUM as it was given in that book. PUER NOBIS ('Unto us a boy is born') is another famous tune from the same source, and DIVINUM MYSTERIUM (Ex. 23, cf. *E.H.* 613), RESONET IN LAUDIBUS (*E.H.* 612) and PERSONENT HODIE (*S.P.* 502) are three more. Many others are preserved in Woodward's *Cambridge* and *Cowley* Carol Books.

The chief characteristics of the seventy-four melodies in *Piae Cantiones* are their extreme waywardness and their adherence to the ecclesiastical modes. Twenty-two of them are (roughly) in the Dorian Mode, twenty-four in the Phrygian, two or three in the Mixolydian, five (perhaps four) in the Hypodorian, and one in the Hypomixolydian; this leaves only nineteen in the Aeolian and Ionian modes.

The three best known tunes from this source, mentioned at the beginning of our short list, happen all to be Ionian in mode. In this respect, they give only a hint of the *Piae Cantiones* atmosphere. But in another respect, they infallibly betray their origin. Not one of them is entirely syllabic. The flourish at the end of PUER NOBIS, the charming expanded turn surviving in our modern setting of DIVINUM MYSTERIUM (*E.H.* 613), and the only too familiar 'swoop' at the end of 'Good King Wenceslas' are the 'signature' of *Piae Cantiones*. A glance at the original version of DIVINUM MYSTERIUM, at Ex. 23, and at the beautifully rambling melody of PARA NYMPHUS ADIENS (Ex. 24a) shows the fondness for ligatures which is so marked in this book. It may be recalled also that in O QUAM MUNDUM,

---

[1] *Piae Cantiones*, edited by G. R. Woodward for the Plainsong and Mediaeval Music Society, 1910.

now familiar in Woodward's carol, 'Up Good Christen men',[1] the phrase now sung to a refrain of 'ding-dongs' was originally entirely given to the syllable 'O' (Ex. 24b).

This book, antiquarian even in 1582, provides, in its diverting mixture of the solemn and the hilarious, the best compendium available to us of the musical heritage of popular religious music which the Lutheran singers were able to take over from the Middle Ages.

B. English and German Styles

This note is less an authoritative statement than a contribution to a discussion of far wider connotation than that of the present study. There is, however, a group of Lutheran tunes, dated about 1600, upon which we may comment, partly in order to sort out the evidence concerning the tunes themselves, and partly in order to provide a small contribution for those who are researching into the relations between English and continental musical schools of the period.

1. Consider the tune FÜR DEIN EMPFANGEN SPEIS UND TRANK (*E.H.* 549),[2] which is found in the Görlitz Collection, edited in 1599 by Praetorius, and later in Praetorius's own collection of 1609. This is remarkable for its period in being indistinguishable in style and metre from the Scottish and English Psalm-tunes of the day. In the 8,806 chorales collected in Zahn's catalogue, only forty-two are in this metre, and eighteen of these date from years later than 1750; two others are English tunes (JACKSON and ABBEY). As we shall later see, this metre is virtually confined to the English ballads (its counterpart in German and French is sevens and sixes). There is some reason, then, for thinking that this tune in Praetorius may perhaps be an importation from Britain.

2. The tune IST GOTT FÜR MICH, Ex. 25, appears as a German chorale first in the Augsburg collection of 1609. But in William Chappell's *Popular Music of Olden Time* (1850–9), it is given, in the second form at the Example, as a melody from *Queen Elizabeth's Virginal Book*, and a note explains that it was associated in the fifteenth and sixteenth centuries with a ballad variously called *Lord Willoughby's March* and *Lord Willoughby's Welcome Home*. The ballad is preserved in Percy's *Reliques* (Series II, Part ii, No. 20) and the Lord Willoughby referred to distinguished himself at the Battle of Zutphen in 1586.[3] The tune is also called ROWLAND, in Queen Elizabeth's Virginal Book, probably from its association with a ballad beginning 'Now

---

[1] *Cowley Carol Book*, 29.
[2] Alter from *E.H.*: omit long initial notes: phrase 1, *nn*. 6–7 in dotted rhythm; phrase 4, *nn*. 1–2 read C-D for D-C.
[3] Chappell, *op. cit.*, Vol. I, p. 114.

welcome neighbour Rowland'. Chappell further states that the tune was as popular in the Netherlands as in this country. Earlier in his first volume,[1] Chappell provides a clue to the traffic in ballad tunes between England and the Continent by telling how, on the occasion of the 'churching' of Queen Elizabeth (the consort of King Edward IV) in 1466 a state concert was given by English musicians which made the greatest impression on a large company of foreign ambassadors who were present. In this tune, therefore, we have a clear link between the popular music of this country and the Continent. At the present time, in its 1609 version, it is a popular chorale in Lutheran congregations.[2]

3. The tune VALET WILL ICH DIR GEBEN (Ex. 26, cf. *E.H.* 622), renowned both here and in Germany, has often been supposed to have some connection with the English folk-dance, 'Sellinger's Round', upon which Williams Byrd wrote a celebrated set of variations. In the Oxford Hymn Book (1908) it is actually attributed to Byrd. Certain important differences make this ascription impossible, chief of which is that the 'Round' (which is in itself not necessarily the composition of Byrd) is in the Mixolydian mode while Teschner's chorale is in the Ionian. But the first two phrases and the beginning of the third are virtually common to both, and it is very possible that the 'Round' had been paid into that common clearing-house from which the composers of the chorales drew their material. Teschner's is an essentially plain and popular melody in the ballad style rather than in the chorale style. It only remains to add that Monk's astounding recension of the tune for 'All glory, laud, and honour', which amounts to turning the melody inside-out, is a vandalism which English hymn books are now beginning rightly to abandon.[3]

---

[1] Vol. I, p. 44.
[2] I am indebted to Mr T. W. Cowap, one of the editors of the *Methodist School Hymn Book* (1950), which prints this tune (No. 329), for directing my attention to its sources.
[3] The inverted form of the tune appeared first in *Hymns Ancient and Modern* (1861). One of the earliest hymn books to defy this convention was *Worship Song* (1905); this defiance is one of its very few claims to musical reliability. Standard hymn books have conceded Monk's version until the *B.B.C. Hymn Book* (1951) and *Congregational Praise* (1951), agreed in renewing resistance to it.

4

THE GENEVAN PSALTERS

THE stream of English hymnody is fed from two great watersheds —the Lutheran and the Genevan traditions of hymnody. But the courses of the two tributaries are different, and the difference is great importance. If English hymnody as we now know it is as rich of in association and historic content, as busy and vital as the Thames at Westminster, then the Cotswold Hills of English Hymnody are the Genevan tradition. The Lutheran chorales, although historically slightly older, form a river which joins the main stream comparatively near its mouth—as if we were to imagine a river the size of the Trent joining the Thames at about Maidenhead. The development of the English psalm tune from the Genevan psalm tune is a clear and uninterrupted evolution. The impact of the chorales was not felt in any great strength until the nineteenth century, when they came to us (as we shall later see) through the redactions of J. S. Bach and other eighteenth-century German editors. All at once, in the mid-nineteenth century, English hymnody received the full force of the German steam. As a result, in our modern books there appear only a few Genevan psalm tunes along with a multitude of English psalm tunes which are their direct descendants; but there appear alongside these a good number of tunes from Lutheran sources, practically all of them dating from before 1750, and many of them, nowadays, in their original versions.

We are, therefore, now exploring the genuine source of our own hymnody, and a brief historical note will not be out of place.

The history of the Reformation, though an exceedingly complex subject for the church historian, falls into a simple pattern which will suffice for the present study. In Wittemburg, on October 31st, 1517, Martin Luther, an Augustinian Friar, threw down his first challenge to orthodox catholicism in announcing his readiness to dispute in public (in a normal academic manner) upon ninety-five heads. This was the 'nailing-up of the ninety-five theses'.[1] It gave rise to the popular religious and political movement which we compendiously call the Reformation. John Calvin (1509–64), a Frenchman, renounced his allegiance to the Catholic church in 1534, published in 1535 the

---

[1] A scholarly and sparkling account of these proceedings, together with an entirely reliable exposition of the principles of the Lutheran Reformation, will be found in Gordon Rupp, *Luther's Progress to the Diet of Worms*, 1521 (Epworth Press, 1951), with which should be read R. N. Flew and R. Davies (Ed.), *The Catholicity of Protestantism* (Lutterworth Press, 1950).

first edition of his *Institutes*, as a defence and declaration of his faith, was called to Geneva in 1537 to lead a popular movement there which combined a kind of civil rebellion with a religious movement against Rome; he left Geneva in 1538 in fear of his life and spent three happy years in Strasbourg teaching and preaching. In 1541, greatly against his inclinations, he was persuaded to return to Geneva. There, not only against Roman opposition but also in the face of a recalcitrant and unbiddable Protestant community, he founded and administered what was virtually a Presbyterian church coterminous with the population of the city. In this colossal experiment in theocracy you may say that he succeeded—religious and civil law were alike administered, in his time, by the presbytery of Geneva.[1] The experiment, which did not long survive Calvin in its original form, broke the health and spirit of its author. The last twenty-three years of his life left him few days that were not darkened with tension and controversy of the kind which issued, in 1553, in the notorious and tragic episode concerning Servetus, who was burnt at Geneva on Calvin's order for heresy.

Luther, we said, was an artist. Calvin was a speculative theologian of the first rank. Luther's Reformation became a popular movement (despite the cavalier manner in which Luther treated the Peasants' Revolt), Calvin's became an ecclesiastical movement. Luther's chorales were ecstatic; the psalm-tunes of Calvin were severely disciplined. Luther was himself a musician, ably abetted by Walther and Weisse. Calvin had only a conventional appreciation of music (although he was not, like Zwingli of Zurich, prepared ever to remove it entirely from the church); but he was fortunate enough to find a superb hymn-book editor in Louis Bourgeois, of whom more in a moment.[2]

Between the evangelical fervour of the Lutheran Reformation and the Biblical dogmatism of the Swiss, there stood, geographically and theologically nodal, the city and the Minster of Strasbourg, whose genius, less picturesque than Luther, less forbidding in learning than Calvin, was Martin Buçer. Buçer was the best statesman the Reformation ever had. Both Luther and Calvin were able to be happy in Strasbourg. It is, appropriately, in Strasbourg that this part of our story must begin.

Two chorale-books were published in Strasbourg in the early days of the Reformation, the *Kirchenamt* (1525) and the *Psalmen* (1526).

---

[1] A good popular account of the life and work of Calvin will be found in R. Carew Hunt, *Calvin* (Centenary Press, 1933).

[2] Luther's natural leaning to the aesthetic and Calvin's neutrality towards it are excellently illustrated in their attitudes to the Mass. Their liturgies may be conveniently compared in W. R. Maxwell, *An Outline of Christian Worship* (Oxford, 1936).

Each of these has contributed to the general treasury of hymnody a famous tune. From the earlier book comes the great chorale which is known with appropriate ambiguity by the chorale-title of O MENSCH, BEWEIN' DEIN SÜNDE GROSS, and by the Genevan title of PSALM 36. It is faithfully preserved at *E.H.* 544.[1] From the 1526 source came AN WASSERFLÜSSEN BABYLON, a setting of the 137th Psalm which never found its way to Geneva (see Ex. 27).

Now this is a different world from that of the typical Lutheran chorale. O MENSCH BEWEIN' is a poised, formal tune, rhythmically quite regular, indulging in melodic repetitions to bind the whole together, easily assimilated by an English congregation. Melodic development is here also in the dramatic substitution of the fifth for the third in the repetition of the seventh phrase. The whole lies within the compass of an octave. AN WASSERFLÜSSEN is a little freer in its movement, not quite syllabic, but it bears a strong family-resemblance to the earlier tune (compare phrase 9 of O MENSCH, BEWEIN' with phrase 7 of AN WASSERFLÜSSEN). The four-note figure which begins its eighth phrase should also be observed; we shall meet it frequently in a later family of tunes.

The composer of O MENSCH BEWEIN' is usually thought to be Matthäus Greiter (*c.* 1500–52), an able musician who had been a monk in Strasbourg Minster but had joined the reformers in Buçers early days. He returned to the Catholic church before his death. Greiter's chief claim to fame is, however, in that he was the musical editor of Calvin's first Psalter of 1539, published at Strasbourg.

It will be remembered that Calvin spent three years in Strasbourg. During his short stay in Geneva he had, with the reforming pastor, Farel, introduced an order of public worship there in which the only public praise was psalm-singing. The French metrical psalm, which was brought to its height in Calvin's psalters, has a rather curious history.

Metrical psalmody began in the court of Francis I of France. Attached to this court, which was composed chiefly of nominal Roman Catholics who looked on the Lutheran reformation as an entertaining novelty worthy of their casual patronage, was a poetaster named Clément Marot (1497–1544). Marot was well known for his wit and his faculty for writing topical verse of a kind agreeable to such company, and from such accounts as we have of him it seems fair to infer that his moral principles were not notably in advance of those of the contemporary French nobility. It became Marot's business to

---

[1] Only one note needs to be altered to restore the original version: the last note in phrase 7 was originally G, not B flat.

provide a regular diet of poetic fancies for the delectation of the court, and in 1533 he presented the Princess Marguerite with *Le Miroir de très Chrestienne Princesse Marguérite de France*. This contained, among other verses of a mildly religious tone, versified paraphrases of the *Pater Noster*, the *Ave Maria*, the *Credo*, and the Sixth Psalm.

Now Marot was by no means of the Reformed persuasion. But he found in the tirades of the Reformers against the corruptions of the monasteries and the papal court excellent material for satire. Incautious use of such material caused him to be identified with certain Huguenot outrages, and on more than one occasion he was imprisoned or banished. But his entertainment value usually procured for him the intercession of the court. And of all his poetic fancies, none pleased the court so much as his Sixth Psalm. Encouraged by this reception, he wrote further psalms in metre, and in 1542 these were published under the title of *Trente Pseaulmes de David, mis in françois par Clément Marot, valet de chambre du Roy*. No melodies appear in the book, but twenty of the psalms carry metrical indexes. In the intervening years these had, of course, been in circulation in the court, and each member had his own personal favourite.[1] And, if we may believe what seem to be reliable accounts, these psalms were by about 1540 being sung around the palace and the fields, at the children's cradles and at the hunt, by all the distinguished entourage of the Royal family and their servants. They were sung to tunes already well known as secular airs.

There is not much doubt that Calvin, in his first impressionable Protestant years, became familiar with this technique of metrical psalmody. It was this that he had in mind when he suggested psalm-singing in the Genevan church; and although the atmosphere of unrelieved psalmody appears austere to modern Christians, it may well have been as popular a form of public praise as Calvin could have laid his hands on. The principle was admirable for the situation —the psalms kept doctrine safe, and their tunes made it popular.

Events which we have already recounted caused Calvin's first psalter with music to be published not in Geneva but at Strasbourg. This consists of eighteen psalms, with versions of the Nunc Dimittis, the Commandments, and the Creed. Calvin took Marot's psalms, had them amended by one Père Alexandre, a renegade Carmelite monk, and caused Greiter to arrange their tunes.

---

[1] Lord Ernle (R. E. Prothero) tells this story in detail, and excellently, in his *The Psalms and Human Life* (Murray, 1903), ch. 7.

Examples of the musical style of these tunes may be referred to at Exx. 28 a, 29, and 30 a, and at *E.H.* 233, where the melody of PSALM 46 has been reproduced with Sir Richard Terry's harmonies. But the reader should, if possible, consult Terry's facsimile edition, which is still reasonably accessible.[1]

The most impressive difference between these tunes and the chorales of Germany is their strict adherence to the syllabic rule. In the twenty-one tunes of the 1539 *Psalter* there are eighteen instances of more than one note being sung to a syllable, and seven of these are in the setting of the Creed, which is a continuous, not a strophic setting. Three others are in the tune for the COMMANDMENTS, and two in the Alleluyas following PSALM 138.

We may take PSALM 2 (Ex. 29) as a very fair example of the 1539 psalm-tune style. It is in the Dorian mode; all the tunes are strictly modal. Its first two phrases are repeated in chorale-style; this also is normal in the 1539 book. But the striking quality in the tune is its substitution of formal devices in the melody for rhythmic variety. The fifth and seventh phrases are nearly identical, but the difference between them is a deliberate movement of musical thought. The sixth and eighth phrases begin with the same four notes; but whereas the sixth takes the melody to the dominant, the eighth brings it down to the tonic; and the very slight variation which we hear between phrases 5 and 7 prepares the ear for precisely this variation from phrase 6 to phrase 8. The whole is a continuous argument.

This kind of melodic formality is to be seen in many of the 1539 tunes. PSALM 1 (Ex. 28 a) is one of the most majestic examples of it. The recalling of its first line at the end is an obvious formal device not unknown in the chorales. The movement of thought between phrases 3 and 4 is subtler but equally persuasive—the gradual expansion of the compass of the musical thought from a third in the third phrase to a fifth in the fourth phrase. PSALM 36 (*E.H.* 544), as we have already seen, uses the same device of repetition. In some of the other tunes different formal devices appear. PSALM 50, for example, has something like a rudimentary sonata-form—a sentence consisting of two phrases followed by an answering sentence bringing the melody to the dominant; then the first sentence repeated, and the answer modified to bring the melody back to the tonic. PSALM 46 (*E.H.* 233) is in the following form—

a. b. a. b. c. c. d. b'.

---

[1] *Calvin's First Psalter*, ed. Sir Richard Terry (Benn, 1932), which includes not only a facsimile of the Psalter but also harmonised versions of the tunes set to English translations, and a learned Preface.

Finally, observe in Ex. 29 the marked phrase of four notes. This rhythm, with a falling interval at the end, is to be found in nine of the twenty-one tunes; in PSALM 138 ten of twelve lines begin with this figure. PSALM 46 (*E.H.* 233) uses the figure with great emphasis. It appears again in the Genevan 134th Psalm (known to us as OLD 100TH, phrase 2). Some other examples will be found at Ex. 32.

Calvin left Strasbourg for Geneva in 1541. In about the same year there settled in Geneva the notable musician Louis Bourgeois (*c.* 1510–*c.* 1561) who became for the next ten years the hero of the Genevan Psalters. He was a Protestant convert who had great facility in the art of the song-writer. He does not stand high in the company of the great polyphonists of the sixteenth century; but his art was just what Calvin was looking for, and Calvin gave him the task of setting music to the *Trente Pseaulmes* of Marot as they appeared in 1542. He became Cantor at the great church of St Peter in Geneva in 1545, and held office until 1557, when he was succeeded by Pierre Dubuisson.

The source for bibliographical information on the Genevan Psalters is Douen, *Clément Marot et la Psautier Huguenot* (1878–9, Paris). It is probable that some editions of the Psalter have disappeared completely, but we know that (a) in 1542 a continuation of the 1539 Strasbourg *Psalter* was published at Strasbourg, with music, falsely imprinted 'by permission of the Pope, at Rome'; (b) a psalter was printed with music in the same year at Geneva, and (c) Marot's work, enlarged to become *Cinquante Pseaulmes*, appeared, without music, in 1542. No music edition appeared between 1543 and 1546. The tunes for the new psalms in the *Cinquante* appear for the first time in Bourgeois' *Cinquante Pseaulmes* of 1547. This work is harmonised in four parts and was published, not at Geneva (where it would have met official opposition) but at Lyons. In 1551, there appeared the most famous edition, containing eighty-three psalms. This was Bourgeois' last work. In 1556, a new edition, of eighty-nine psalms, the six new ones written by Theodore Beza, appeared. The *Psalter* was completed, with music, in 1562, perhaps by Dubuisson. (He may have edited the 1556 edition; although Bourgeois was still in office, his name does not appear in the book.) This 1562 edition contains 125 tunes, in 110 metres, for the 150 psalms. In 1565, Claude Goudimel (*c.* 1510–72) published a four-part edition of the whole *Psalter*.[1] It is an error, therefore, to ascribe the composition of any of the tunes to

---

[1] *Les Pseaulmes mis en rime par Clément Marot et Theodore de Bèze, mis en musique a quatre parties par Claude Goudimel* (1565).

Goudimel. His was only the work (brilliantly carried out) of harmonisation.

We must now examine in some detail the technique of Bourgeois. He is the father of the modern hymn tune in a more complete sense that we could apply to any composer or editor of the chorales. Tunes in which Bourgeois had a hand may be examined in their original versions at the following numbers in *E.H.*: 114 (PSALM 124), 200 (PSALM 42), 277 (COMMANDMENTS),[1] 269 (NUNC DIMITTIS), 512 (PSALM 3), 564 (PSALM 12), 305 (PSALM 118), 538 (PSALM 110) and 640 (PSALM 86). No. 637 (PSALM 117) can, with slight adaptation,[2] be read in its original form. The OLD HUNDREDTH (*E.H.* 365) is Bourgeois' most famous tune in this country; but let it be remembered that in 1551 it was set to Psalm 134, and that in Geneva it was sung with three long notes at the beginning of its last line. All these tunes have what we may popularly call an admirable 'congregational' quality, a universality of appeal and an enduring dignity that is surpassed nowhere in the literature.

In order to analyse this generalisation, compare the two versions of PSALM 1 which appear at Ex. 28. The first is the Strasbourg version, perhaps the work of Greiter; the second is Bourgeois' version of 1542. Note what he has done. (1) He has matched the last line exactly with the first. (2) He has altered the second phrase, placing its highest note sixth instead of fifth; the *caesura* of the words comes naturally after the fifth note, and the alteration thus places the highest note in an emphatic position. (3) He has begun the fourth phrase on the mediant instead of the supertonic; this marks the development between phrases 3 and 4 more clearly by confining it to the last seven notes. (4) He begins the fifth phrase on the mediant, again making a more conventional melody lying comfortably on the notes of the common chord.

If we look at Ex. 30, (cf. *E.H.* 252), and examine there another redaction of Bourgeois, we shall see exactly the same process at work. Here he makes one drastic alteration—that of raising the whole of the second phrase by a fourth. This brings the tune within a more practicable compass, and (to modern ears) keeps the first two phrases safely in key. In phrase 5 he again slightly alters the melody so that its emphatic notes fall on the common chord. The alterations in phrases 4 and 8 are very slight, the last a matter of rhythm alone; but they are enough to make the tune run more smoothly for the modern ear.

---

[1] The triplet-marks in *E.H.* are misleading, so are the bar-lines.
[2] In the last phrase remove the slur over notes 6 and 7 and tie (as a semibreve) notes 5 and 6.

This is the impressive fact about Bourgeois, that, working in 1542, he so precisely judges what congregations for the next four centuries will find easier to sing. In every case of his editing, you find that his result is more 'congregational' than the original. In technical terms this means that Bourgeois brings the ancient tunes, by the merest touch here and there, into line with the new dimension in which music is being heard—the dimension of harmony. Now that the polyphonists of Flanders and Italy are making their mark, it is impossible for the cultivated musician to hear melodies otherwise than as implying harmony. That has the consequence in Bourgeois' case of urging him to rewrite modal and purely melodic tunes in a way that brings out their harmonic implications; and this in turn produces a tendency to approve for popular singing those melodies which lay discreet emphasis on the notes of the common chord. An examination of the Bourgeois tunes in the *English Hymnal*, or of the larger selection to be found in *Songs of Syon*,[1] confirms this point.

Further examples of Bourgeois' work may be found in our Examples. Ex. 31 shows the Strasbourg (1539) tune to the *Nunc Dimittis* for which Bourgeois in his 1547 (harmonised) book substituted an entirely new tune (*E.H.* 269). What objection he had to the 1539 tune we do not now know; but his own tune is known to be founded on a popular melody, so perhaps he thought that would go down better at Geneva.   PSALM 6 (Ex. 33 a) is a singularly beautiful example, one of the very few of Bourgeois' tunes that breaks the syllabic rule. The secular original of this, again, has been found.[2] At Ex. 36d will be found Bourgeois' recension of a tune in the 1542 (second) Strasbourg *Psalter* for Psalm 104. Here he has extended the tune to double its original length. We shall have more to say later about the curious history of the 104th psalm-tunes. It will be observed for the present that the Strasbourg tune goes back through a popular song published by Attaignant in 1530 to an ecclesiastical plainsong original; this is a good illustration of the traffic between secular and sacred in the Renaissance period.

Before we leave the Genevan psalters we may refer to Ex. 34, which is one of the new tunes (PSALM 23) in the final edition of 1562. It is interesting in being clearly related to a famous tune by Crüger (see below, p. 72), but it does not belie the view expressed by scholars that in the new 1562 tunes there is a marked falling-off from the standard of Bourgeois. Some of the 1562 tunes (cf. *E.H.* 258 and 377) are as good as the 1551 tunes, but none is better and not a few are

---

[1] *Songs of Syon*, ed. by G. R. Woodward (Schott, 1910).
[2] 'Si la nature en sa diversité', published by Attaignant in 1530. (*Hymnal* (1940) *Companion*, U.S.A., 1949, p. 137, Hymn 192). The identification was first made by Douen.

downright dull. Even here (Ex. 34) we find the pervasive four-note phrase of Strasbourg surviving in phrase 3.

Bourgeois, then, is the architect of the modern hymn tune because he anticipates the modern principle of 'harmonic melody'—melody whose pivot is the common chord. With this goes the principle of modulation—of the juxtaposition of related common chords extended into melodies; and as a consequence of this we have the principle of the continuous melody carrying an uninterrupted argument from beginning to end and shaped to a climax. PSALM 1 (Ex. 28b) is a perfect and complete example of this principle. Its melody is continuous throughout, and its climax in phrase 5 is rhetorically placed just where it normally appears in modern hymn tunes.

There is another respect in which we find the principles of hymn-tune architecture permanently laid down in the Genevan Psalters. This principle of harmonic or tonal melody means a breaking-away from modality. But the modal scheme leaves one permanent legacy in what we may call the 'polarity' of the melodies.

Students of plainsong and medieval music are well acquainted with the distinction between the 'plagal' and the 'authentic' form of each mode in the Gregorian system. The mode itself is determined by relating the 'final' (to which the melody always falls at last) to the scale of whole and half tones which the melody uses. But a mode may be employed in two different ways, the difference lying between two different relations which the final may bear to the *range* within which the tune is written. First Mode Authentic has its final on D and its range of operation between low D and high D; First Mode Plagal has its final on D and its range between its two dominants, A and A. (The Dominant is not, of course, necessarily the fifth of the scale; it happens to be the fifth in the First Mode.) The distinction, then, is between those tunes whose final lies at the bottom of their compass, and those whose final lies in the middle. The notion of a tune ending on its high tonic is foreign to modal music, and only appears in hymn tunes when the harmonic principle is fully established. The first psalm tunes to end on a high tonic are in the works of Henry Lawes (1637) which we shall find, when we come to them, to be highly experimental. The exceptions to this generalisation are all to be found in the German chorale tradition, which we have already observed to be quite independent of the Genevan at its beginning.

We find in Genevan tunes, and in all those tunes which follow the Genevan pattern (that is to say in the bulk of English tunes from 1562 to 1900) that this same pattern is accepted. PSALM 1 (1542) is obviously in the 'plagal' position; PSALM 101 (Ex. 43a) equally clearly in the 'authentic'. Taking random examples in *E.H.*, Nos. 393, 394 and 395 are 'authentic', Nos. 397, 398 and 399 'plagal'. In the case of minor keys, whose polarity is formed not on the pattern tonic-dominant-tonic, but on that of tonic-mediant-dominant-tonic (because of the peculiar importance in any minor key of its relative major) we find some 'authentic', lying between their two tonics, and two forms of 'plagal', those lying between dominants (such as PSALM 86, *E.H.* 640) and those lying between their mediants (such as PSALM 61 from Geneva, 1551 or MEINE HOFFNUNG, *C.P.* 417, or ST AELRED, *E.H. Appendix* 62). When, however, we find a tune in a *major* key imitating this concession to minor modes and lying between its two mediants, we find that it is, unless it comes from Germany (as ALL SAINTS, *E.H.* 204), liable to be an unsuccessful melody (like NATIVITY, *E.H. Appendix* 48 or GOSHEN, *E.H. Appendix* 70).

This last legacy of modality is proved and transmitted in the Genevan tunes. Of the thirty-one Genevan tunes accessible in *Songs of Syon* only one or two leave any doubt as to their modal position. The reason for the comparatively rare appearance of minor tunes lying between mediants and the rare appearance of good tunes on the same pattern in major keys is simple enough, and recalls the other principle established at Geneva. In any melody there is a rhetorical power in high-pitched notes. The good melody (like PSALM 1) isolates its highest notes and uses them only once or twice at most in places of rhetorical emphasis. The tune with no conspicuous climax is dull; the tune with too many high notes is hysterical. The rhetoric of the tune is, then, in its few high notes; its argument in its majority of lower-pitched notes. But if rhetoric plus argument have to be packed into the interval of a third, as they do in a tune between mediants (since the end of the argument is, ex hypothesi, a descent to the final) the composer must use great artistic skill to balance his tune. Tunes in a minor key using this pattern have the better chance of success because of the higher rhetorical content of minor tonality (derived from the fundamental tension between the minor common chord and the natural harmonics of the keynote). Tunes in the major key using this pattern must work hard to sustain the interest in these parts of the tune which lie below the tonic. German technique, which (as we saw earlier) lies mainly in the effective and pungent single phrase, serves better for this special pattern than Genevan or English. Therefore, Bourgeois instinctively avoided it, and the pattern was most generally followed in the Victorian age of England, which is distinguished by the disorganisation of its musical vocabulary.

This chapter may be concluded by giving expression to a disagreement with the late Sir Richard Terry, whose work in bringing to light and expounding the Strasbourg Psalter of 1539 and the Scottish Psalter of 1635 we cannot sufficiently praise. But at the end of his Preface to the 1539 Psalter, he wrote this:

> 'The Lutheran chorale may be likened to a fertile spreading tree, shedding abundantly the seeds from which other trees were to spring. The Genevan psalm-tune remains in its primitive aloofness, like a noble marble statue; incapable as a statue of propagating its species; pathetic in its frozen grandeur.'

One of the chief contentions of this present study, which the next chapter will substantiate, is that that judgment is the reverse of the truth. It will be our thesis that while the Genevan canon was closed in 1562 it propagated its species in England; and that conversely although the chorales increased mightily in quantity through four centuries, yet the stock degenerated through in-breeding after 1715, and there are signs much earlier than that of a sorry confusion of its original clarity.

5

ANGLO-GENEVAN PSALMODY, 1549–62

The Old Version

The credit for the inception of English metrical psalmody is due to Thomas Sternhold (*c.* 1500–49), Groom of the Wardrobe in the courts of Henry VIII and Edward VI. The following account of its origins was set down in *The Musical Times,* in 1865, by the Rev. C. Powell:

> There can be no doubt that the primary mission of the metrical psalm was purely social.   It was proposed as the godly antagonist of the profane and ribald ballads which, to the sorrow of the wise and good of our land, filled the mouths and defiled the minds of the people in the days of the Reformation. By its aid it was desired that Englishmen should comply with St Paul's injunction, even by their firesides: 'If any be merry, let him sing psalms'. Hence, was the well-known ballad measure, the measure of 'Chevy Chace' at first exclusively adopted; hence, did the tune embrace as many of the well-known ballad tunes' characteristics as accorded with its change of service from human to divine.[1]

It is clear, then, that the tunes which Sternhold had in mind from the first were those very folk songs which, during the last fifty years or so, have been diligently sought out and revived by scholars for the enrichment of the English repertoire of hymns and carols. A glance at the many English folk songs thus revived in *E.H.* and in the *Oxford Book of Carols* will show that the great majority of them are in English ballad metre—eights and sixes or sevens and sixes. The story of English psalmody is determined by the ubiquity of this ballad metre and one or two derivative metres.

By the time of his death, Sternhold had versified forty-four psalms. In these he departs only three times from ballad metre, the 25th in short metre,[2] the 120th, in six sixes, and the 136th (if this be his) in sixes and fours. Thus, we have one metre for forty-one psalms and four for forty-four, in contrast to the Genevan Psalter's 110 metres for 150 psalms.

It is important to note that ballad metre is only approximately interpreted by the metrical index 8.6.8.6. Until quite late times the

---

[1]   This is quoted in J. S. Curwen, *Studies in Worship Music* (undated: about 1889), p. 3. Curwen's book is an excellent critical study of Victorian English hymnody and its history.
[2]   S.M. is ballad metre minus one foot. It was revived, in triple rhythm and with an internal rhyme, in English limericks by Edward Lear and his imitators.

conventional printing of the psalms in this metre was not thus:

O God, my strength and fortitude,
Of force I must love thee;
Thou art my castle and defence
In my necessity,

but thus:

O God, my strength and fortitude   Of force I must love thee;
Thou art my castle and defence   In my necessity.

The ballad metre is properly described as the 'fourteener'. The ballad tunes are composed in two or four phrases of fourteen syllables each, and the movement in the mind of the metricist was therefore the free flowing phrase of KINGSFOLD (*E.H.* 574) or FOREST GREEN (*E.H.* 15) rather than the broken-up phrases of the later C.M. psalm tune.

The later history of the first metrical psalter in English is briefly told. In circumstances into which we shall go in a moment, new and expanded versions were published in Geneva in 1556 and 1558, and further editions in this country in 1560 and 1561. The last, published in 1562 (the same year as the complete Genevan psalter) was the com-edition, containing the whole 150 psalms done into metre, six of them twice over (Psalms 23, 50, 51, 100, 125 and 136). Of these 156 versions, forty-four are by Sternhold, sixty-three by John Hopkins, twenty-eight by John Norton, fourteen by William Whittingham, and seven by William Kethe (including 'All people that on earth do dwell'). One hundred and thirty-four of these are in C.M., five in S.M., and three in Long Metre. One, the 148th, imitates Hopkins's 136th in sixes and fours. The remainder, thirteen psalms, appear in peculiar metres of Genevan origin.

This complete Psalter came to be known later as the *Old Version* (thus distinguished from the *New Version* of Tate and Brady, published in 1696). It was the norm of English hymn-composition until the Methodist revival, with a few small though important exceptions. Tunes associated with psalms in the Old Version came to be known in England and Scotland in the form OLD HUNDREDTH or OLD EIGHTY-FIRST. And hymn writers down to and including Isaac Watts (1674–1748) and Philip Doddridge (1702–51) did not deviate in their compositions from the metres of the psalms. The complete list of metres accepted in congregational hymnody down to 1800, with the exception only of a few devotional books and of the Wesleyan tradition, was this:

Common Metre (8.6.8.6, sometimes doubled), so called because a tune in it could be sung to practically any psalm in the Old Version.

Long Metre, or 'As the 100th Psalm'—four eights with alternate rhymes.

Short Metre, or 'As the 25th Psalm': 6.6.8.6.

'As the 136th (or 148th) Psalm'—four sixes and four fours, later modified to four sixes and two eights.

'As the 50th Psalm'—four tens and two elevens (Genevan).

'As the 112th Psalm'—six eights.

'As the 113th Psalm'—six or twelve eights, grouped in threes.

'As the 120th Psalm'—six sixes.

'As the 122nd Psalm'—6.6.8.6.6.8 (D).

Anglo-Genevan Music

The development of the Old Version was carried out partly in Geneva. This was the result of the persecutions in this country which drove many Protestants to the Continent during the reign of Queen Mary (1553–8). Some of these found their way to Geneva, and were greatly impressed by the metrical psalmody in use there. Their Genevan contacts had two immediate results; one was in that they composed some of the remaining psalms in Genevan metres in order to accommodate certain Genevan tunes that especially appealed to them, the other was in that they adapted other Genevan tunes to set psalms in their own metres. PSALM 111 (Ex. 39) is an example of the first process—one of Bourgeois' simplest and most attractive tunes for which Hopkins wrote a version of the same Psalm in English in the same metre. Examples of the second process we shall study in a moment. In one case they took over with only a slight alteration a Bourgeois tune for one psalm and set it to another; this, of course, was Genevan PSALM 134, which became the OLD HUNDREDTH.

The best original sources for a survey of the complete effect of the Genevan exile are, of course, the 1562 Psalter with music, or the four-part version published in the following year by John Day, together with the Scottish Psalter of 1564, a complete Psalter along the lines of the Old Version, but independently translated and having scarcely any versions in common.

In these sources, and especially in the Scottish, will be found certain tunes adapted from Genevan tunes, sometimes not set to the same psalms. One of these will be found at Ex. 33b. Here is the sixth Genevan Psalm adapted to the metre of the 85th Scottish Psalm (a metre not used in the Old Version). It will be noticed how each seven-syllable line has been lengthened to eight syllables; this is to accommodate the characteristic accentuation of the English language which does not, as the French does, abound in 'feminine endings'. The simplest expedient is used—of doubling the penultimate note in the longer phrases. In this tune the effect is unusually unfortunate, in that the haunting effect of the original cadences in lines 4 and 5, dropping a third and a fourth, is entirely lost. A more celebrated example is the transformation of PSALM 107 into the OLD 107th. The original may be found at *Songs of Syon*, 300, or in Charles Wood's anthem, 'God omnipotent reigneth'; the 1564 revision at *E.H.* 493; the revised version is a grand tune, but the alteration of its cadences makes it a trifle gawky, and the loss of the metrical inversion in phrases 5 and 6 is unhappy.[1]

Examples 36 and 37 provide one unusually curious case. Here we have a Bourgeois tune (on whose earlier history we commented on page 32 above) which was taken over as it stood for a psalm-version which appeared to be in the same metre but, in fact, was not. Bourgeois' tune was in tens and elevens, strictly iambic throughout. The English version, also in tens and elevens, is anapaestic (as in 'O worship the King', a later version of the same psalm). Thus, at regular and frequent intervals the singer has to negotiate a disastrous mis-accentuation. Ravenscroft's noble and famous tune (Ex. 37) was pro-vided in order to remedy this defect; but even Ravenscroft swings into iambic rhythm in the last line, breaking across the accentuation of the words and causing the ambiguity of versions in the last phrase with which we are familiar in modern books.

Ex. 38 shows, or seems to show, that traffic between the Genevan and Lutheran traditions was even at this date in existence. This version of Psalm 149 in the unusual metre of six fives in the Anglo-Genevan Psalter of 1558 carries a tune which looks suspiciously like VOM HIMMEL HOCH (*E.H.* 17).

The most disastrous, and the most persistent, of English adaptations from Geneva is that recorded at Ex. 43. The original is a Bourgeois tune of curious and delightful asymmetry. The appended examples show its subsequent history, how an English editor in the Anglo-Genevan psalter of 1561 hit on the notion of dividing its first phrase into two, and of making a S.M. tune out of it for the English Psalm 134. The story thereafter is musically too discreditable to detain us long. One editor after another tried to make it work; it was thrust into this mode and that, and the last line turned up and then turned down. After 1595 it disappeared, only to be revived in its modern form by William Crotch in 1836, and to have 'gathering-notes' conscientiously

---

[1] The versions may also be compared by the use of the *Handbook to the Church Hymnary* (1929), at Hymn 151, *Songs of Praise Discussed* (1933), at Hymn 512, or the *Companion to Congregational Praise* (1953), at Hymn 53.

added by the editors of *E.H.* What remains, ST MICHAEL (*E.H.* 27) is a pathetic twisted torso, no more.

There were many cases, however, in Day's complete musical edition of the Psalter (1562) where tunes appear either for the first time, or are not traced behind the Anglo-Genevan psalters of 1556 and '58. A few of these tunes have survived, or been revived. One of these is OLD 25th (*E.H.* 149). Another, perhaps the most celebrated, is OLD 137th (Ex. 35: only approximately transcribed at *E.H.* 404). This noble tune appears first in the 1556 book, and corresponds to nothing in Genevan sources. But its musical language, if we allow for the effect of English D.C.M. on the vocabulary, is Genevan all the way. One theory, not impossible, is that Bourgeois wrote it to show the English exiles what could be done in D.C.M. with the Genevan style—but that is only a critical conjecture. But there is one very interesting and important difference between this tune and the Genevan tunes. It falls quite clearly into two halves, coming to a full close at the fourth phrase. The same thing happens in the OLD 22nd (*E.H.* 163), and in the OLD 132nd (*Oxford Hymn Book*, 152 (i)). This last tune proves the point conclusively; its first half has survived, altered only in small details, in the modern tune ST FLAVIAN (*E.H.* 161).

This amounts to a common characteristic of Anglo-Genevan tunes. It is very frequently possible to make a good four-line tune by using their first half. They often have, as in OLD 137th, a certain monotony of cadence throughout. But the proof that they are none the less coherent and continuous tunes is in that normally their second halves make much less satisfactory four-line tunes. The second half of OLD 132nd would stand on its own; that of OLD 137th would make a passable tune; that of OLD 22nd would not work at all. Despite this, we may judge that their monotony of cadence and their tendency to fall apart at the middle is a clear consequence of the adaptation of the flowing Genevan style to the stiff rhythm of ballad metre.

Some of the tunes in the psalters of 1556–62 come clearly from other sources. OLD 44th (*E.H.* 211), if the conventional long initials be dropped,[1] sounds more like an English carol tune than anything from Geneva (it has even a snatch of 'God rest you merry' in its sixth phrase). OLD 81st (*E.H.* 461)[2] with its persistent, and (for the period) unusual triple rhythm, and its A-B-B-C melodic form[3] suggests a

---

[1]   See below, p. 55 ff. for a discussion of the significance of long initials (commonly and inaccurately called 'gathering notes').

[2]   Also known as OLD 77th. In 1562, it is set to both psalms, to the 77th in duple time.

[3]   Compare for A-B-B-A form, KING'S LYNN (Norfolk, *E.H.* 562) and CORMAC (Irish, *S.P.* 495) and HOLY WELL (English and possibly Irish, *Oxford Book of Carols*, 56) for A-B-B-C form, 'C' being an answer to, not a repetition of, 'A', ST SECHNALL (*S.P.* 268, Irish).

ballad origin even more strongly. The delectable NUNC DIMITTIS (Ex. 41), modal and mostly in triple rhythm, may also come from an English source.

Some other tunes of 1562, on the other hand, were never notable successes. MAGNIFICAT (Ex. 40) is an example of a tune which is obviously modally ambiguous, and which, although the later psalters persevered with it for a time, did not commend itself warmly to English use. Its intervals are oddly unvocal; and not a few of the 1562 tunes give the impression that an attempt is being made, but not yet with success, to coin a new church-idiom native to England[1]. The triple rhythm of OLD 81st and the NUNC DIMITTIS was considered secular and vulgar in puritan circles, and it is only the superb melodic flow of these tunes that kept them in favour. The rule was common time with rhythmic modifications.

---

[1] For an unusually impressive tune that seems deliberately to exploit modal ambiguity, being composed on tonic C but dominant F, see OLD 136th (or OLD 148th), from the 1556 source (*S.P.* 197 (i)), which is the main subject of Sir Ernest Bullock's anthem, 'Give laud unto the Lord'.

6

ENGLISH AND SCOTTISH PSALMODY,
1562–1677

THE *Old Version* of 1562, published with music by John Day, contained, as the last chapter was designed to show, a series of tunes, mostly in Double Common Metre, some of which were Genevan, some of which were Genevan-derived, some of which were survivals from the ballads, and the remainder of which were new tune struggling to find a fresh church-style. The books with which we shall now deal, being the chief of the music-editions during the Psalter period, are these:

1563. Day's edition, with music in four parts. For reproductions of their harmony, adapted for use with the melody in the treble (see *E.H.* 149).

1579. Daman's first psalter (see Exx. 44 and 45, *E.H.* 77[1] and 209[2]).

1591. Daman, revised by Este (see *E.H.* 332).

1592. Este (see *E.H.* 30, 109, and (for harmony) 209).

1621. Ravenscroft (see *E.H.* 6 (2 versions), 30 (2nd), 43 (2nd), 140 161 (2nd), 267 (2nd), 365 (2nd), and 472 (2nd), and Ex. 37, and for harmonies, Exx. 46 and 47).

1644. Barton's *Psalms* (see Ex. 48 (*E.H.* 492)).

1671. Henry Playford, first psalter.

1677. Henry Playford, revised (see *E.H.* 394, and Ex. 39 b). These are the chief English landmarks. We shall fill in the picture with references to a few others of the many tune-books published in the period. To these we add the chief Scottish tune books:

1564. Scottish Psalter with tunes (see Exx. 33 b, 38, 42, and *E.H.* 493).

1615. Psalter, edited by Andro Hart (see *E.H.* 43, 64, 291, 445, 449,[3] 472 and 525, and Exx. 49 and 50).

1635. Psalter newly edited by Hart's heirs (see *E.H.* 354 and 451, and Exx. 51 and 52).

Here again, we shall refer in passing to certain other sources.[4]

---

[1] To read the original melody, sharpen the C's in phrase 3.
[2] To read the original rhythm, transpose semibreve and minim at the beginning of phrases 3, 4, 5 and 6. The tune appeared earlier in the *English Psalter*, 1570.
[3] In 1615, the two semibreves in the middle of phrase 1 are minims.
[4] N.B. All the harmonised psalters in this period that are here mentioned give the melody to the tenor. The earliest to give it to the treble is Allison's *Psalter* (1599).

These books cover the classical period of English and Scottish psalmody. Indeed, they more than cover it, for the greatest of our puritan psalm-tunes all date from years before 1621 in England and 1635 in Scotland.

The tunes with which we shall almost exclusively deal here are tunes in Common Metre, that is, tunes which set four lines, or two lines of 'fourteeners', to a verse. The 1562 group are all Double Common tunes. We have not yet encountered a Common-metre tune.

It is impossible to say with certainty which is the first of the Common-metre tunes. Three candidates present themselves. One is Tallis's ORDINAL, published about 1561 (*E.H.* 453), with which we shall deal later. Another is the 23rd PSALM in the Anglo-Genevan Psalter of 1556. A third is the group of very ancient tunes which are first printed in Daman's 1579 book, and of which we reproduce two at Exx. 44 and 45. There are some (for example, Millar Patrick[1]) who conjecture that these are the oldest of all, dating from before the exile of 1553. These speculations need not detain us; dates of publication do not in these primitive years indicate dates of composition. Suffice it to say that Common-metre tunes are first found collected in Daman, 1579. The principle of the 'Common tune', that is, a tune which may be sung at pleasure to any psalm, distinguished from the 'Proper tune' which is always sung to its own psalm, is firmly established in the Scottish psalter (Hart) of 1615, which prints twelve 'Common tunes' at its end, the tunes applying to whatever psalm the precentor chooses. From the practice of common tunes grew the practice of distinguishing tunes by names, first used by Este and first systematically applied by Ravenscroft (1621). The names, usually taken from the place of the tune's supposed origin, are an obvious expedient when the 'proper' psalm number cannot be applied.

The genesis of the Common tune in popular use is clear enough. It was one thing for Bourgeois to train his highly disciplined congregation at Geneva to sing his noble and expansive melodies. It was quite another for the congregations of the scattered puritan churches and meeting houses of England to assimilate these tunes, or tunes constructed on their plan. The consequence was inevitable. Alongside the 'proper' tunes in D.C.M. there grows up a popular hymnody in tunes of half their length, tunes consisting mainly of stock phrases, which are as elementary in their musical demands as they can be. Indeed, at a later stage the 'proper' tunes virtually disappeared from general use in favour of a handful of 'common' tunes.

---

[1] Millar Patrick, *Four Centuries of Scottish Psalmody* (O.U.P., 1949), pp. 66 ff.

These 'common' tunes are an impressive treasury of popular praise. The venerable OLD COMMON (Ex. 44) is, if not demonstrably the earliest, the most primitive of them all. It is hardly more than an ejaculation—plainsong-like in its austerity. Its half-articulate power suggests once again an idiom in the process of being coined. The same is true of LOW DUTCH TUNE (Ex. 45), often called CANTERBURY or LONDON TUNE. A similar example in Short Metre can be examined in LONDON OLD TUNE at *Oxford Hymn Book* 222. LONDON OLD is sometimes called SOUTHWELL; but alongside it is another S.M. tune in Daman (1579), now called SOUTHWELL —a much more shapely Dorian tune (*E.H.* 77 plus sharpened sixth in the third phrase); perhaps this is an attempt by Daman to improve on the older tune.

It is, however, only a few years later, in 1592, that we find the 'common tune' in its full flower. Este's great Psalter of that year, whose harmonies were contributed by musicians of the standing of John Farmer (sixteen tunes), John Kirby (eleven), Richard Allison (ten), George Farnaby (nine), and John Dowland (six), contains many of our most familiar psalm-tunes, among them WINCHESTER OLD (*E.H.* 30) and CHESHIRE (*E.H.* 109). WINCHESTER OLD is a perfect example of the inspired commonplaceness of the psalm-tune— every phase is a stock-phrase, and yet the whole is powerful, popular, and lasts for ever. CHESHIRE is much more dramatic, especially in its second line.

Este's was the first of a long series of psalters whose bibliography we shall not here discuss.[1] All of them except that of Allison (1599) are harmonised in four parts with the melody in the tenor; Allison's has its melody in the treble.

The early period of invention in psalmody is closed in England by Ravenscroft's Psalter of 1621. This is a comprehensive book containing four-part harmonisations of all the 'proper' tunes of 1562 and a selection of 'common' tunes at the end, including some tunes from Scotland and Wales. Among these last are BRISTOL (*E.H.* 6), LINCOLN (*E.H.* 140), DURHAM (*C.P.* 257), NORWICH (*S.P.* 577) and the four-line version of TALLIS'S CANON (as at *E.H.* 267) from English sources. There are also some psalm-tunes from other sources making their first appearance in an English book, like DUNDEE (*E.H.* 43), ST. DAVID (*E.H.* 166) and YORK (*E.H.* 472). Examples of the skilful harmonisations to be found in this book are Exx. 46 and 47, the latter being of Ravenscroft's own.

---

[1] Frere in the Introduction to the Historical edition of *Hymns A & M* (1909), has a good summary of the English Psalters. Maurice Frost, *English and Scottish Psalm Tunes*, 1525–1677 (S.P.C.K., 1953) is the most scholarly and complete work ever done on this aspect of the subject.

The tune we now call OLD 104th (*E.H.* 178), but which, as we have explained, is not the original tune to Psalm 104 (Ex. 37) is thought by many to be Ravenscroft's own composition.

After Ravenscroft there is very little publishing until after the Restoration. Ravenscroft's book becomes definitive for England. It was hardly a decade before the country was entering upon that great controversy which culminated in the execution of King Charles I; and the Commonwealth period which followed was not a time favourable to much enterprise in the field of church music. Two English books from those fifty years will have to come into our story. One is Barton's *Psalms*, a book compiled just before the Westminster Assembly of 1645, submitted unsuccessfully as a candidate for the office of official Presbyterian psalter, and used thereafter very widely among the newly-formed Independents or Congregationalist group. It was almost certainly the inadequacies of Barton that spurred Isaac Watts to the writing of his hymns. Barton's book contains the tune COLESHILL (Ex.48), which will be the occasion of a general comment in a moment.

After the Commonwealth come two psalters from the celebrated publisher, Playford. He had during the Commonwealth period published several notable music books, and was responsible (1658) for the invention of the 'new ty'd note' which is the technique of grouping crotchets and notes of smaller value by substituting a common line for the individual tails. In 1671, Playford published an experimental psalter in three parts, which was not a success. In 1677, he published another in the normal four parts; and this book had great success and influence. Playford was virtually the first English editor to apply systematically the technique of simplification and popularisation of existing tunes. He was an 'improver' who anticipated by two centuries the often nefarious activities of Monk. LONDON NEW (*E.H.* 394)[1] and ST DAVID (*E.H.* 166)[2] are examples of older tunes which Playford altered and which have become exceedingly popular in their altered versions; in both we can judge Playford to have made genuine improvements. Many tunes, on the other hand, he reduced to pale ghosts of themselves. One example is PSALM 111 (Ex. 39 b). He has the unenviable distinction of being the first of the many editors who have tampered with Gibbons's ANGEL'S SONG (see Ex. 57 (c–d)). Playford was no composer, and had not Bourgeois' sureness of touch in reducing unusual melodies to a congregational idiom. None the less, Playford's psalter became the basis for many of the tune-books published in association with the New Version after 1700.

---

[1] Originally in the third phrase, D-D-D-C-A-B-D-C- (*Songs of Praise Discussed* at No. 503).
[2] For the original version in Ravenscroft see *Oxford Hymn Book* 128, or *S.P.D.*, at 301.

In Scotland, the story runs along parallel lines. We have said enough already to indicate the general lines on which the 1564 Psalter was compiled—chiefly D.C.M., with occasional variations—rather more frequent than in the *Old Version*[1]—derived from Geneva; the tunes, Genevan, Genevan-derived, or native, with a few from foreign sources. Ex. 42b shows one of the foreign tunes in the Scottish Psalter of 1564. It comes from a late medieval German processional, probably originating in a source comparable to that of the *Laudi Spirituali*, on the borderline between secular and sacred. This tune has persisted since the Reformation in many forms. One is to be seen at *E.H.* 534, and another drastically altered, at *A.M.*(*S*) 305 (ii). Ex. 42a shows how the same editors further boiled down Genevan PSALM 107, which they had already reduced to D.C.M. for their own 107th.

The other two Scottish Psalters which concern us are those of 1615 and 1635. The importance of the 1615 edition is in that it contains the twelve 'common tunes' in addition to the 'proper tunes'. Officially an innovation, these tunes had obviously become the normal practice of congregations during the previous generation or two. OLD COMMON had appeared in the 1565 edition, marked for Psalm 108. In 1611, two more C.M. tunes were added, LONDON TUNE and ENGLISH TUNE (Ex. 45), each marked for several psalms. But in 1615 the following appear as 'common tunes':

KING'S TUNE

DUKE'S TUNE (*Scottish Psalter* (1929) 50).

FRENCH TUNE (*E.H.* 43).

STILT TUNE (in England, YORK), (*E.H.* 472).

DUNFERMLINE TUNE (*E.H.* 64)

DUNDEE TUNE (in England, WINDSOR), (*E.H.* 332)

ABBAY (ABBEY) (*C.P.* 397).

GLASGOW TUNE (Ex. 49)

MARTYRS (*E.H.* 449).

OLD COMMON TUNE (Ex. 44).

LONDON TUNE (Ex. 45).

ENGLISH TUNE (Ex. 46).

Of these twelve common tunes, seven are in regular use to-day, and only GLASGOW TUNE disappeared from common use in the tune-books before the mid-nineteenth century.[2]

---

[1] The figures are these: C.M. 99, L.M. 11, S.M. 5, and peculiar metres (twenty-seven different metres), 35. These may be compared with the *Old Version* figures on page 37.

[2] SCOTTISH 67th (*E.H.* 291), is the only new tune that survives from the 1615 book, apart from the Common Tunes.

Neil Livingston, in his edition of the 1635 Psalter[1] writes thus:

> The rise of this description of tunes is not difficult to account for. The proper system required a large assortment of tunes, and most of those actually selected were of considerable dimensions; so that, though confessedly superior when practicable, it must have formed too heavy a burden for the majority of congregations, amidst the disadvantages of those early times.

Rather than wait, in those times of religious violence, to master what they must have thought to be the jaw-breaking periods of Genevan diction, Scottish and English puritans preferred the simple 'common tune'.

It was precisely the aim of the 1635 psalter to check the dispossession of the 'proper tune' by the 'common tune'. Its editor, Edward Millar, wrote in his preface—

> 'The motives moving me hereunto, are chiefly GODS glorie, the advancement of this Art, the saving of paines to Teachers thereof; the incitation of others to greater acts of this kind, the earnest desire of some well affected, the imployment of my poor talent; together with an abuse observed in all churches, where sundrie Trebles, Bases and Counters set by divers Authors, being sung upon one, and the same Tenor, do discordingly rub each upon another, offending both Musicall, and rude ears, which never talked of this art: which unhappie fault I thought might happily bee helped, and the church Musick made more plausible by publishing this Book.[2]

Millar was a cultivated musician, and was one of the earliest Scotsmen to raise fairly and squarely the tension between popular practice and expert precept. His psalter therefore falls into three parts.[3] The 'common tunes', now thirty-one in number, come first. These include some that were published since 1615 and some, like ELGIN (*S.P.* 665), NEWTOUN (the original of *E.H.* 394), MELROSE (*E.H.* 451), GLENLUCE (*C.P.* 284), and COUPER (Ex. 50), never before published. Then there are the 'proper tunes', harmonised in four parts, in the editing of which Millar allowed himself a certain licence of selection; here and there (e.g. Psalm 66) there is a brand-new 'proper tune'. A striking innovation is a new tune to PSALM 124, replacing the celebrated Genevan tune, and now called GREYFRIARS (*Church Hymnary*, 635). It has been thought that this tune may be Millar's own composition. It cannot conceivably have been more familiar or popular than the Genevan tune.[4] Ex. 51 shows a typical example of the harmonic treatment of the Common Tunes.

Thirdly, standing between the 'common' and the 'proper tunes,' there are some 'tunes in reports', upon which a word must be said. A

---

[1]   *The Scottish Metrical Psalter*, ed. N. Livingston, 1864, p. 140, col. i. The Dissertations which preface this work are of the greatest value for a study of the Scottish Psalter.

[2]   Livingston, *op. cit.*, p. xvi.

[3]   Those who have not access to Livingston may consult *The Scottish Psalter*, of 1635, ed. R. R. Terry (Novello, no date, about 1935). This book has excellent preface and notes.

[4]   Millar Patrick, *Four Centuries of Scottish Psalmody*, pp. 64–5.

good example is the OLD 137th in reports, Ex. 52. The earliest tune of this kind is BON ACCORD (*Scottish Psalter* (1929) 192) from the Aberdeen Psalter of 1625. These are tunes of C.M. pattern either elongated by a rudimentary imitative fughetta at the third phrase, or treated in counterpoint with the melody as *canto fermo*. In the 1635 book, Psalms 6, 12, 18, 21, 113, 116, 120 and 137 are thus treated; Psalms 12, 21 and 120 receive new 'reporting' tunes; the others have counterpoint added to their tenor melodies. Livingston comments that, on the evidence of Edward Millar's preface, these tunes were designed chiefly for the pleasure of cultivated musicians; but that a few of them may well have been sung in the churches. There are two in the 1633 edition of the *Psalter*, and these, significantly, are classed with the 'common tunes'.

Edward Millar spent a good deal of his life in the Chapel Royal in London, where, since 1617, the English Service had been maintained 'with the singing of choristers, surplices, and playing on organs'. It is Dr Millar Patrick's view[1] that both the unusual elaboration of the work and its complete failure to achieve its aim in Scotland are due to this connection of its editor with an institution with which Presbyterian, Puritan Scotland could have had so little sympathy.

Millar Patrick, *op. cit.*, p. 69.

7

THE PURITAN DISCIPLINE OF PSALMODY

SO far we have dealt with the bare outline of the picture. Were we to attempt to fill in the details with any completeness we should need a much larger book than this; in any case, Dr Frost's monumental work[1] has done this work from the bibliographical point of view. That work is indispensable for the serious study of the present subject. But this chapter will be designed to fit the picture of Christian hymnody in the post-reformation period over the picture of church history in that period; in the process we shall mention certain tune-sources which have not yet appeared in these pages.

In the Lutheran chorales of the period 1524–1615 we found an urgency of rhythm, a dependence on the emphatic short phrase, a rule of unison singing which correspond very well with the evangelical fervour of the Reformation, with Luther's prophetic, explosive and magnetic personality and influence, and with the popular nature of the movement. In the Genevan psalter tunes we found a discipline, poise and serenity, coupled again with a unison congregational rule, which correspond, not indeed with the external tensions and troubles of Calvin's Geneva, but with the essential serenity and poise of his theology of God's sovereignty, and with the popular puritan nature of his church order. Just as the chorales express not the roughness and barbarity of Luther at his worst, but that spiritual vitality which led both to his errors and to his greatness, so the psalm tunes of Geneva give us not the ruthlessness of Calvin's later doctrine of predestination[2] or the hardness and inflexibility which produced the Servetus tragedy, but, with the help of Bourgeois' expansive humanity, the essential firmness and certainty which gave Calvin in his best years his majestic grasp of theology. Psalm and hymn tunes, we shall find, express what is best in their ages, and, if their composition becomes indiscriminate and their coinage debased, the worst also. There are no bad Genevan tunes because they were all in the hands of Bourgeois and Dubuisson, and there are in any case only 125 of them. There are few bad chorales in the first period because they continue to have the primitive and crude virtues of folk-song for popular use.

---

[1] See preface, page 3.
[2] This doctrine, which to so many represents all that Calvin had to say, is elaborated only in the last (1559) edition of his *Institutes*. In the first (1536) and second (1541) and in his *Instructions* of 1537, there is no sign of its final harshness.

Now in English psalmody the picture is broader and more complicated, because the issues at the English Reformation were in their own way so curiously complex. Psalm and hymn tunes express the popular religious mind. Therefore, those issues which do not take fire in the popular mind do not have any reflection in hymnody. We cannot deduce the whole story of our Reformation from its hymnody, but we can find in the hymnody many clues to the popular forces at work.

The deepest-seated of these forces was undoubtedly the new conception, born of the Renaissance, of the rights and powers of the common man. This led to an insistence in Germany, Switzerland, and England especially, upon the congregational element in worship; hence chorales and hymns and, hence their simplicity and popular nature. The difference between the popular and partly individualistic piety of early Lutheranism and the hierarchical ecclesiastical system in Geneva produces the difference between the ecstatic chorale and the poised psalm-tune.

The ecclesiastical system in England, however, was not, as in Protestant Germany and Switzerland, a clear-cut and unified force opposing the Church of Rome. Protestantism in England did not equal Puritanism. The issue against Rome was for the ordinary Englishman largely an issue of patriotism, arising out of the new nationalism, the chief necessity being to confound the politics of Philip of Spain. The internal ecclesiastical issue was, after Queen Mary had died, between those who could and those who could not accept the supreme governorship of the Crown over the church. The question all through the puritan controversies was, 'How does Christ rule in his church?', to which the answers came variously, 'through the Sovereign', 'through bishops', 'through the Pope and his legates', 'through Presbyters', 'through the church members gathered in church meeting'. Now and again the controversy flared up in such incidents as the executions of the Brownists (Barrow, Greenwood, Penry and their friends) in 1593, the Cromwellian Protectorate, and the Ejectments of 1662.

How, then, was society popularly divided in the years of the psalters (let us say, from 1562 to 1621)? It was religiously divided between the High Churchmen, who accepted the Elizabethan Settlement and the episcopate, and the puritans (some of them anglicans, some renouncing their loyalty to the church of England) who rejected it in favour of more radical Reformation. Beside this controversy the controversy between Rome and Canterbury became comparatively insignificant, so that although there were sporadic persecutions of

Roman Catholics by Protestants, a man like William Byrd was able to live to be eighty without any kind of molestation for his Catholic faith. Secondly, England was socially divided between the old landed and new mercantile classes, and the labouring folk of rude education to whom especially the extreme reforming faith appealed, and who were taking a lively interest in the reformation because of its sympathy with their own rights and needs.

Corresponding with this picture we have the overall acceptance of psalmody as popular praise in Protestant England diversified between on the one hand the tradition of unison singing and of the 'common tune', expressing the extreme democratic emphasis, and on the other a series of psalters in harmony, such as Cosyn's Psalter in five-part harmony of 1585, William Hunny's *Seven Sobs of a Sorrowfull Soule* (1583), and the Psalter of F. R. Tailour (1615), in which the psalms are set in elaborate counterpoint throughout. In Scotland, by the same token, we have on the one hand the austerity of the unison psalter of 1615, and on the other the elaboration, the attempt to raise standards, the appeal to the educated and the rebuke of the philistine, in Millar's 1635 psalter.

The Protestant principle, in sum, produced a musical form in which all is subservient to melody; the puritan principle adds to this the unison rule and the insistence on what is simple and popular; the cultivated and High Church principle, less tolerant of rude education, more apt to set before the less educated the work of the more educated and urge them to accept it, adds the elaboration of counterpoint and the composition of new tunes.

We may take this further if we answer the question, who wrote the psalm tunes? The answer is, of course, that they are, one and all, anonymous. But more than this, they are formed from a common treasury of popular song upon which each composer drew as he would, without a thought that there was anything discreditable in using a phrase that had been used before. The psalm-tunes are all formed of clichés, and yet the best of them have a power that makes a virtue of their very commonplaceness. In the absence of any evidence, it is a reasonable guess that these psalm-tunes were improvised by precentors and people from the popular musical vocabulary of the time. The congregation, unable to obtain or (in many cases) to read hymn books, sung by dictation; the precentor 'lined out' the psalm two phrases at a time, and the congregation followed. How much easier, for an average congregation, to sing a simple tune of commonplace yet compelling idiom, than to struggle through the classics of 1562. It mattered not to them that stock-phrases came up again and again. The point was, in cathedral and in meeting-house, that the people should praise.

The only vice in psalm-tunes, then, is that of dullness, resulting from the concatenation of phrases which do not produce a rhetorically powerful tune. There are surprisingly few of these. DUKE'S TUNE (*Scottish Psalter* (1929) 50) is certainly one, and SALISBURY (*ib.* 124) is another. But these are accidents. Most of the tunes which did not show some virtues passed out of use, and are only to be seen in the ancient psalters. The body of 'common tunes' thus refined by popular and editorial criticism remains a priceless heritage, combining more surely than even the chorales or the Genevan psalms the virtues of utter popular simplicity with indomitable staying-power.

This, then, is the legacy of English puritanism, the religious speech of the common man of the great sixteenth century of England and Scotland. But lest it be too easily assumed that the distinction between puritan and high-churchman is a rigid one, that no puritan would sing in harmony and no anglo-catholic in unison, consider the strange case of the tune COLESHILL (*E.H.* 492). This is the one new tune in Barton's Psalter of 1644 that has survived into modern use. But it is obviously very like WINDSOR (DUNDEE) (*E.H.* 332). A clue to the relation between these two tunes is given in the note appended to COLESHILL in Moore's *Psalm Singer's Delightful Pocket Companion* (1762), the first Scottish book to include the tune. The editor there directs 'Sing DUNDIE Bass and Counter to this tune'. Now it has already been seen how the practice of harmonising tunes for private or choral use led to the composing of a descant-part which was later found more attractive than the original tune (see above, page 19 f.); this, the consequence of contrapuntal traditions of harmony, happened again in the 1635 Scottish Psalter, where the original PSALM 46 is made subsidiary to a new tenor melody for the same psalm. But this is not precisely what happened to DUNDIE. Nobody could call COLESHILL a very good counterpoint to DUNDIE, if one be sung in the bass and the other in the treble. But if the two are put on the same stave, as at Ex. 48, you immediately have an excellent example of amateur congregational harmonisation. The differences between the two tunes occur at the cadences and at a few other points where an enterprising singer might be expected to add his third or a root-bass. That, undoubtedly, is how COLESHILL grew out of DUNDIE—not by any scholar's counterpoint, but by harmony improvised on the spot.

Here, indeed, is a working compromise between the unison rule and the native pleasure in harmony (or the native propensity for improving on, or making easier, or not troubling to learn correctly, a given melody), a compromise between fighting philistine puritanism and scholarly, precise orthodoxy which one may expect of the English character in the seventeenth or any other century.

One other detail must be added to this picture, which will help to redress any grievance the reader may yet feel that we have over-simplified the issue between the puritan and the high-church attitude to worship. There is one source to which we can trace some of the psalm-tune clichés with some certainty. In 1553 there appeared a curious work by Christopher Tye (1497–1572), organist of Ely Cathedral and Gentleman of the Chapel Royal, called *The Acts of the Apostles*. Tye, a Protestant, did not join the exiles on the Continent but remained undisturbed in his quiet home at Ely. *The Acts* is a continuous setting, designed for domestic devotion and edification, of the first thirteen chapters of *The Acts*, done into abominable English C.M. The music is very mildly polyphonic, but it runs throughout in square quadruple rhythm, and contains in its tenor line a series of simple vocal phrases. The characteristic cadence-phrase of psalmody (the last line of 'While shepherds watched') comes again and again. Some sections of the work have in modern times been formed into simple anthems, though not with their original words.[1] Cowan and Love[2] were the first to point out that WINCHESTER NEW (*E.H.* 30)[3] reproduces two phrases from the setting of Chapter viii of *The Acts*. WINDSOR (DUNDEE) likewise can mostly be got from the same source.

Tye must be regarded as the source and inspiration of some of the psalm-tunes. And yet—it is not to be thought that *The Acts* had so wide a circulation as this might seem to imply. It is rather to be conjectured that Tye himself was drawing on the common speech of the Protestants of England—writing what he knew they would find easy rather than what would best delight the connoisseur—and that he was therefore a means of canalising rather than of creating the psalmodic technique. No doubt a publisher of the eminence of Este would know Tye, and be inclined to make psalm-tunes out of Tye's work, but there is something so persuasively reminiscent of the ballad in Sunday dress about Tye's tunes that we ought to be reluctant to give him credit for too much in this direction.

When we survey the whole scene as we now have it, then, we see not only the puritan principle over against that of orthodoxy anglican

---

[1] 'Laudate nomen Domini' (Novello), and 'O God of Bethel', *Church Anthem Book* (O.U.P.), 64.
[2] *The Music of the Church Hymnary* (1901), p. 163.
[3] Note that although *E.H.* 30 reproduces the tune faithfully from Este, Tye's melody has the now familiar dotted note in phrase 3 (see *S.P.D.*, at 82.)

churchmanship reflected in the psalm-tunes, but also their interaction one upon another. We see in public use the chorally harmonised psalm-tunes here and the unison settings there; but in the domestic devotion of cultivated families be they puritan or high-church, we find the madrigals and glees and catches replaced by more or less elaborate and always delightful polyphonic versions; only those less educated would be averse to these songs and would be content with their 'common tunes'. The great divisions of English society, social and religious cutting across each other, are thus faithfully reflected in the psalmody of the time.

8

TWO GENERAL NOTES

1. On Rhythm in the Psalm-Tunes

Before we close this section on the psalm-tunes, we would take up from where we left it in discussing the Lutheran chorales the matter of rhythm. Our text may well be R. O. Morris's pregnant dictum that plainsong is 'rhythm and little else'[1]. The psalm-tunes share with the chorales the insistence on melodic interest; like the Lutherans, the English puritans regarded four-part harmony as an indulgence to be used sparingly and not to be encouraged; they objected not to four-part harmony as such, but to four-part harmony as a symptom of professionalism and artificiality. So that where people could without rehearsal and training sing in four-part harmony they did so; but to be led or, what would be worse, silenced by a choir singing elaborate harmony was abhorrent to them.

Now certain Lutheran composers, we saw, exploited the possibilities of rhythm in many ways. They used in the same chorale semibreves and quavers, varying the tempo and the movement of the music within the space of the chorale as the words or their musical sense dictated. Psalmody, on the other hand, limited itself virtually to notes of two values.

The Genevan psalms are, however, distinguished by the subtlety of the rhythm which with these limited resources they were able to achieve. No Genevan tune is ever four-square; it can never be intelligibly divided into four-beat units—there is always the odd pair of beats that require the occasional six-beat bar. Even the OLD HUNDREDTH in its Genevan form has six long notes in its final line and four in all the others.

Now this is musical rhythm, not divorced from or militating against the rhythm of the words, but not, of course, so completely guided by the subtleties of verbal rhythm as plainsong had been. And the music of the Genevan psalms is seriously damaged if their rhythm is altered. The result of such surgery may be a serviceable tune, simply because the tunes had not only rhythmic but also melodic shape; but their essential beauty, when rhythm is replaced by metre, is marred because the very fibre of their character is removed.

---

[1]   Morris, *Contrapuntal Technique* (O.U.P., 1932), p. 72.

This fact was not hidden from the English psalmists during their exile in Geneva. The result of this influence can be clearly seen in the rhythmic shape of the early psalm-tunes.

But the issue on this point has been somewhat confused by the introduction of a term which is almost always used learnedly but inappropriately; we mean the word 'gathering note'.

This expression refers to the practice of lengthening the initial note of a line in order to give the congregation time to take up the line; it corresponds to the lengthened initial chord which an organist of the present time is obliged to play when he is accompanying hymns sung by an untrained congregation.

The necessities of 'lining-out' ensured that in performance a psalm-tune would have been in this way discontinuous, and each line would have a slow start. There would have been, in this sense, a 'gathering note' each time the congregation made a new start in singing.

But this is a point of practice not of musical technique in the composer. It is true that the very old tunes like OLD COMMON (Ex. 44) appear in their earliest versions simply with the first note and (for symmetry) the last of each line lengthened. Thus far, and no further we may speak of gathering notes.

For the tunes which derived from the Anglo-Genevan family—that is all psalm-tunes that came into currency after 1556—were *conceived as continuous tunes*. True, they are not always technically continuous, but they were undoubtedly conceived as whole tunes, not as aggregates of unrelated phrases. And when we turn to their early versions we find, not a simple system of

𝅝 𝅗𝅥 𝅗𝅥 𝅗𝅥 𝅗𝅥 𝅗𝅥 𝅝 ‖ 𝅝 𝅗𝅥 𝅗𝅥 𝅗𝅥 𝅗𝅥 𝅝

but something more like this:

𝅝 𝅗𝅥 𝅗𝅥 𝅝 𝅝 𝅗𝅥 𝅗𝅥 𝅝 ‖ 𝅗𝅥 𝅝 𝅗𝅥 𝅗𝅥 𝅗𝅥 𝅝

The narrow confines of Common Metre do not give the scope for rhythmic subtlety enjoyed by the Genevan tunes with their long and irregular lines. But the tendency in early English psalmody was all away from rhythmic regularity and woodenness. We find, of course, that with the advent of four-part harmony, especially in its more elaborate forms, the tune is given a new kind of rhythmic regularity by the use of harmonic passing-notes under the long notes of the melody, which keep up a steady movement of minims.

Two examples from Daman (1579) will make the point clear. His version of WINDSOR (DUNDEE) is clearly based on Tye's *Acts*. In Tye the rhythm is straightforward enough. It is when the tune is adapted as a psalm-tune that the characteristic syncopation in the second line is introduced. Again, the old S.M. tune called SOUTH-WELL (not the newer tune) *begins* with precisely such a syncopation.[1]

These long notes, then, are integral to the melodies; they are part of the rhythm. Modern editors may have to choose between varying arrangements of them, as in the case of MARTYRS, which as printed in the 1615 Scottish Psalter (its first appearance) has its first line in this rhythm:

𝅝 𝅗𝅥 𝅗𝅥 𝅗𝅥 𝅗𝅥 𝅗𝅥 𝅗𝅥 𝅝

which in the 1635 Scottish Psalter—the Genevan sympathiser—its first line reads rhythmically thus:

𝅝 𝅗𝅥 𝅗𝅥 𝅝 𝅝 𝅗𝅥 𝅗𝅥 𝅝

But the dismissal of the long notes from the older tunes robs them of their character and cannot be explained away by describing the long notes as an outdated practical expedient.

In the case of tunes appearing after 1621, the issue is not so keen. Tunes like BRISTOL (*E.H.* 6), which have never appeared otherwise than in simple initial trochaic rhythm, lose less by the elimination of the long initials than they would if long notes appeared at other points in the melody. But, in general, it must be recognised that the practice of printing, and singing, psalm-tunes in regular minims throughout is a modern practice quite foreign to the psalm-tune idiom.[2] It is the product of that musical age which was enslaved by the four-bar unit of dance measures; and any experienced organist will agree that it is very much more difficult to make a large congregation sing a psalm-tune or modern hymn-tune in strict minims throughout and keep together, than it is to manage that same congregation when the tune contains a judicious mixture of long and short notes in quadruple time. The congregational idiom of puritanism is not the idiom of the dance-measure—who would expect it to be? It is the idiom of Geneva and of the German psalm-tunes, melody and rhythm, without harmony or accompaniment.

2. *On Family-relationships*

It cannot have escaped the most casual student of hymn and psalm tunes that in this early period there is a great deal of community in phrases between various tunes of different dates and countries of origin. Conversely, it is only too well known how in modern times, when the sense of property in printed words and music is so highly

---

[1] One modern English hymn-book has courageously returned to the ancient psalm-tune rhythm in a few places (see the *B.B.C. Hymn Book*, 293 and 378.)

[2] R. Bridges is slightly astray, as our examples will show, in writing (*Yattendon Hymnal* (Clarendon Press, 1899), p. 7, *n.* 10), 'The practice was to write all the C.M. tunes with long notes at the beginning and end of every line'.

developed, and copyright laws so strict, and plagiarism so deeply frowned upon, the frantic efforts of modern composers to write what has never been written before have brought into hymnody a distractingly arty and difficult idiom. It is worth pausing upon this point.

The clearest and most impressive example of family relations in hymnody is presented by considering the following tunes:

> PSALM 68 (1525), *E.H.* 544, *C.P.* 713.
> PSALM 138 (1551), *S.P.* 661, *C.P.* 430.
> OLD 22nd (1556), *E.H.* 163, *C.P.* 605.
> LASST UNS ERFREUEN (1623), *E.H.* 519, *C.P.* 31 (cf. Ex. 176).
> MIT FREUDEN ZART (1566), *E.H.* 604.

together with these from later sources:

> INNOCENTS (1850), *E.H.* 37, *C.P.* 242.
> ST JOHN (1851), *Rev. Church Hymnary* 710.
> TROAS (1889), *A.M.(S)* 554.

Observe how frequently, in these tunes of diverse origin, the following three phrases occur:

It is obviously useless to try to trace derivations all the way from 1525 to 1889. These tunes come from Strasbourg, Bohemia, Geneva and England. But there are three stages through which our argument can pass.

(i) If we take the first or ancient group all together, we can say at least that the stock-phrases tend to appear in them verbally repeated and without melodic development. And if we analyse these phrases themselves, we find, without much trouble, that they are in fact very simple extensions of the elementary constituents of diatonic melody, thus:

As soon as we observe the emergence of a new harmonic tradition in the manner which we described above on page 18 f., a harmonic tradition, that is, which is added to an already ancient melodic tradition, we may expect to find melodies developing harmonically. The framework of the new harmonic tradition is the common chord, and in that compendious and enormously significant phrase which has just been quoted (*c* above) we have not only the elementary components of the common chord extended into melody (*a*), but also the beginning of a modulation at the second appearance of the fifth of the scale (*b*). All this was happening, we may say, without its being directed by any composer's conscious effort. Behind the production of these several tunes was the 'minting' process that turned out the archetypes of most of the hymn tunes of the next three centuries. In particular, the theory I wish to advance here of the genesis of this group of ancient tunes is that the vocabulary had formed itself and that the anonymous composers, Protestant and Catholic (for LASST UNS ERFREUEN is from a Catholic source), Swiss, German, French, and English, helped themselves to what they required.

(ii) The two tunes of 1850 and 1851 appear after a gap of three centuries after the minting of the common coin of hymnody. Nobody has been rash enough to suggest that either is derived from a Genevan source. But it is extremely significant, I believe, that both these tunes, ST JOHN and INNOCENTS, appeared anonymously in an age of rising artistic individualism. Both appeared in the magazine, *The Parish Choir*, of which in 1850 and 1851 W. H. Monk was editor.[1] Neither is stylistically anything like Monk's work, but, on the other hand, Monk, that careful and learned student of sources, gave no indications of the sources of these tunes. The plain fact remains, then, that these tunes, using this ancient material, are two of the anonymous tunes of the nineteenth century, and that Monk either composed them out of phrases with which his work had made him familiar or heard them in the circumstances of informality and improvisation that marked the composition of the original psalm-tunes. This is not direct derivation: but we can, perhaps, see a young composer here (Monk was born in 1823, and his work on *Hymns A & M* did not begin until the late 'fifties) picking up an ancient idiom and being unwilling to claim for himself the origination of the tunes he set down.[2]

(iii) The last tune, a perfectly innocent new composition by Archbishop Maclagan for the 1889 edition of *A.M.*, contains

---

[1] It ceased publication in 1853 ; Monk was editor from its fortieth number to the end.

[2] INNOCENTS is often ascribed to one Joseph Smith (1800–73). This composer wrote a song entitled 'The Sun' whose first and third phrases are the same as those of INNOCENTS; but there the resemblance ends. Monk does not acknowledge Smith but calls INNOCENTS 'An ancient Litany'. (*Songs of Praise Discussed* (O.U.P., 1933), p. 203, at Hymn 366.)

verbatim two of the stock phrases under review. There is no reason to suppose that the Archbishop was aware of any of the tunes in the older group. Here, then, in a signed nineteenth century tune combining two lines of traditional material with four that could only have been written in the nineteenth century.[1]

We could take this much further. Consider, for example, the first line of the folk-song MONKS GATE (*E.H.* 402), which adds but one note to stock phrase (*a*). Or compare LÜBECK (*E.H.* 552), TRURO (*E.H.* 420) and DUKE STREET (*E.H.* 167); consider PSALM 107 (*E.H.* 493), which has stock phrase (*c*) in the minor mode. For other melodic patterns consider the group of tunes founded on a secular song from Attaignant (1530)[2]—NUN LOB', MEIN SEEL (*Songs of Syon*, 302), OLD 68th (*Scottish Psalter* (1929) 153), and the OLD HUNDREDTH. Or consider a celebrated pair of which the later has often been described as derived from the earlier—WACHET AUF (*E.H.* 12) and NICAEA (*E.H.* 162).

Here we have, as a matter of fact, two tunes, separated by 250 years, both derived ultimately from a common source. Here are the first and last phrases of WACHET AUF:

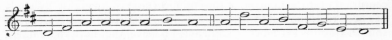

and here the first and last of NICAEA:

The germ of both is the ancient plainsong chant, fifth tone, third ending:

This chant, though, of course, to a medieval ear in the Fifth mode with a flattered fourth, sounded to the developing harmonic sense of later days in D major. It was developed in decadent Roman Catholic music into an extra-liturgical chant known as the 'Parisian Tone', which simply added the upper tonic:

---

[1] An interesting line of speculation is suggested by the name of DUNDEE (*E.H.* 43), which the Scots call FRENCH before Ravenscroft gave it its English name. Why did the Scots call it FRENCH but because it is a C.M. summary of the material worked out in this Genevan family? If its conventional second and fourth phrase be removed, the remainder of the tune makes this at least plausible.

[2] 'Il me souffit de tous mes maulx'.

That was one simple development of 'Fifth and third'. In **WACHET AUF** we have exactly the same material much more highly developed. In NICAEA we have another, and simpler development. It is not a case of direct derivation, of Dykes arranging Nicolai or of either arranging plainsong. It is just another case of the free use of traditional material by the composers of these religious folk-songs which are hymns. Nicolai's other great tune is not far from the same root, and Dykes's NICAEA is perhaps the only really great and timeless tune that he wrote. Other near relatives of this family are the late plainsong **ADORO TE** (*E.H.* 331) and a virtually anonymous tune of 1923 called **CHRISTMAS** (*C.P.* 640).[1]

We may say, then, that this early period of hymnody and psalmody was the period of the establishment of the vocabulary from which later composers have drawn their material quite freely. Later we shall see the effect on tune-writing of the ages of artistic individualism which invented the sin of plagiarism, and in which (notably the early nineteenth century) it was thought better to ascribe a tune to any composer rather than to none. In the great days of psalmody it was more important that the words of the Scriptures should be placed in the mouth of every member of the congregation than that the composer of some ancient tune should not be slighted by a later plagiarism. In that climate the psalm tune took firm root; we shall see what storms that sturdy plant had to survive.

---

[1] See page 136 below for the interesting history of the group of tunes from which this comes.

9

COMPOSERS OF THE PSALM-TUNE PERIOD

THE golden age of psalmody is adorned round its borders by three of the most distinguished names in English music. The signed psalm-tune is the rare exception in the puritan period, and the signed tunes are in style and technique well removed from the anonymous psalm-tunes. It is only recently that these signed tunes have come into anything like common use. Their use in their own day was for various reasons severely restricted; in later times their style or metre told against their chances of popularity. But the revival of early hymnody under Robert Bridges, G. R. Woodward and Dr Vaughan Williams (for which see below, Chapter 19) has brought all three composers into the standard books. The three are Thomas Tallis (*c*. 1505–85), Orlando Gibbons (1583–1623) and Henry Lawes (1596–1662).

Beside these there appear many distinguished names in the great psalters of Este and Ravenscroft (as we said above, page 44). Then there are the religious part songs of William Hunnys (*E.H.* 79 and Ex. 53, cf. *E.H.* 403), Thomas Ford (Ex. 54), Thomas Campian (*S.P.* 587 and 639, *Oxford Hymn Book* 51, approximately reproduced at *E.H.* 487) and William Leighton (melody at *E.H.* 180). These stand half way between the psalm tunes and the signed melodies. They are infinitely delectable though never intended for congregational use. But in these three great composers we have a remarkable, though not extensive, treasury of new tunes.

TALLIS

Tallis's output, so far as we can be sure, runs to eleven tunes, of which one is doubtfully ascribed to him. One of these, TALLIS'S LAMENTATION (*E.H.* 235) appeared first in Day's harmonised edition of the *Old Version* (1563); another, the dubious one, was first used as a hymn tune in *E.H.* (VENI CREATOR, *E.H.* 153). The other nine appear in Matthew Parker's Psalter, whose date is uncertain, but may be placed between 1561 and 1567. Matthew Parker (1504–75) was Master of Corpus Christi College, Cambridge, in 1544, an opponent of Henry VIII's policy of spoilation, but a sympathiser with the more radical Protestant reformers in England. During the Marian persecution (about 1555) he went into retirement and wrote his metrical psalter.[1] He became Archbishop of Canterbury in 1559, and soon after this his psalter was printed without date; it was probably never distributed by normal publication.[2]

This psalter, whose versification singularly lacks grace, carried a musical appendix of nine tunes composed by Tallis. Of these the first eight are each in one of the eight modes (subject to the modifications of modality that polyphony necessarily imposed), and the ninth is the ORDINAL (*E.H.* 453), always associated with the C.M. paraphrase of *Veni Creator* in the *Book of Common Prayer*.

Only one of the other eight achieved continuing popularity. This was the eighth tune, written in canon. It is preserved in its original version, each line being repeated, in the *Yattendon Hymnal* (No. 72) and in the *Revised Church Hymnary* (291). Ravenscroft was the first to print the now familiar four-line form. Smith and Prelluer, *Divine Harmony* (1733) was the first book to mark it for Ken's evening hymn.

Tallis's tunes can be consulted at the following sources:

FIRST MODE MELODY (D.C.M.), *E.H.* 78, *Y.H.* 2.
SECOND MODE MELODY (D.C.M.), *E.H.* 3, *Y.H.* 78.
THIRD MODE MELODY (D.C.M.), *E.H.* 92, *Y.H.*
FIFTH MODE MELODY (D.S.M.), (Ex. 55), *S.P.* 483, *Y.H.* 98.
SIXTH MODE MELODY (D.C.M.) (Ex. 56), *Y.H.* 68.
SEVENTH MODE MELODY (eight sixes), *E.H.* 496.
EIGHTH MODE MELODY (L.M.), *E.H.* 267, *Y.H.* 54–5).
ORDINAL, *E.H.* 453, *Y.H.* 14.
TALLIS'S LAMENTATION, *E.H.* 235, *Y.H.* 59.
(VENI CREATOR), *E.H.* 153.

These tunes are dark, insistent and immensely dramatic to modern ears. The obsessive repeated notes of the FIRST, SECOND, THIRD and SIXTH melodies, and the almost hypnotic rhythm, irregular within its four-bar units but in its whole pattern perfectly symmetrical, carry us into a world very different from that of the psalm-tunes. The shaft of light thrown across a sombre background in the FIRST and THIRD melodies (in the third long phrase of each) is the kind of dramatic effect after which composers of three hundred years later strove in vain.

---

[1] Julian, *Dictionary of Hymnology* (1892 and 1907), p. 882, s.v. *Parker*.
[2] R. Bridges, *Yattendon Hymnal* (Clarendon Press, 1899), page 6 of notes, at Hymn 2.

We have in these tunes the art of the song-writer and of the contrapuntist. Only a song-writer, sensitive to words, could so faithfully interpret the internal rhymes of the verses as Tallis does in his SIXTH tune (Ex. 56) and in his THIRD. Only a contrapuntist, skilled in cross-rhythms and thinking in the vocabulary of Tudor polyphony, would have composed so effortless a canon as the EIGHTH, would have so uncannily handled the rhythm of the THIRD and SEVENTH, would have produced so gloriously happy a song-tune as the FIFTH (Ex. 55) or would have craftily used in his melody the changing-note cliché of polyphony, as in the third phrase of the FIRST:

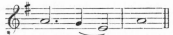

And only a master of musical form, of the continuous song-style, would have cast his simplest tune, the ORDINAL, in clear simple binary form.[1]

All the dark grandeur of Tallis's style can be seen in his LAMENTATION (*E.H.* 235). The VENI CREATOR (*E.H.* 153) is so dubiously ascribed to him that we had better not use it as evidence of his style.[2]

GIBBONS

The tunes of Orlando Gibbons form a musical companion to the first hymn-book published in English—George Wither's *Hymns and Songs of the Church* (1623). These hymns, anticipating by two generations Isaac Watts's great gesture in bringing the New Testament into public praise, are free compositions based on the Scriptures of both Testaments. Although King James I granted Wither a patent for printing the book, the Company of Stationers, jealous of the patent, succeeded in virtually suppressing the book. Very few copies of it now exist (there is one in the British Museum and one in Christ Church, Oxford), but a reprint edited by Edward Farr (1856 and 1895) is still accessible.

There are fifteen of these tunes of Gibbons, together with a sixteenth which has been thought to be his but is now known not to be.[3]

---

[1] Cf. Scholes, Oxford Companion to Music (1st edition, 1938, page 334).

[2] It will be observed by students of these sources that while the majority of Tallis's tunes in modern use take his original tenor part for the melody, *E.H.* 78, 453 and 235 use his original treble part. It is clear that in 453 he intended the treble part to be the melody: in the others it is natural to think that he meant the tenor to have the melody, but the impressiveness of the tunes as they stand in the modern versions allows doubt on this point. Here, at all events, is further evidence for Tallis's contrapuntal skill.

[3] See below, p. 66 for bibliographical notes on Songs 41, 47 and 67.

Observe their metres as well as their accessible sources in the following list:

SONG 1: (six (eight) tens),[1] *E.H.* 384.
SONG 3: (D.C.M.)
SONG 4: (four (six) tens), *E.H.* 113.
SONG 5: (L.M.), *E.H.* 483[2].
SONG 9: (six eights) (Ex. 57b), *Oxford Hymn Book* 233.
SONG 13: (four (six) sevens), *E.H.* 413[3].
SONG 14: (seven eights).
SONG 18: (886.886), *E.H.* 357.
SONG 20: (S.M.), *E.H.* 442.
SONG 22: (four tens), *E.H.* 438.
SONG 24: (four (six) tens), *E.H.* 430.
SONG 31: (six sevens).
SONG 34: (L.M.) (Ex. 57a), *E.H.* 259, Ex. 57a.
SONG 41: (six eights) Ex. 58.
SONG 44: (eight eights) (SONG 9 with last phrase repeated).
SONG 47: (nine tens) (seven tens plus a chorus) Ex. 59.

In this list we find the first appearance of several metres which later came into common use—six tens (OLD 50th metre modified), four tens, and sevens. We also find, in SONGS 34 and 9, a probably unique case of a tune being elongated by its composer, the process producing a second tune just as satisfying as the original.[4]

The tunes are, of course, provided for those songs which either would not go to a psalm tune because of their metre, or for which no existing psalm-tune was suitable. Wither provides a metrical index to make existing psalm-tunes available for the other songs. Hence, the discontinuity of Gibbons's Song-numbers—which are the serial numbers of the Songs in Wither—and the paucity of psalm-metres to be found in them.[5]

The tunes divide themselves naturally into two groups—those written in major keys and those written in minor. The major key tunes show a strong family-likeness to each other (see Ex. 60); three of them are so to speak, 'triplets'—9, 34 and 44. They have long, continuous, and unusually graceful melodies, even in rhythm, persuasive in melody, with a melodic climax practically invariably on subdominant

---

[1] i.e. six tens plus a repetition of the first two phrases, discarded in modern books. So with succeeding metres noted in this form.

[2] This tune originally began on the last beat of a bar, the first melody note being tied over to the first beat of the first bar: in effect a dactylic start in four-minim rhythm.

[3] The sixth note in the version at *E.H.* 413 is highly doubtful. It was probably F in the original.

[4] Sydney Nicholson's CUMULUS (*A.M.(R)* 622) employs a similar device; but here the tune is lengthened to accommodate an expanding metre in one hymn, not made into another tune.

[5] Note that L.M. was still very ill supplied with tunes at this date; hence, SONGS 5 and 34.

harmony. Most of them are still in use, but SONG 47, one of the most skilful of them all, has as yet not found a hymn to carry it (see Ex. 59).

The minor-key tunes are much more individual. Among them is the one Gibbons tune that is really awkward and lacking in his usual vocal power; perhaps it is an interloper (SONG 41, Ex. 58). It is omitted from Farr's reprint. These minor-key tunes have a strong dash of modality in them.

All the tunes are written in two parts—melody and bass. Despite the disadvantages of their first publication, many of them are now popular.

A Bibliographical Note

It is necessary here to make a note of one or two current misunderstandings about certain tunes of Gibbons, which are derived from the use by well known authorities of Farr's reprint; this has led to a certain amount of confusion.

1. SONG 41 is altogether omitted from Farr. This is (see Ex. 58) no great loss; but the existence of the tune should not be overlooked. It was revived in Chope, *Carols for use in Church* (*c*. 1860), set to Wither's Song xlix.

2. The form of SONG 34 (or ANGELS' SONG) at *E.H.* 259 is not correct. The tune is there printed as the first four lines of SONG 9, whose first four lines are otherwise identical with SONG 34. Originally, SONG 34 runs, as at *A.M.*(*R*) 336, in minims throughout except at the beginning and end. The mistake originates in Farr.

3. SONG 46 (*E.H.* 468) is mis-numbered. This two-line tune is the first two phrases of the last tune but one in the 1623 source, which, *though marked by Farr* for SONG 46, metrically fits not that Song but the next, SONG 47. A vexatious complication which at this time of day editors can hardly rectify without inducing confusion.

4. SONG 67 (*E.H.* 197) is not by Gibbons. It appeared two years earlier in Prys's Welsh Psalter (1621). Wither's is the first English book to include it. Ravenscroft missed it, although he included ST MARY (*E.H.* 84) from Prys. Obviously, Gibbons included it as a serviceable C.M. which the others had missed, but there is no reason to think it was his composition. Gibbons is not likely to have penetrated to the wilds of North Wales.

This information is entirely owed to the Reverend Maurice Frost, who includes it in his book, *English and Scottish Psalm Tunes*, 1525–1677, at various points in the section on Gibbons, together with other important bibliographical material.

LAWES

Henry Lawes's tunes appear with their words in G. Sandys' *A Paraphase upon the Divine Poems* (1637), commonly known as Sandys' Psalms. This was a selection of free psalm-versions in metres more like those of Wither than those of the Psalter. Lawes provided tunes for twenty-four of them more or less on Gibbons's principle of setting tunes to psalms that could not be sung to existing tunes. Sandys' work has not the springing distinction of Wither's, and not much of it survives.[1]

---

[1] 'All from the sun's uprise', *Worship Song* (1905) 190, from Psalm 100, is probably the last survivor.

The following table shows the metrical scheme of the tunes and their accessible sources:

PSALM   1: Four tens (also 31, 72).

PSALM   2: Six eights (rhyming a.b.b.a.c.c.).

PSALM   3: L.M. (also 8 and 9).

PSALM   4: 8.8.4.4.6.

PSALM   6: Six eights (a.a.a.b.b.b.) (also 46).

PSALM   7: 7.4.7.4.8.8. (Ex. 61).

PSALM   8: L.M. (WHITEHALL, *E.H.* 234).

PSALM 10: 8.8.4.4.8.6.6. (as Psalm 121 in the *Old Version*) (also 136).

PSALM 12: Six eights (a.b.a.b.b.a.) (also 22, 111).

                    FALKLAND, *E.H.* 219.

PSALM 13: Six sixes (as Psalm 120 in *Old Version*).

PSALM 14: Four eights (a.b.b.a.). (The first example of 'In Memoriam' metre).

PSALM 15: Four sevens (also 29).

PSALM 31: Four tens (BATTLE, *E.H.* 432).

PSALM 32: Four sixes (*E.H.* 505).

PSALM 34: 8.8.6.8.8.6. (as Scottish Psalm 85).

PSALM 39: 8.4.8.4.8.8.

PSALM 47: Sixes and fours, as OLD 148th (*C.P.* 128).

PSALM 72: Four tens (FARLEY CASTLE, *E.H.* 217).

This composer represents a school of English music far less productive of great material than that represented by Gibbons. Gibbons comes into the golden age of polyphony, Lawes into the age of English song-writing. He was a professional singer, and earned celebrated praise from Milton. His tunes do not, like Gibbons's, rest contentedly upon the treasury of vocal melody laid up by the polyphonists. Their frankly experimental idiom remains the subject of controversy. Robert Bridges disliked them.[1] The editors of *E.H.* thought him well worth singing. Those of the *B.B.C. Hymn Book* (1951) included nothing but PSALM 47.

The accessible tunes of Lawes, together with Example 61, will indicate how unwilling Lawes was to follow anything like a beaten track. To some, his melodies are haunting, to others irritating. Even more impressive is evidence offered in Ex. 62 of Lawes's predilection for unusual turns of phrase, and especially for that four-note phrase which we now associate with ST ANNE ('O God, our help in ages past'). Ex. 63 tells the same story in terms of Lawes's final cadences.

---

[1]   *Yattendon Hymnal* (1899), page 21 of notes, Hymn 73, where he dismisses PSALM 47 as a 'somewhat sentimental tune' and judges Lawes unworthy of Milton's encomium.

In the last two tunes of Ex. 63, PSALMS 136 and 72 (one of which is the familiar FARLEY CASTLE, *E.H.* 217) Lawes ends his melody on the high tonic, not having previously sounded any higher note. This is still an extreme rarity, and these are the first English tunes to have it. (It is found in some early chorales and in one tune of Heinrich Schütz.) It is, oddly enough, also found in ST ANNE, which is the only standard psalm-tune in the literature written on this pattern.

There can be no clearer indication than we have in these two qualities—markedly disjunct melody and high endings—that Lawes belongs not to the polyphonic tradition but to the new tradition of opera and aria. Polyphony breeds smooth melody; and melody naturally falls to its final. The contradiction of the natural fall implies a bass, which will supply for the ear that aesthetic sensation of falling to the final that the melody does not here give. By instinct, neither the Genevan nor the English psalm-tune composer could have constructed his melody in this fashion. Sing ST ANNE in unison unaccompanied, and its incompleteness will be at once demonstrated, and this in turn demonstrates the principle that a high finish needs a bass, and the particular contention that Lawes was a song-writer of the new school.

None of these three great composers achieved any sort of popularity before 1906. Appearances of their tunes, with a few exceptions, are only sporadic. Tallis's CANON is to be found in books of all periods, sometimes grotesquely revised. Gibbons's ANGELS' SONG (SONG 34) is to be found, usually unrecognisably edited, all through the eighteenth and nineteenth centuries. Lawes's PSALM 8 (WHITE-HALL), turns up, slightly altered, in Green's *Psalmody* of 1715, and the *Anglican Hymn Book* of 1871 began the custom of singing his PSALM 47 to 'My song is love unknown'. The restricted circulation of their sources, the unusual metres of the tunes of Gibbons and Lawes, and the curiously unvocal and capricious turns of phrase in Lawes, provide the causes of their virtual silence during two centuries and more until modern antiquarians brought them to life again. Their tunes have in common a distinction which is denied to the psalm-tunes, and a corresponding deficiency of homespun commonplaceness. Of the three, Tallis produced the profoundest tunes, Gibbons the easiest, Lawes the most intriguing.

10

THE LUTHERAN CHORALE, 1615–1715

THE century covered by this chapter falls naturally into two parts which are divided by the year 1662, in which Johann Crüger died. Crüger, the greatest name in German hymnody, will dominate the scene by his influence during his lifetime in establishing the Lutheran church style, by his notable championing of the restrained style of writing in face of mounting opposition from new secular styles, and by the manner in which after his death the chorale gave way almost without further resistance to these secular styles.

We shall pass through country of rapidly changing scenery. We begin on the eve of the Thirty Years' War, from whose depths of suffering some of the noblest German hymns, those of Löwenstern and Paul Gerhardt, were born. We pass from this into an age of individualistic and domestic piety, and of failing ecclesiastical prestige. That operatic style of music, with its emphasis on individual prowess and virtuoso technique, on captivating melody and subservient harmony, which began with Peri and Caccini at the beginning of the century, is the chief influence at work to modify, and in the end to overthrow, the traditional conception of the chorale, and to turn it into a song. At the beginning of the period we see the chorale, under the influence of the Genevan style, growing away from the popular folk-song style into a dignified and solemn church style. At the end it has abandoned that church style for a new kind of secular style associated not with folk-music but with professional music—an altogether new idea. The church style grew out of the folk-song style through a process parallel to that which turned the popular movement of the Reformation into an established church; the church style gave way to the professional style by a process consequent upon the recession of the congregational principle of churchmanship in favour of the domestic and private principle. These generalisations we shall now substantiate.

First, concerning the Genevan style. The Reformed churchmanship of John Calvin found its way into German-speaking communities before the seventeenth century was out. It never established itself widely, and its two greatest hymn writers, Joachim Neander and Gerhard Tersteegen, fall into the period of pietism which had little in common with Calvinism. But A. Lobwasser's translation of the

Genevan psalms into German in 1573 brought many of the Genevan tunes into German currency, and the greater part of the 1551 tunes therefore find a place in Zahn's catalogue. This style of hymnody had a certain influence in 'taming' the chorale. MACH'S MIT MIR, GOTT (Ex. 64, cf. *E.H.* 138 (i)) is a good example of the chorale-idiom influenced by the discipline and shapeliness of Genevan style. Its rhythm is Lutheran, its shape Genevan. We find the Genevan influence more pronounced in such tunes as Crüger's SCHMÜCKE DICH (*E.H.* 306), which is pure Genevan in idiom. Schein's style is always restrained and powerful. HERR GOTT, DU UNSER ZUFLUCHT BIST (Psalm 90) (Ex. 65) is an example of his minor-mode style, and ALLEIN NACH DIR (Ex. 66) of his skill in coping with a characteristically wayward Lutheran metre. Johann Schein (1586–1830) was, like Selnecker before and J. S. Bach after him, cantor at the Thomaskirche at Leipzig, and his tunes were published in his *Cantional* (1627).[1]

A more normal chorale style is seen in ACH GOTT UND HERR (Ex. 67), which began in a form very different from that in which it appears at *E.H.* 329. It was Christoph Peter who in 1655, possibly through a mere error, transposed it into the major key, and Bach who removed its rhythmical subtlety. But it had lost its flourish in the last line—characteristic of primitive chorales but not of the new, more severe style, by 1640, when Crüger pruned its last line as indicated at the Example. This tune first appeared at Leipzig in *As Hymnodus Sacer*, 1625. An interesting story hangs by another tune from the same source, HERR JESU CHRIST, MEIN LEBENS LICHT, which was metamorphosed through two centuries into the tune we now call BRESLAU (*E.H.* 484). For the history of this see *Songs of Praise Discussed* at Hymn 132.

Proceeding across the centre to the far limits of experimental music in the new style, we come to the psalm-tunes of Heinrich Schütz (1585–1672) published in his *Psalmen Davids* (Meissen, 1628).[2] Here, contemporary with Schein, we have a composer of the first rank in larger forms showing his skill in hymnody; and here also we have the beginning of that secular style to which we referred above. These psalm-tunes should be carefully studied; they deserve a book to themselves. We must be content with quoting only four. PSALM 138 (Ex. 68) is one of the few of his tunes that survive in contemporary Lutheran use. It is square and straightforward and we include it to

---

[1] Ex. 64 was published with another tune on a two-page leaflet associated with this book, printed in the following year (1628).
[2] Since this was written, Schültz's Psalms have become available in Volume 6 (*Der Psalter*) of *Heinrich Schültz, Neue Ausgabe sämtlicher Werke* (Bärenreiter-Verlag, Kassel und Basel, 1955).

offset the eccentricities of the others. PSALM 15 (Ex. 69) shows a very free vocal melody, high pitched and, in its third phrase, far from congregational in texture. Its last phrase has a flourish in the old style, but within that flourish is a rhythmical ambiguity suggestive of a Tudor madrigal—a device, indeed, for which no school of musicians is so celebrated as the English. This is not the crude flourish of religious 'animal spirits' that we associate with the primitive chorale, but a subtle and sophisticated embellishment taken straight from the vocabulary of the secular part song. PSALM 84 (Ex. 70) is a piece of pure word-painting, a melody which makes no sense without supporting harmony, a beautiful choral setting of 'My soul longeth, yea fainteth . . .'. PSALM 45 (Ex. 71), one of the most remarkable even in this astonishing collection, combines a bewildering archaism of notation with a device that we shall meet often in the succeeding period—a change of time-signature, and with it a change of note-values[1]; this is a reflection of the new experiments in overture and suite, another consequence of the new view of musical argument as being sustained not by interplay of rhythms and melodies but by their juxtaposition. Many of the tunes of the florid type have this 'overture and first movement' form, though most of them give the greater space to the 'overture'.

There would be a case for saying that Schütz wielded a disastrous influence on the chorale; but such a contention would not be just. The extravagances of Schütz's psalms are certainly developed in later devotional music. But Schütz's psalms were never in wide popular use; and it is true even of the most extravagant of them that, considered as motets for choral use they are superb music. But their style, with all its subtlety and dramatic power, when applied to hymn-tunes and chorales makes them appear over-written. There is in Tovey a revealing paragraph, written in the context not of church music but of opera, which can be brought to bear precisely on this point. We dwell on it because here we meet for the first time the bogey of over-writing which haunted so many later composers. Contrasting purely instrumental music with music for opera (and we shall change the scene to a contrast between purely vocal music and music for congregational use) Tovey wrote:

> Purely instrumental music is not less, but enormously more dramatic than any music for which situations can be found on the stage . . . If it were possible to put on the stage anything so dramatic as the first movement of Beethoven's D minor sonata, the result would make not every existing opera, but every existing drama, seem cold. It could not be great drama, for its temperature would be insupportable . . . Mozart uses with complete

---

[1] In the Bärenreiter-Verlag edition the note values after the first (repeated) pair of phrases are halved—minim for semibreves, etc.

adequacy (sc. in *Don Giovanni*) formulated musical gestures which are far too cold to find a place in the development of any symphony he wrote at a later age than seventeen.[1]

And again:

Theatre-music is like theatre-scenery; it is a medium in which simple resources and methods produce immediate and vivid effects.[2]

Tovey is saying that since in opera music is only one of many means used to make an impact on the senses and the mind, it not only can afford to be, but must of necessity be written at a lower pressure than the 'absolute music' which he contrasts with it. It not only may but positively must sound a trifle 'thin' when taken out of its full context. *Mutatis mutandis* this is precisely so with chorales and hymn tunes. The hymn tune must be homespun and durable. It must be, judged by symphonic standards, the apotheosis of platitude. It must, to recall our opening simile, recall domestic architecture rather than a mono-lithic style. The truth is that Schütz's psalms are over-written for use as congregational hymns, and he never intended them for that use. What we shall especially execrate, however, is a style different from this, namely, the style which is over-written but, at the same time, trivial; to this style religious fervour of a certain kind has very frequently offered generous hospitality.

These three groups—the tunes of Schein, of the 1625 source and of Schütz, then, set the scene upon which we may now usher the weighty figure of Johann Crüger (1598–1662), Cantor of the Cathedral of St Nicholas, Berlin from 1622, his twenty-fourth year, until his death. Crüger is chiefly to be honoured for initiating the monumental *Praxis Pietatis Melica*, whose first edition appeared in about 1644 (it has now entirely disappeared), and which continued, in successive editions spanning a century, to be long after his death the classic source for Lutheran praise. But Crüger's earliest tunes appear in the *Volkommlicher Gesangbuch* of 1640. The most famous of these is HERZ-LIEBSTER JESU (Ex. 72, cf. *E.H.* 70). It is what will presently appear to be a typical Crüger tune, simple, syllabic, rhythmically decisive but not, in the primitive way, subtle. It establishes him as a Genevan sympathiser by containing what seems to be a direct quotation from PSALM 23 of 1562 (cf. Ex. 34).

We cannot now tell what tunes were in the first edition of *Praxis Pietatis*. The earliest surviving edition,[3] the second of 1647, gives us NUN DANKET ALLE GOTT (*E.H.* 533).[4] A credible tradition says

---

[1] D. F. Tovey, *Essays and Lectures* (1949), p. 172.
[2] *Ibid.*, p. 342.
[3] If it does survive. It was in the hands of Frere when he prepared his *Introduction* in 1909. It may not have survived two world wars.
[4] The tune has suffered many minor alterations in modern use. The *Companions* (*S.P.D.* at 350, *H.C.H.* at 29, *C.C.P.* at 42) give the original version.

that it was sung at the Peace of Westphalia which ended the Thirty Years' War in 1648.[1] It is not inappropriate that *Praxis Pietatis* should be ushered in by this tune, which epitomises all that that collection stood for, suavity, vitality and universality.

The third edition of 1648 contained AUF, AUF, MEIN HERZ, a tune made famous, and without alteration, by Bach (Ex. 74). Another collection of his, *Geistliche Kirchenmelodien* (1649), gives us the magnificent melodies, SCHMÜCKE DICH (*E.H.* 306) and HERR, ICH HABE MISGEHANDELT (Ex. 73). The fifth edition (1653) of *Praxis Pietatis* brings to light JESU MEINE FREUDE (*S.P.* 544)[2] and NUN DANKET ALL UND BRINGET EHR (*E.H.* 421). In the same year he contributed to Runge's *Christliche Lieder* JESU MEINE ZUVERSICHT (*E.H.* 282)[3] and HERR DEINEN ZORN (*E.H.* 223).

Of the same school as Crüger was Johann Schop (*d.* 1664), town director of music at Hamburg. Schop's most celebrated tunes are WERDE MUNTER (*A.M.* 500/276, cf. *E.H.* 418), which became the chorale in Bach's 'Jesu, joy of man's desiring', and ERMUNTRE DICH, which was used by Bach in his *Christmas Oratorio* (post-Bach version at *C.P.* 551). These, with LASSET UNS DEN HERREN PREISEN (Ex. 76), seen in their original versions, show a freer rhythm than Crüger usually employs, but the same melodic coherence and shapeliness; this last characteristic can be discerned equally from the modern post-Bach versions. In WACH AUF, MEIN GEIST (Ex. 77), however, we have an idiom which Crüger did not affect. Here is one of the many chorales of this period which, forsaking the primitive rhythmic subtlety, replace it by the juxtaposition of two different rhythmic schemes. This, upon which we commented under Schütz above, is exactly parallel to the new style of juxtaposed melodies.

Christoph Peter, Cantor of Güben (1626–69) makes his first appearance in 1665 with *Andachts Zymbeln*, from which come IHR GESTIRN, known here as CHRISTOPHER (*E.H.* 304), and a delightful alternative for JESU MEINE FREUDE (Ex. 78). From his later *Arien*, of 1667, comes a springing tune, DAS HERRLICH, preserved without alteration at *E.H.* 182. We have here still Crüger's discipline, but a freer and more popular idiom in line with the developing technique of song-writing.

---

[1] Not to these words, but to 'Herr Gott, dich Loben Wir', translated in the *Chorale Book for England* (1863), No. 183, *H.A.M.* 509, 'Lord God, we worship Thee'.
[2] Not vitally altered (see the Companions).
[3] A tune with a long history (see *H.A.M.* at No. 4).

When Crüger died in 1662, the authorities at St Nicholas, Berlin, followed their fathers in appointing another young man, Johann Georg Ebeling (1637–76) to succeed him. In Ebeling we have perhaps the finest flower of the gracious and poised song-style that the Crüger school produced. Ebeling's tunes, published in 1666 with a book confined to hymns by Paulus Gerhardt, have an attractive and youthful brightness (see VOLLER WUNDER, *E.H.* 256, WARUM SOLLT ICH, or BONN, *C.P.* 81, and MERKT AUF, Ex. 79).

Crüger's successor as editor of *Praxis Pietatis* in its eleventh (1664) and twelfth (1667) editions was Christoph Runge. He was succeeded by Peter Söhren, who was in charge from the thirteenth (1668) to the nineteenth (1678). DIES IST DER TAG (Ex. 80, cf. *E.H.* 138 (ii) is a bold tune preserving certain ancient rhythmical conventions; its first phrase (repeated) is in the primitive ambiguous rhythm, its last pair in modern triple rhythm. This and GUTE BÄUMEN BRINGEN (*E.H.* 72)[1] are examples of Söhren's own style. NUN LASST UNS GEH'N (Ex. 81), which may be compared with the lovely Dresden setting at *E.H.* 104, is an example of what he included in his book from other hands—it is not marked as his.

Johann Rudolph Ahle (1625–73) of Erfurt and Muhlhausen is celebrated as the composer of LIEBSTER JESU (Bach version at *E.H.* 336), originally called JA, ER ISTS, DAS HEIL DER WELT. His greatest tune, also immortalised by Bach is ES IST GENUG (Ex. 82), from *Arien Dritte Zehn* (1668)—an extremely simple tune deriving an almost overpowering rhetorical force from its first phrase, consisting simply of four slow notes ascending in whole tones. Many other composers set this hymn, but none with such economy. The force of the first phrase will be appreciated if the reader realises that ES IST GENUG is a hymn written on the sixth word from the Cross, 'It is finished'.

Of the more flexible kind, but still superbly economical in resources, is HAST DU DENN, LIEBSTER (*E.H.* 536),[2] from the Stralsund book of 1665, set in *Praxis Pietatis* (1668) to LOBE DEN HERREN, by whose title it is usually known. This tune is too celebrated to need further comment. A great tune in the old Crüger style from the 19th (1678) edition of *Praxis Pietatis* is Jakob Hintze's ALLE MENSCHEN MÜSSEN STERBEN (*E.H.* 128).[3]

---

[1] Original version reads the last line A-F-E-E-D in triple minim-crochet rhythm (*S.P.D.* 466).

[2] The version in *E.H.* is from the *Chorale Book for England* (1863), the harmony by Sterndale Bennett. Originally, bar 4 ran G-A-B, and bar 11, F-E-D; the fourth phrase was B-A-G-G-F-G-A. But the rhythm is unchanged except for dotted rhythm in bars 2, 3, 8 and 9.

[3] Originally in 8.7.8.7.8.8.7.7, adding low D at the end of phrase 2 (4), and repeated notes at the ends of phrases 5 and 6.

These tunes show the manner in which the austere but not forbidding style of Crüger was perpetuated in *Praxis Pietatis* and associated books.

Other tunes showing the characteristics of the Crüger school will be found, virtually unaltered, in *E.H.* as follows: AUS DER TIEFE (73), HEIL'GER GEIST (76), CHRISTE DU BEISTAND (160),[1] SEELENBRÄUTIGAM (272), JESU, JESU, DU MEIN HIRT (655), and GOTT DES HIMMELS (132).

Mysticism and Pietism

The qualities we have specially observed in the Crüger school of chorales—strong, syllabic melody, and firm metrical rhythm, while they make up a noble and catholic hymnodic diction, both lyrical and strong, represent a reaction against certain tendencies whose beginning we have already encountered. This school of composers accepted an idiom far more lyrical and song-like than that of the primitive chorales; but the song-quality in such tunes as GOTT DES HIMMELS (*E.H.* 132) and SEELENBRÄUTIGAM (*E.H.* 272) is the popular song not the professional song, the song of public praise rather than of amusement.

But another style was gaining ground, and ultimately defeated the Crüger style. This we have called the style of professional song or song for amusement, and it was greatly encouraged by the remarkable development in Lutheran piety after the Thirty Years' War.

The effect of that war was, of course, to break down the national organisation of the Lutheran church, to throw the local church, and to a great extent, the family and the individual, upon their own religious resources. This gave great encouragement to the cultivation of mysticism, pietism and later quietism, those essentially individualistic forms of piety which, in turn, gave rise to curious sects and enthusiasms.

First came mysticism, of which the pioneer was the German philosopher Jakob Boehme (1575–1624). His most distinguished works were *Aurora* (1612) and *Der Weg zu Christo* (1624). The thesis which involved him, after the publication of the former book, in proceedings for heresy, was that true religion lay in a direct personal intellectual revelation from God. Man's last end was 'unification' with God; man and God are basically of the same substance. This cut clear across Lutheran teaching and Lutheran churchmanship. For Luther, the

---

[1] Matthaus Appelles von Löwenstern (1594–1648), composer and author of this hymn, was one of the heroes of the Thirty Years' War (see *S.P.D.* at No. 349). To read the original of this tune from *E.H.* (i) delete all triplet-marks, (ii) omit the suspended note at the ends of phrases 2 and 3 and in phrase 4, (iii) read phrase 4—F-G-G-F-G and phrase 5, E-F-D-C-D, each in the pattern minim-crotchet alternating. For Löwenstern, see S. H. Moore, *Sursum Corda* (Independent Press, 1956) ch. 2.

pilgrim's road leads from the state of *Ungnade* (not-grace) to that of *Gnade* (Grace)—that is, he must travel from familiar country across a frontier into wholly unfamiliar country. For Boehme, the journey lies in a straight line to a goal within the familiar country. There is in his theology a denial of that 'otherness' of God which Luther, following Augustine, so sternly stressed; and there is also a virtual denial of the necessity of the Church.[1]

The divisive effect of the Thirty Years' War added to the attractiveness of this approach for many Lutherans, and the result was a wave of mysticism, a surge of popular devotion to Christ, which is excellently exemplified in the hymns of Paul Gerhardt (1607–76), the 'Charles Wesley of Germany'. Another effect of this was for a time to open the frontier between Protestant and Catholic, so that in the 1650's we have a spate of music and verse from Protestant and Catholic books whose religious affiliations are not deducible from their styles; one of the outstanding Catholic-convert poets of this generation was Johann Scheffler (1624–77), who became known as 'Angelus Silesius' and, in collaboration with Georg Joseph, produced a collection called *Liebesflamme* (1657), to which we shall have to attend.

Only a little later came the movement of Pietism under Philip Spener (1635–1705). Spener was an ordained Lutheran pastor, who founded in 1670 the 'Collegium Pietatis' in Frankfort; this was to be the focus of his movement, whose aims were, briefly, the study of scripture in domestic bible-classes ('*ecclesiolae in ecclesia*') emphasis on philanthropy, missionary effort, and good works in general, a large share in church government for the church members, a sympathetic and uncensorious attitude towards unbelievers, a training which placed personal piety above doctrinal orthodoxy, and a preaching method which exalted the homely and practical above the rhetorical virtues. The theology of pietism thus fell away from high churchmanship, fled from contradictions, ignored tensions, and concentrated upon goodwill. As a result, the 'ecclesiolae in ecclesia' became, even during Spener's lifetime, so unruly in enthusiasm and so prone to indiscipline and even moral laxity that he had to suppress them.[2]

It happened that one of the most enthusiastic followers of Spener was Joachim Neander (1651–81), with whom we shall have something to do. This brought together pietism and the Reformed (Calvinistic) church in Germany. During the next century the persistence of

---

[1] Encyclopaedia Britannica, s.v. *Boehme*, 11th edn., Vol. IV.
[2] *Encyclopaedia of Religion and Ethics*, s.v. *Pietism*.

pietism produced a climate in which Moravianism was able once again, after two centuries of relative obscurity, to flourish under Zinzendorf.

The public praise of Germany was thus very strongly influenced by pietism and its attendant forms of devotion; and just as pietism was essentially private piety, so pietist music was essentially private music, the music of the cultivated music-room, derived from that of the salon and the opera-house.

The way was already prepared. Ex. 83, DIE GÜLDNE SONNE, indicates what was going on in the byways as early as 1648. In this tune we have every evidence of the new operatic technique. M. Weyda published in 1643 a version of EIN KIND GEBOR'N (*E.H.* 44) with a similar extensive flourish at the end (Zahn 592).

The most distinguished figures of the 'mystical' period, the period of the ascendancy of Gerhardt before Spener appeared on the scene, were Georg Neumark (1621–81) of Hamburg, Georg Joseph (fl. 1657), Johann Scheffler (1624–77) of Breslau, and A. Hasse of Frankfort.

Neumark we know best for his strongest and most congregational tune, WER NUR DEN LIEBEN GOTT, which we call NEUMARK (*E.H.* 458). You would hardly suspect from that tune that UM DEN LIEBEN FRIEDEN (Ex. 84), with its melodic breakdown and trifling chromaticisms, lay in the background. Joseph we know as the composer of the original of our ANGELUS (*E.H.* 266—named after Angelus Silesius, of course);[1] but that comparatively demure tune has to join hands with the astonishing overture-and-first-movement melody, GEH AUF (Ex. 85). It is seldom even in this style that we hear dotted breves and quavers in the same tune. Scheffler included in his *Liebesflamme* the original of 'O Love who formest me to wear' (*E.H.* 460) and, also, some popular melodies, no doubt arranged by himself. Of these we have CULBACH (*E.H.* 286) and KEINE SCHONHEIT (*E.H.* 586).[2] But when the Muse was seriously at work, Scheffler wrote in the style of DEIN EIGNE LIEBE (Ex. 86). Hasse produced another, and quite distinct, *Liebesflamme* in 1659, from which we quote two tunes, WIE SCHMECK ES SO LIEBLICH (Ex. 87), with its preposterous *coloratura*, and O ELEND JAMMER (Ex. 88), a remarkable experiment in tonality.

It will be obvious why we describe all this as 'private music'. It was never intended to be congregational; it is domestic sacred song. But the point here to be stressed is the poverty of the craftsmanship in so many of these tunes. This we have not encountered before. The

[1] See *H.A.M.* at Hymn 30, *S.P.D.* at 42, *C.C.P.* at 632.
[2] Cf. HELFER MEINER ARMEN SEELE, *E.H.* 648, a simple example of the two-movement style.

ancient idiom of the chorale is now far behind, and the attractive idiom of the opera is more difficult to use than these ecstatics realised. These are melodies whose architectural and tonal defects are only thinly veiled by added harmony.

Our sketch of the history of Lutheran devotion will have prepared the reader to be told that it was this pietistic style, with flowing and song-like melody, which eventually won the day. Most fortunately, it fell into the hands of a group of really capable musicians, and although the chorale, in the form in which we have known it from Luther to Crüger, is doomed, we have in the next generation a series of religious songs of quite unparalleled grace and beauty.

Joachim Neander, the firebrand of Reformed pietism,[1] published in 1680, within a year of his death at thirty, his *A und Ω Glaub- und Liebesübung* ('*A.B.C. of Faith and Love*'). This contained over sixty tunes of his own, mostly in a simple, square and unsophisticated style. Best known to us are UNSER HERRSCHER (NEANDER, *E.H.* 380),[2] MEINE HÖFFNUNG (*S.P.* 442, *C.P.* 417), and WUNDERBARER KÖNIG (GRÖNINGEN, *C.P.* 224).[3] O SÜNDER DENKE WOHL (Ex. 89) is a noble tune in more serious vein.

But in J. W. Franck (1621–88), doctor of medicine and musician at Hamburg, we have a genuine master of the dance-like and lyrical style. His KOMM SEELE (*E.H.* 486) is now well known in this country; although we always set it to confident and happy hymns, it was originally a Passiontide melody, clearly intended to be sung quite slowly. DAS GROSSE LICHT (Ex. 90) is more flexible and more obviously a solo song. SEHT, WIE WECHSELN (Ex. 91), from a later collection, is more complex, with a rhythmic break near the end which jerks the tune out of its tranquillity.

ZEUCH MEINEM GEIST (Ex. 92) is worth quoting both for its exquisite lyrical melody and also because few would suspect it as the origin of a very square and uncompromising tune known to us as ST GREGORY (*E.H.* 49).

The solemn style returns in WER NUR DEN LIEBEN GOTT from the Hamburg book of 1690, which is the original of WIN-CHESTER NEW (*E.H.* 9: compare Freylinghausen's version at *Church Hymnary* 377) and in O GOTT DU FROMMER GOTT (Meiningen, 1693), the original of our BREMEN or MUNICH (*E.H.* 195 and *C.P.* 351). From the *Dresden Kirch- und Hausbuch* of

---

[1] Do not fail to read his biography in the *Companions*.
[2] Originally, the last two lines break into triple time, minim and crotchet alternating regularly.
[3] Originally, phrases 7 and 8 were written in notes of double length, making them an inverted development of the opening phrase; and the last phrase repeats the penultimate, but an octave lower (in key C).

1694 we have NUN LASST UNS GEH'N (*E.H.* 104), SO GIEBST DU (*E.H.* 515), and STRAF MICH MICHT, the original of our WURTEMBURG (*E.H.* Appendix 12).[1] The great Darmstadt *Gesangbuch* of 1698 gives us ZEUCH MICH, ZEUCH MICH MIT DEN ARMEN (original of *E.H.* 204)[2] and the arrangement of DIE WOLLUST DIESER WELT which appears as O GOTT DU FROMMER GOTT at *S.P.* 621[3] and in the Bach Cantata of that name. JESU DEINE LIEBESFLAMME (Ex. 93) is quoted in order to show the fallibility of these later sources; its initial dignity is sadly let down in its penultimate phrase.

Along with these the reader may turn to ES IST KEIN TAG (*E.H.* 521), LIEBSTER IMMANUEL (*E.H.* 41, founded on a dance), ST LEONARD (*E.H.* 527), WURZBURG (*E.H.* 127), SCHÖNSTE HERR JESU (*E.H.* 323) and to Gastorius's famous WAS MEIN GOTT THUT (*Church Hymnary* 544) for further examples of the smooth and rounded style of the chorale in this period.

This song-style was brought to its finest fruit by two composers, Johann Anastasius Freylinghausen (1670–1739) and Johann Sebastian Bach (1685–1750). Freylinghausen must close this chapter; Bach must have one for himself. Freylinghausen, like Neander and many others, was a minister-musician. He allied himself with the younger generation of Pietists, and became their greatest hymnodist. His fertile genius was capable of tunes in many styles, and a glance at his *Geistreiches Gesangbuch* in its early editions between 1704 and 1714 shows his versatility. The tunes of his known best to us are, of course, those written in his more public and dignified style, and many of these are arrangements by him of older tunes. DAS IST MEINE FREUDE (*E.H.* 97), DEN DES VATERS SINN GEBOREN (*E.H.* 218) and JESUS IST DAS SCHÖNSTE LICHT (*E.H.* 247) are his own; JESU MEINES GLAUBENS ZIER (*E.H.* 118), NICHT SO TRAU-RIG (*E.H.* 358), MORGENGLANZ (*E.H.* 374) and GOTT SEI DANK (*E.H.* 552), come from other hands but are known to us in his versions.

But characteristic of lyrical style in which the great majority of his tunes are written are the tunes we quote at Exx. 94–7. These tunes are in pairs. The first two are settings of WAS DER GOTT THUT, published respectively in 1704 and 1708. The earlier tune is delectable, but misses a metrical subtlety in the words—a change from three-pulse to two-pulse measure. This is rectified in the more solemn later

---

[1] Originally, in 7.6.7.6.3.3.6, repeating first phrase, omitting penultimates in phrases 2 and 4, and fourth note of phrase 3, and adding passing note between notes 2 and 3 of phrase 1, and antici-patory notes at cadences of phrases 2 and 4.
[2] See *S.P.D.* at 210.
[3] See *S.P.D.* at 621. The first two notes in the first quotation should be semiquavers.

tune. His provision of two tunes for MORGENSTERN, IM FINSTERN NACHT (Exx. 96–7) seems to be pure generosity, for although they are so different in style, it is impossible to judge which is the more attractive. The earlier tune has the undoubted distinction of packing more music into twenty-seven syllables than any other successful tune in the repertory.

We have now set the stage as best we may for the appearance of J. S. Bach. The song-idiom now holds the field undisputed. Bach's arbitration between the chorale and the song provides a notable scene in the story of hymnody.

11

JOHANN SEBASTIAN BACH

THE truth about Bach may be broadly told by saying that, contrary to popular belief, he never composed a chorale. Two kinds of hymn tune come from Bach—his original songs and his chorale-arrangements. But Bach will only be understood in this context if it be made clear at the beginning that his technique and vocabulary of composition had nothing whatever in common with the traditional chorale technique. He follows and crowns Freylinghausen; that is, he moves in the tradition of the sacred song which has been for two or three generations in clear opposition to that of the chorale. Bach must be thought of as a consummate composer who, with the true humility of the great, knew when he was not wanted. Clearly conscious that he had nothing to add to the rich store of popular hymn tunes, he added nothing.

Bach's original tunes, of which Ex. 98 is characteristic, and three more of which are to be found at *E.H.* 100 (NICHT SO TRAURIG) and 499 (ZUM FRIEDEN) and *A.M.*(*R*) 422 (LAUS DEO), are all from the Schemelli *Gesangbuch* of 1736. Of the sixty-nine tunes in that book, forty come from earlier sources, and the number of tunes wholly to be given to Bach is variously estimated at twenty-nine (Spitta), twenty-four (Wüllner) and twenty-one (Eitner and Sanford Terry). One of the dubious ones is ICH HALTE (*E.H.* 644), but its irresistible 'My heart ever faithful' style suggests *prima facie* a case for giving it to the master. These tunes will best be studied in C. Kennedy Scott, *Fifty Sacred Songs, Taken mainly from the Schemelli Hymns* (*O.U.P.*, 1944); in the Preface to that work Kennedy Scott pays tribute to Franz Wüllner (1832–1901) who added mean parts with exquisite propriety to Bach's treble and bass in his edition of 1901. The flexible and poised melodies, the work of the world's greatest melodist, are so well known and so outstanding in their technical achievement that they need no further comment here. Let it simply be understood that this is Bach's native style. It was imitated by a whole school of song-writers, and examples of these appear in our collection at Exx. 130 and 131.

But it is Bach's chorale-arrangements that are usually referred to as 'Bach chorales'. These were collected by C. P. E. Bach in a definitive edition of *Choralegesänge* in 1769, and can be obtained in a number of modern editions. The Peters edition of 371 chorales is very service-able. They originate in the oratorios, Passions, and cantatas. In the larger works they correspond to the 'chorus' in Greek tragedy, bring-ing the congregation 'on to the stage' in causing them to utter a commentary on the drama which is being enacted. The connection between this and the practical devotion of Pietism is as clear as that between their words (and for that matter the words of the Schemelli songs) and the private devotion of that tradition. These elaborate chorales are arrangements of popular hymns, and his use of HERZLICH THUT MICH VERLANGEN (*E.H.* 102) in both the *Passions* and in the *Christmas Oratorio* suggests that it was one of the most popular at the time.

The cantatas take various lines; sometimes a chorale is introduced at the end of a cantata to provide a congregational response. Some-times the cantata (as JESU MEINE FREUDE) will be an extended commentary on the chorale in variation form. Whether the chorale be the subject, or a summary of the cantata, it is not an ordinary hymn tune designed for liturgical use.

Consider now WACHET AUF as it is given at *E.H.* 12 and at Ex. 17, and observe what Bach does with it.

(1) The tune appears in a steady four-in-a-bar rhythm.

(2) It is harmonised tonally in the major scale.

(3) The harmony is in the contrapuntal style of the eighteenth century, not of the sixteenth.

(4) The melody is slightly modified.

To take the fourth point first, observe how Bach introduces a passing-note before the highest note of the melody in both cases where it occurs ; and how he brings the melody down step-wise at the end of the second phrase, eliminating Nicolai's drop of a fifth. Both modifications tend in the direction of congregational ease, and may be derived from popular inaccurate use.[1] On the other hand, Bach removes the small ligature from Nicolai's opening; in the eighteenth century context (in which the common chord has so much more prominence in musical architecture) this sounds more dramatic; it would not have done so to Nicolai's ears.

Diatonic counterpoint is characteristic of Bach's easier arrange-ments, and it may be examined in many chorales preserved in *E.H.* (see Nos. 36, 68 70 (i), 86, 102 (i), 118, 128, 138 (i), 148, 232, 329, 417, 478 and 510.)

---

[1] Note that Mendelssohn in *St Paul*, having no thought of congregational use, keeps the older form of the melody in the second phrase.

On other occasions, in contexts of heightened tension and pathos, Bach uses chromatic counterpoint, of which examples can be seen at *E.H.* 70 (ii), 102 (ii), 110, 462 and 622. More dramatic than any of these is Ex. 67b. We will pause upon this.

Making bold to summarise Bach's profound grasp of harmonic diction in a sentence or two, we suggest that Bach's versions must always be looked at as counterpoint, not as a series of passionate chords. The four chords closing the first phrase of Ex. 67c, containing that curious sliding alto part, can be broken down into the following contrapuntal paraphrase:

The alto part is chromatic because four parts have to do duty for five, and the alto here has to jump from the alto to the second treble in the paraphrase. But in the paraphrase all five parts are entirely logical, their combination of the tonalities of B flat minor and major producing the tension between them. The whole tune could thus be broken down into simple phrases; we must not do that here, but we will ask the reader to observe that in the fifth phrase of the elaborate setting of HERZLICH THUT MICH VERLANGEN (*E.H.* 102(ii)), what is really happening is this:

the other parts filling in appropriate harmony between these major and minor scales in contrary motion. This contrapuntal technique is

the heart of Bach's pregnant harmonic effects. Chromatic harmony, so greatly abused in the nineteeth century, has no inherent vice, but that if it be not sound counterpoint, as was Bach's, it will sound like a man asking his neighbour, in accents appropriate to *King Lear*, to pass the mustard. Of this we shall have more to say in its place.

Bach's treatment of a modal tune is well exemplified in Ex. 8b. This was his normal method of harmonising a Phrygian tune; the ambiguity of its tonality remains, but the moving parts under the final chord (cf. *E.H.* 102 (ii)) are an assertion of classical orthodoxy; Bach compromises in the Phrygian cadence by making two cadences, the first primitive, the second classical:

But although Bach's idiom often removes much of the salt from the modal scale, his bold juxtapositions of major and minor tonality are his compensation for this.

In sum, then, Bach removes rhythmic irregularities and modal archaisms, compensating this by counterpoint and by rich use of tonalities. He never alters the internal structure of the tune; he clothes a sixteenth century melody in eighteenth century court dress. It was later editors, admiring the rhythmically square versions of Bach, who performed operations for prefrontal leucotomy on the chorales, radically altering their very personality. The results of this are listless tunes like NARENZA (*E.H.* 518), ST MICHAEL (*E.H.* 27), FRANCONIA (*E.H.* 370) and DIX (*E.H.* 39). Neither this kind of unscrupulous editing nor chromatic inanity can be paralleled in Bach; but both were abuses of techniques in which he was a master.

12

ENGLISH PSALMODY FROM THE RESTORATION TO THE EVANGELICAL REVIVAL

THE Restoration of the English Monarchy in 1660 marked a decisive victory for those political and religious forces to which Puritanism had been implacably opposed. The sympathies of King Charles II were cosmopolitan and anti-Protestant; he and his court were less interested in that intense English patriotism of Elizabethan puritanism than in the importation of the riches of Continental culture. The same predispositions which caused the King to send his choirboys (like Pelham Humfrey) to study in France caused his courtiers to lay upon the Puritans persecutions comparable with those which the Puritans had lately laid upon the Royalists.

Psalmody, therefore, suffered first an eclipse and then a transformation. Very little invention is to be found after Ravenscroft (1621); the Puritans were too busy with the Civil War to need new psalm-tunes. After 1660, the Puritan congregations, dispersed under the Clarendon Code of 1662–4, were naturally content with their musical heritage; indeed, in some localities hymn-singing of any kind would have attracted undesirable and dangerous publicity. The new music of the Restoration held the field.

This new music, technical descriptions of which will be found in any textbook of musical history, was 'new' in construction, in technique, and in social atmosphere. It employed less the devices of polyphony, or contrasting and concurrent rhythm and melody, than those of 'monody', the contrast being between melody and bass, and between melodies treated consecutively. It was 'new' in technique because of the new prominence given to instruments playing solo or in 'concert', at the expense of voices. It was 'new' in social implication because of the new attention directed at the individual singer or player. The new music writes a full-stop to the age of anonymity and of amateur chamber music; from now on it matters who wrote the music and who is singing it. The immediate distinction between the verse-anthems of the Restoration composers and the often anonymous polyphony of the 'school of Tye'[1] in 1560, points this contrast.

This had a considerable effect on the practice of psalmody. It was indirectly responsible for a new concession to humanism in the composition of hymns, from Benjamin Keach (1673) and Isaac Watts

---

[1] E.g. the anthem of disputed authorship, 'Lord, for Thy tender mercies' sake'.

(1707) onwards. It means that we find an increasing number of signed hymn and psalm tunes. It imparts at once a new technique of psalm-tune writing. And yet the old anonymous principle dies hard, and whereas among the Restoration group and the singers of the Evangelical Revival we find the tunes mostly signed, in the psalm-books of the Anglicans and Puritans we continue to identify tunes chiefly by their sources until close on 1800. But, conversely, we frequently find, as the eighteenth century advances, a concession to professionalism in the more or less indiscriminate ascription of tunes to distinguished composers—HANOVER to Handel, for example, and BURFORD (*E.H.* 447) and WALSALL (*E.H.* 13) to Purcell.

Hymns in the Seventeenth Century

We may now recapture the atmosphere of the *Old Version* by recalling the rule that public praise must be confined to the psalms. The exceptions to this are few, but they were important. In the *Old Version*, in 1562, the following compositions were added to the Psalms:

> The Ten Commandments (C.M.).
> A Prayer following the Commandments (4 verses, C.M.).
> The Athanasian Creed (C.M.).
> The Twelve Articles (Nicene Creed) (C.M.).
> A Prayer to the Holy Ghost to be sung before the Sermon (5 verses, C.M.).
> The Humble Suit of a Sinner (C.M.).
> The Lamentation of a Sinner (D.L.M.).
> The Lamentation (C.M., slightly adapted at *E.H.* 84), 'Preserve us, Lord' (Prayer for defence against Pope and Turk, always sung to the original of ERHALT'UNS, HERR, *E.H.* 68).

The last is omitted, and four other pieces are added, in the Scottish Psalter of 1635. Ravenscroft adds, in 1621, certain 'Hymns Spirituall', including 'A Psalm before morning prayer', a similar psalm for evening, and a hymn beginning 'Give peace in these our days'. In 1677, Playford adds these : 'After Communion' (C.M.), 'For Sunday', 'Morning Hymn' (translation of 'Iam lucis', *E.H.* 254), and the curious hymn whose melody and first three verses we quote at Ex. 99, 'On the divine use of Musick'. It should be noted, however, that none of the seventeenth century compositions now used as hymns (*E.H.* 93, 411, 427, etc.), were in use as hymns during that century.

The *Old Version* with these additions continued unchallenged until 1696, when Tate and Brady produced their *New Version* (from which come *E.H.* 367 and 502, and, from the additional material after the psalter, *E.H.* 30). The *New Version* makes no advances on the *Old* in metrical scheme, but its appearance was the beginning of a resistance to the infallibility of the *Old Version* which was soon carried further in defying the all-sufficiency of the Psalms. During the next decade or so there appeared *The Divine Companion* (1701, 2nd edn. 1707), *Tune-Supplement to the New Version* (1708) and John Bishop's *A Set of New Psalm Tunes* (about 1711). *The Divine Companion* was a hymn-book containing several original pieces for devotional singing, with some important new tunes.

Hymn Tunes, 1685-1738

One of the earlier Restoration composers to come into our story is Benjamin Rogers (1614–98), whom we know for his HYMNUS EUCHARISTICUS (*E.H.* 328), written while he was organist at Magdalen College, Oxford, for the 'Magdalen Tower Hymn'. He may also be the composer of O GOD OF LOVE (*E.H.* 446), ascribed in the *Divine Companion* to 'B.R.'. A new psalm tune of this period that has become very popular is ST JAMES (*E.H.* 341), from the special edition of the *New Version* printed for St James', Westminster. But the Restoration style is most nobly epitomised in DAVID'S HARP (*E.H.* 378), from the *Divine Companion* (1701 edition); its third phrase is a characteristic Restoration utterance, and the graceful dignity of the whole is worthy of Humfrey and Wise at their best. Michael Wise himself is credited with an austere tune of psalm-like diction called CONGLETON (*E.H.* 312).[1]

The most celebrated composer of the *Divine Companion* group is Jeremiah Clarke (1659–1707).[2] His tunes are always perfectly regular in rhythm, and often have a very free and captivating melody. The most striking melody is his KING'S NORTON (*E.H.* 419)—forty-four notes for twenty-eight syllables spread over an octave and a half. UFFINGHAM (*E.H.* 434) is another lovely example. ST MAGNUS (*E.H.* 147, not quite certainly his) and BROCKHAM, its first cousin (*E.H.* 220) are in the syllabic idiom, but more quick-moving and continuous than the psalm-tunes. BISHOPTHORPE (*E.H.* 408), not published until 1786[3] is another characteristic flowing tune. BROMLEY (*C.P.* 297) contains the first example (separated by many

---

[1] *La Scala Santa* (1681), which gives us COLERAINE (*E.H.* 333) is a collection of devotional renderings of the Psalms of Ascent, translated by Hugh Hare, first, Lord Coleraine, from the Italian of Loredano, with a translation, also of Loredano's commentary. It stands therefore outside the main tradition of psalmody, but is an excellent example of the new Catholic sympathy of Restoration England. COLERAINE was set in L.M. to Psalm 122.

[2] His birth date is variously recorded in hymn books 1669 or 1670. Dent's *International Cyclopaedia of Music and Musicians* gives 1659 with evidence.

[3] H. Gardner, *Select Portions of the Psalms of David* (1786).

years from the next) of a key-change within a hymn tune. TUN-
BRIDGE (*E.H.* 88), unpretentious in appearance, is full of pregnant
Restoration idiom, especially at the end of the third phrase.[1]

By contrast, William Croft (1678–1727), whose tunes appear in the
Supplement of 1708, affects a more staid and psalm-like idiom.
EATINGTON (*E.H.* 639) is commonplace enough. CROFT'S 136th
(*E.H.* 565) has a psalm-like solidity and change of rhythm. HAN-
OVER (*E.H.* 466) is a springing tune in the new-found triple measure.
BINCHESTER (*E.H.* 398) is more yielding, like Clarke. ST ANNE
(*E.H.* 450) seems to be thrown together from phrases in Lawes (see
above, page 67), and is, despite its popular associations, an al-
together less satisfactory tune. Its ascription to Croft is uncertain.[2] [3]

John Bishop, the eldest of the three (1665–1737), is different again.
Three tunes show the range of his technique. ILLSLEY (*E.H.* 61) is a
suave psalm-tune in the new style, but beginning and ending with
double-length notes. LEICESTER (BEDFORD) (*E.H.* 322) is a
massive tune on the largest scale in the 'Old 112th' metre.
CHICHESTER (Ex. 100) is a charming, dance-like measure for the
122nd Psalm, marked in 1719 for Watts's 'How pleased and blest was
I', one of the comparatively few tunes in our Examples for whose
revival and popularity we could plead with eloquence. It will be
observed how frequently we have already encountered the device of
melodic sequence, a new and serviceable device for extending a
melody in continuous style which becomes useful once the devices of
irregular rhythm have been lost.

Finally, we must mention the EASTER HYMN as it appears,
monumental and Croft-like, in *Lyra Davidica* (1708), and as it is
retained at *E.H.* 133 (i).

During the years 1711–1738 several important collections were
published. The early collections contain a great deal of fine music;
these contain music of a more variable merit. In the psalter of John
and James Green (Nottingham, 1715), the standard of psalmody is,
on the whole, notably debased. ECKINGTON (Ex. 101) shows a
typical C.M. tune from that source—supremely dull by psalm-tune
standards. Another, FERRY, appears at *S.P.* 39. From later
editions come serviceable new tunes, CROWLE (1724, *E.H.* 463)
and ALTHORP (1744, *A.M.*(*R*) 249). But a glance at Exx. 102 and
103 will show how the Greens conceded to popular taste a line of

---

[1] Also from this source—LAMBETH, *E.H.* 340.

[2] See *C.C.P.* at 52.

[3] Also from the *Supplement:* ALFRETON (*E.H.* 240), and FOLKINGHAM (*E.H.* 558) and
Croft's (probably) ST MATTHEW (*E.H.* 526).

east resistance when dealing with the more austere forms of ancient psalms. Many old tunes are roughly handled in their book.

Perhaps the finest of these psalters in Chetham's (1718), which gives us BURFORD (*E.H.* 447), and a large number of other springing tunes in the new square idiom. Chetham does not deal much in triple time. His setting of PSALM 98 (all his tunes are unnamed) to be seen at Ex. 104 looks like a rewritten version of ST MATTHEW (*E.H.* 526, perhaps by Croft); in its own right it is a fine tune. His new tune for the *Old Version*, PSALM 126, in its very extended Genevan metre (Ex. 105) is a fine example of continuous and clean melody in the new style. He has also a curious new tune which uses HANOVER as an alto part.

In the 1720's we have Anchors's Psalter of 1721 (WALSALL, *E.H.* 13), John Church's *Introduction to Psalmody*, *c.* 1723 (SURREY or CAREY'S, *E.H.* 491, with those words), Timbrell's *Psalms*, *c.* 1725 (BEDFORD, *E.H.* 83), Wilkins' *Psalms* (STROUDWATER, *E.H.* 158), and the appearance of odd single tunes like LONDON (*E.H.* 297), published separately *c.* 1720 with Addison's 'The spacious firmament'.

In the succeeding decade there is Tans'ur's great collection of 1735, which gives us some familiar tunes, BANGOR (*E.H.* 300), EPSOM (*E.H.* 506)[1] and ST ANDREW (*C.P.* 393). Gawthorn's *Harmonia Perfecta* of 1730, compiled for the Presbyterians at King's Weigh House Chapel, London (now a Congregational church), contained many melodies of the more florid kind, but among them two tunes of great dignity, ELTHAM (Ex. 106) and BUCKLEBURY (*S.P.* 189). Then there is the collection of the Dorset precentor, William Knapp, of Wareham, which gives us WAREHAM (*E.H.* 475), SPETISBURY (*C.P.* 396) and DORCHESTER (or WESTON FAVELL) (Ex. 107), one of the earliest of the florid tunes from which the Methodist tunes took their lead.

These tunes show the movement from the surviving psalm-tune idiom, successfully revived in Croft, played-out in Green, to the flowing, dance-like tune of the Evangelical Revival. We have not yet entered on the period of that revival, but Knapp has prepared the way in his WESTON FAVELL, which, after singing the verse conventionally indulges in a repeat of the words for the sake of the tune. In our next chapter we shall find the music taking charge completely, at the expense of any kind of literary sense. But for the moment let it be established that the period between the Toleration Act, of 1689,

---

[1] *E.H.* has not traced it to its first source.

and the conversion of Wesley, in 1738, was a period of tension for the psalm-tune in which, just as in Germany (where Lutheran piety had in a precisely parallel way swung away from theological churchmanship towards individual devotion) the lyrical and in the end the irresponsible style won. But we had no Freylinghausen, and no Bach to redeem for us the graces of secular melody.

13

THE EIGHTEENTH CENTURY, 1738–1801

The Evangelical Revival

All great historical figures are sons as well as fathers; they grow out of history as well as influencing it. John Wesley was raised up for two purposes—to awaken the conscience of the nation from the moral and religious apathy into which it had fallen since the days of religious civil war, and to fight the gross and gloomy Calvinism which had overtaken so many of the best religious minds. The eighteenth century was a time when religious neurotics abounded; document after document tells of the enthusiasms, the holy terrors, and the fundamental tensions and perplexities of religious minds. On the one hand, Presbyterianism was degenerating into an arid unitarianism which could not save a sinner: on the other, fanatical Calvinism, emphasising reprobation and diminishing divine love, removed from many sinners the notion that they could be saved. These were the things against which Wesley saw in himself the champion.

His message, Lutheran rather than Calvinist, that upon an act of faith any man could be sure of salvation, cut clean across classical artificiality, social snobbery, ecclesiastical immobility, and the despair of the poor. It stimulated, over two generations, the souls of the poor to self-respect and those of the wealthy to compassion. Himself an industrious and widely cultivated man, Wesley offered a challenge to the source of emotion and action rather than to the intellect. He dealt neither in philosophical theology nor in gentle mysticism. The country was ready for revival. Men were ready for direction. John Whitefield, Martin Madan, John Cennick, Selina, Countess of Huntingdon and, of course, his own brother Charles were waiting for the word from John Wesley.

Apart from divine providence and human helpers, the strongest agent for the propagation of Wesley's message was music. Here again, Wesley found waiting for him just the material he could best use. WESTON FAVELL (Ex. 107) is a musical herald of the evangelical Revival.

A message that is to be forced home to individual men can be immensely strengthened by simple, melodic music; this is especially true of a message which proclaims certainty and safety rather than the

91

answers to sophisticated intellectual problems. Exuberant melody is the natural accompaniment and expression of that ecstatic individualism which was the popular reaction to Luther and Wesley.

The parallel between Luther and Wesley is here not accidentally drawn. Wesley was in close touch with the Moravians of Herrnhut, who, under Count Nicolaus von Zinzendorf (1700–61), had in the 1730's been bringing alive Luther's message in a new way. 'If you want to hear pure psalmody', said Wesley 'go to Fulneck and hear them sing "Think of thy Son's so bitter death" '. And although that particular hymn was associated with VATER UNSER (*E.H.* 462), the music which he heard when he visited the Moravians must have had much in it of the lyrical felicity of the lately-developed sacred songs of Germany. He translated many German hymns for English use; his brother Charles made some interesting experiments with German metres in his hymns (such as 'Come, let us anew', *C.P.* 639).

And, in this country, Wesley had two musical inheritances to draw on; one was psalmody, which he used and used gladly. But to replace the dying art of psalmody there was the Restoration music to be drawn on, and, even more potent for his particular ends, the new Italianate operatic style of Handel. That which was mediated to Lutherans by Scheffler and the mystics was mediated in a maturer form to Englishmen by Handel and his followers. So, just when he wanted it, here was a fresh, entertaining, full-blooded musical idiom waiting for him.

Now Handel himself only touches the fringe of our story, in as much as he wrote three tunes for hymns of Charles Wesley—GOPSAL (*E.H.* 476), CANNONS (*E.H.* 66) and DESIRING TO LOVE (*Methodist School Hymn Book*, 1950, 33). But his influence far transcends these three tunes. The point at which it bears most heavily on the style of hymnody is in that it presupposes the complete ascendancy of music over verbal rhythm. Plot, libretto and verbal stress, each at its own level is subjected to the demands of music; and the music is now fully wedded to dance-rhythms in square and symmetrical units, cast in monodic form, and impregnated with the atmosphere of virtuosity. English drama is only now beginning to recover from the assault made by opera upon its verbal resources.

So the music develops autonomous forms, and the words fit in where they can, bound by dance-measure on the one hand, and clogged on the other by long coloratura passages. Handel's genius can compensate the great loss that this entails by his superb grasp of large musical forms and his keen appreciation of the dramatic power of the new music. The music may distort the rhythm of the words, but it always illuminates their general sense. In the hands of lesser men this illumination is frivolous and irrelevant; in Handel it is as good as a spiritual commentary.

The first Wesleyan tune book, in which immediately we shall see Handel's influence, is the *Foundery Collection* of 1742. It is a small collection of forty tunes, designed to supplement the available psalm tunes. It gives us our first anglicised versions of WINCHESTER NEW (*E.H.* 9) and SAVANNAH (*E.H.* 135). But it also gives us ISLINGTON (Ex. 108), a magnificent piece of music which introduces a verbal repetition of four syllables near the end. Another remarkable tune from this book is JERICHO TUNE, covering sixteen lines of Short Metre (see *Methodist H.B.* 819, or, for an abridged version, *E.H.* 381); it is the earliest of many Wesleyan adaptations from Handel (taken from the march in *Riccardo Primo*, 1727).[1] In this collection we have a zestful vigour which only later degenerated into triviality.

In 1745, John Wesley met a Covent Garden bassoonist of German extraction named J. F. Lampe (1703–51). He writes thus in his *Journal* under 29 November, 1745:

> I spent an hour with Mr. Lampe, who had been a Deist for many years, till it pleased God, by the *Earnest Appeal*, to bring him to a better mind.

In 1746, Lampe edited the music of a slim book entitled *Hymns for the Greater Festivals;* he shows himself in this a first-class musician. Two of his tunes are still in common use, KENT (or DEVONSHIRE or INVITATION) which in its unornamented form (*E.H.* 347) is a striking piece of musical architecture,[2] and DYING STEPHEN (*Methodist H.B.* 411). Ex. 109 furnishes an example of his work in its original form. He has the instrumentalist's fondness for ornament, but the bones of his tunes are always strong enough to carry any weight. In this tune we see at once the instrumental tradition and the operatic-aria technique, which are so characteristic of Methodist tunes. But we shall find few in later collections to complete with these for solid and serious musical content.

Now this technique, applied by a master, produces music of surpassing grace. But there is another side to the picture, which we begin to see in contemplating Ex. 110, which shows what Whitfield's *Divine Musical Miscellany* of 1754 made of TALLIS'S CANON.

---

[1] ST THOMAS (*E.H.* 11) is the second quarter of another tune in S.M.D.D. called HOLBORN (A. Williams, *The Universal Psalmodist*, 1763: the abridgement was in *The New Universal Psalmodist*, 1770). HOLBORN, repetitive and discontinuous, but not repeating any words, is a tune of much less merit than JERICHO TUNE.

[2] See *C.C.P.* at Hymn 395 for an extended comment.

The contrapuntal magnificence of the CANON was lost on a constituency which had become entirely melody-minded. BRENTWOOD, as the tune is called in the Methodist age, became a most popular tune, and survived a hundred years in this form. It wears its new clothes, you may say, rather gracefully; but you may question the legitimacy of taking it out of Tudor costume at all.

With CARLISLE (Ex. 111), from Madan's *Collection* of 1769, (not to be confused with the CARLISLE, *E.H.* 190, which appeared in a later collection of his), we begin the steep descent. Madan's greatest work was done at the Lock Hospital, one of the great charitable institutions founded under Wesleyan influence. This one was founded in 1746; the Foundling Hospital in 1741, and the Magdalen Hospital in 1758. This philanthropic work paid a dividend in the direction of hymnody. Here and at other such institutions were gathered numbers of young people who provided excellent material for singing-classes. The tune under review comes from a collection of psalms and hymns made for the Lock Hospital, which was expanded into the celebrated *Lock Hospital Collections* of 1769 and 1792. If you want to see Methodist practice in hymnody, you can hardly do better than examine the contents of the Lock Hospital book and see what Madan tried out, with great success, on his ready-made congregations. CARLISLE is jaunty, entertaining, and youthful in spirit, but entirely lacks that profundity which would come from a less inert harmonic scheme.

Never mind. The rhythmic singability of the tune is the thing. Ex. 112, RONDEAU, is a good extreme example (1769) of a tune in a dance-form accommodating the words at their own risk. PASTORAL HYMN (Ex. 113) takes things further by producing a lovely tune which grossly mis-accentuates its words. Its slight chromaticism and its very slow-moving bass made Carey's original tune for these words (*E.H.* 491) look old-fashioned. But try to sing *E.H.* 491 to it.

Another example of classics in modern dress (one of a very large number in the 1769 book) is BRIGHTHELMSTONE (Ex. 114). The reader who is familiar with the atmosphere of post-Handelian England will appreciate how much more entertaining this version would seem to the popular taste than the original. It must be remembered that the ordinary man could not have known Bach's *St Matthew Passion* version at that date.

In MANSFIELD (Ex. 115) we have a totally irresponsible tune, much melody over minimal harmony, amiable part-singing but intellectual stagnation. Things are getting worse for the musically sensitive.

94

But the grand climax comes in DENMARK (Ex. 116), one of a number of anthem-hymns which appeared in this and subsequent collections. Here at last the musician throws restraint to the winds. Each verse goes to a different tune, and the tunes are varied as one might expect them to be in a cantata. It is all cast on a tonic-dominant scheme, and there are dozens of these extended tunes in the Wesleyan repertory of the day. DENMARK is one of the earliest and one of the most celebrated. Another similar tune is AMESBURY, of which we quote simply the last verse (Ex. 117). How revealing are those honeyed parallel sixths and thirds. Here are harmony and counterpoint taking the line of least resistance. Here is a speedy flight from all challenge and tension.

Lest it be thought that the unfortunate children of these institutions were brought up on nothing better than this watery diet, we may recall some classics that have come from these sources. MOSCOW (*E.H.* 553) and CARLISLE (*E.H.* 190) are in Madan. The first mention of AUSTRIA (*E.H.* 393) as an English hymn tune is its being marked as the proper tune for 'Praise the Lord, ye heavens, adore him' in a leaflet appended to the 1796 edition of the *Foundling Hospital Collection*. William Riley edited *Parochial Harmony Corrected*, including tunes of his own and others by distinguished contemporaries, so that that book becomes the source for ST BARTHOLOMEW (*E.H.* 81), WESTMINSTER, by Nares (*A.M.* 267/334), ST EDMUND, by Gilding (*E.H.* 171) and ST BRIDE, by W. Howard (*E.H.* 74). BATTISHILL, reduced to a shadow of its former glory at *E.H.* 596,[1] comes from the same source. Barthélémon's MORNING HYMN (*E.H.* 257), altogether more questionable in merit, comes from another Asylum book.

Now John Wesley was not personally pleased by the developments of Wesleyan music in the direction of irresponsible vulgarity. Taste travels far between the *Foundery Collection* (1742) and even Thomas Butts's *Psalmodia Sacra* (1753), the classic ordinary source for Methodist music. In 1761, John and Charles Wesley published *Select Hymns for Christians of all Denominations*—one of the later original collections of Charles's—and in its Preface, John counsels his readers to 'learn *those* tunes before any others', referring to those in the *Foundery* book and in Butts. 'Sing them exactly as they are printed', he goes on, 'sing lustily; sing all of them; sing modestly; sing in tune; above all sing spiritually.' Later, in the Arminian

---

[1] See *S.P.D.* at 538 for its delicious original.

Magazine for 9 June, 1779, Wesley writes more sorrowfully:

> 'There is no Timotheus of modern times to excite us to fury of tears, or calm us to sleep by his art . . . The grand reason seems to be that the whole nature and design of music is altered. The ancient composers studied melody alone, the due arrangement of single notes, and it was by melody alone that they wrought their wonderful effects. But the modern composers study harmony, which, in the present sense of the word, is quite another thing—namely, a contrast of various notes, opposite to, and yet blended with, each other . . . Ever since counterpoint has been invented it has altered the grand design of music, so it has well-nigh destroyed its effects . . . Our composers do not aim at moving the passions, but at quite another thing: at varying and contrasting the notes a thousand different ways. What has counterpoint to do with the passions?'

This is the shrewd comment of an amateur. Do not press his technical terms. By counterpoint he means, you may be sure, tonic-dominant bass, fugal interludes, and complicated melodies. By counterpoint not touching the passions (and by the passions he means, as he goes on to make clear, the judgment, the will, the source of decision and action) he means the notable facility with which this flamboyant but trivial music by-passes the intellect and induces a false sense of spiritual well-being. And we may well pause over the rubbish that appears in later Methodist books and wonder, if this was thought fit to print, what popular underworld of religious music there may have been, what were the ARIZONAS and DEEP HARMONYS and RIMINGTONS of Wesley's day that may have added fuel to his wrath.

But we must accept the fact that the generous and hospitable Gospel of the Wesleys allowed a good deal of bogus music to slip in. That which found apt expression in the confidence of LEONI (*E.H.* 646) and the superb yet popular grandeur of HELMSLEY (*E.H.* 7) may well have slipped into a vulgar idiom before noticing that it had done so.

Wesleyan hymnody, in general, runs to repetitive melody—sometimes requiring the repeating of four syllables, sometimes repeating whole groups of lines.[1] This was sometimes varied by attaching to the verses, or to the hymn, a coda of Alleluyas or 'Praise the Lords'. For an example of this, see the originals of FALCON STREET (*S.P.* 635)[2], and HARTS (*E.H.* 177)[3]. Its melodies were often instrumental in contour, making melodic use of the common chord and introducing the rising major sixth as a vocal interval. The earliest tune we have found employing this interval, now such a commonplace, but in Palestrina's time so unheard-of, is WINWICK in the *Lock Hospital*

---

[1] MILES LANE (*E.H.* 364), BROMSGROVE (*E.H.* 144) and HELMSLEY (*E.H.* 7) show that repetition does not always lead to triviality.
[2] *S.P.D.* at 635.   [3] *S.P.D.* at 520.

Collection (1769). Another 1769 tune, EXETER (not *E.H.* 528, which however, also appears under another name in the 1769 book) includes a bassoon obbligato (a tribute to the late Lampe?).

There are high spirits in all these tunes; but when one reads a series of them, and imagines them in use in large numbers, the borderline between high spirits and hysteria, between the warmth of the Gospel and the fever of enthusiasm, becomes more and more difficult to trace.

Non Wesleyan hymnody

The influence of this idiom was, of course, widely felt. There was in those days no Methodist denomination. The official prohibition against singing hymns, not removed in the Church of England before 1821, was in those churches which sympathised with Wesley quietly ignored. The dissenting denominations eagerly embraced the new music from the beginning. And so, alongside the development of the 'straight' psalm tune we have the spreading of the Methodist idiom.

Throughout the century the tradition of the strong psalm-tune continues. At each stage we can see new examples of psalmody, influenced by post-Restoration music only in its metrical discipline and melodic freedom, and by its increasing use of triple time. A quick glance at the following well-known tunes will show how bravely the tradition is maintained.

YORKSHIRE (*E.H.* 21), (*C.P.* 82), 1750.
MONTGOMERY (*E.H.* 632), (*C.P.* 503), 1762.
ISLEWORTH (*E.H.* 557), 1765.
DIBDIN (*E.H.* 433), doubtful.[1]
ABRIDGE (*E.H.* 369), (*C.P.* 53), *c.* 1770.
DARWALL'S 148TH (*E.H.* 517), (*C.P.* 5), 1770.
MANCHESTER NEW (*E.H.* 168), (*C.P.* 49), 1774.
LEWES (*E.H.* 250), (*C.P.* 86), 1774.
JACKSON (*E.H.* 210), (*C.P.* 277), 1780.
BLACKBOURNE (*E.H.* 456), *c.* 1784.
WARRINGTON (*E.H.* 263), (*C.P.* 255), 1784.
TRURO (*E.H.* 420), (*C.P.* 57), 1789.
ST STEPHEN (*E.H.* 337), (*C.P.* 47), 1789.

More remarkable and interesting in their various ways are UNIVERSITY (*E.H.* 93), the new version of EASTER HYMN (*E.H.* 133 (ii)), OXFORD NEW (*A.M.* 522/196),[2] HARINGTON (*E.H.* 85, originally a glee), and certain tunes carrying the names of distinguished

---

[1] This has been found in an undated and at present unidentifiable early copy of Watt's *Divine and Moral Songs* set to music. It is obviously about a century older than it is stated to be in *S.P.D.* at 254.

[2] Originally, this melody was embellished with many more passing notes and anticipatory notes. Its last line was marked for repeat, and for the 'second time' of singing the last two bars lead down to the low keynote. The original will be found in Smith. It is only hinted at in the elaborate version at *B.B.C.* 528.

composers—William Hayes's MAGDALEN COLLEGE (*E.H.* 457), NEW 113th (*E.H.* 298) and HAYES (*Oxford Hymn Book* 16) and Boyce's PORTSEA (*A.M.* 767/124), CHAPEL ROYAL (*A.M.* 262/316), KINGSLAND (*E.H.* 554) and HALTON HOLGATE (*A.M.* 640/186).[1] The Common time tunes among these observe the syllabic rule, conceding a few passing-notes; the triple time tunes move freely within their regular bars; but there is no repetition. They are all in the direct descent from Clarke or Croft.

But if we look at Isaac Smith's *Collection of Psalm Tunes* (undated, *c.* 1770), one of the classic sources of the time, the first home of ABRIDGE and OXFORD, we find alongside these powerful and gracious eighteenth century tunes a whole series of tunes in the Wesleyan idiom. DENMARK (Ex. 116), for example, is there. PUTNEY HEATH (Ex. 118) is among those which appear there for the first time—a florid and hearty tune whose only claim to interest is its unusual rhythmic ellipsis on the first 'Alleluia'. There is also the first appearance of the tune PROSPECT (known to us as 'Drink to me only') set to 'There is a land of pure delight'. The 5th edition of 1790 contains FOUNTAIN (Ex. 119).

The indications that we gain from this quite undenominational source are that the same congregations, Methodist and non-Methodist, would be content both with the older and with the newer idiom. But what we also find in these books is that they were impatient of the classical, irregular, gaunt psalm-tunes of the Ravenscroft period.

Ex. 120, RICHMOND, in its truncated form a famous tune (*E.H.* 375: Edward Miller in 1802 is responsible for the short version) is a clue to contemporary practice. Composed by the Rev. T. Haweis (1734–1820) for his own hymn, 'O thou from whom all goodness flows'[2] has a certain haunting beauty; but its repetitions come naturally to its composer. Haweis was an anglican clergyman of Methodist sympathies (one of the founders of the London Missionary Society); he is the typical source of this kind of music.

John Rippon's tune book of about 1796 is the first tune book of the Baptists. It takes over much of the material we find in Smith, Harrison, and other sources. Its taste is catholic. Of its new tunes, TIVERTON (*C.P.* 271) is a restrained example, and HEPHZIBAH (Ex. 121) a florid one; it is not without its deficiencies as a setting of 'There is a land'. SOUTHWARK NEW (Ex. 122) is an example of the operatic, decadent Handelian style. MANNING, (Ex. 123) for

---

[1] Originally, in sevens, as *E.H.* 201, but with the suspensions and passing notes as in *A.M.*
[2] An altered version is at *E.H.* 85. The original is at *C.P.* 766.

'When I survey', arranged from 'He shall feed his flock' is one of a group of tunes taken from Handel in this book; another is MESSIAH, from 'I know that my Redeemer liveth'; they indicate the continuing ascendancy of Handel.

Ralph Harrison's collection of about 1784 and *Psalmodia Evangelica* of 1789, the 1792 *Lock Hospital Collection*, the collection made by Milgrove for the Countess of Huntingdon's congregation at Bath, *c.* 1769 (HARWICH, *S.P.* 161, MOUNT EPHRAIM, *E.H.* 196, HARTS, *E.H.* 177), these, together with the works of individual composers like John Hatton (DUKE STREET, *E.H.* 167) and Sir George Smart (WILTSHIRE, *E.H.* 502) are other sources which show side by side the restrained and the florid idiom.

Thus, then, runs the story of the Methodist descent into triviality and the valiant defence set up by the traditional style as mediated by the Restoration composers.

North of the Border

Dr Millar Patrick called the eighteenth century in Scotland 'The Great Eclipse'.[1] By this he meant the failure of the 1635 *Scottish Psalter* in its object of raising standards and enlarging the repertory. Indeed, the reaction in the other direction was immediate. The Psalter was revised in 1650, and its first tune book, printed at Aberdeen in 1666, contained only twelve tunes, which are the twelve Common tunes of 1615 (page 79) adding BON ACCORD and ELGIN, and omitting LONDON TUNE and GLASGOW.

> By the end of the century these twelve were canonised as embodying the accepted and inexpansible musical tradition of the Church of Scotland. At that point the canon was closed, and it remained fixed for a long time subsequently.[2]

Some attempt was made to introduce more of the classical tunes in Bruce's Psalter of 1726; but despite this Dr Patrick writes elsewhere that Highland churches at that time restricted their range to no more than five tunes.[3] The only Scottish psalm tunes in common use dating from the mid-eighteenth century are ST PAUL (ABERDEEN) (*E.H.* 561) and GLASGOW (*C.P.* 322). Another recently revived is THE BURGHER'S RANT or MONTROSE (*C.P.* 33), first published in 1793, but probably (as is noted in *C.C.P.* at that number) dating back to about 1746. This tune employs the same device of far-striding melody that is notable in BALFOUR (*E.H.* 186), another Scottish tune of the same date.

---

[1] *Four Centuries of Scottish Psalmody* (O.U.P., 1949), chapters x and xi.
[2] Millar Patrick, *op. cit.*, p. 111.
[3] Millar Patrick, *Handbook to the Church Hymnary* (O.U.P.), *Supplement* (1935), p. 94, under the tune YORK.

This sufficiently indicates the climate of Puritan worship in eighteenth century Scotland. No influence was brought to bear on Scottish hymnody from South of the Border until at a late stage the Methodist hymnody began to make its impact. The result of this was a gradual awakening of Scotsmen to the possibilities of revived psalmody. The early precentors and choirmasters, of whom the pioneer was Thomas Channon,[1] had a hard fight of it; but eventually the revival came. Some of its effects will be seen in three groups of tunes. First, there are the frankly Methodistical tunes.[2] Then there are regular psalm-tunes in the milder style, like MARTYRDOM (*E.H.* 367), possibly of secular origin, STRACATHRO (*E.H.* 445) and ORLINGTON (*Scottish Psalter* 93), all of the early nineteenth century, and between them forming a family from which in the next generation (*c.* 1872) sprang the now ubiquitous CRIMOND (*C.P.* 729).

Thirdly, there are a few anthem-like tunes from the distinguished partnership of the minister, Andrew Mitchell Thomson (1778–1831), and precentor, Robert Archibald Smith (1780–1829) of St. George's Church, Edinburgh. Thomson contributed ST GEORGE'S, EDINBURGH (*C.P.* 730) to the book he edited in 1820 for his church before Smith came as precentor. To the later 1825 edition, Smith, then in office, contributed INVOCATION (*Scottish Psalter* (1929) 189). The former of these, a classic in Scotland, is an astonishing combination of platitude and power. The latter is rather more sentimental and Methodistical in its diction. ST GEORGE'S, however, wonderfully combines the high spirits of Methodism with the dourness of Scottish puritanism. Another celebrated precentor was Neil Dougall (1776– 1862), who wrote among other things the magnificent pentatonic tune KILMARNOCK (*E.H.* 542) in the early nineteenth century, thus bringing back into use the scale of traditional Gaelic music, which has since been put to powerful use by the modern composer Kenneth Finlay (1882–   ), in such tunes as AYRSHIRE (*C.P.* 388), FINNART (*A.M.*(*R*) 583) and GLENFINLAS (*C.P.* 704).

But Scotland was able to withstand Methodist excesses more stoutly than England; the historical and theological reasons for this are obvious, and the whole story is too well told by Dr Patrick to need repetition here. Scottish hymnody is now very much alive, as the revised *Church Hymnary* (1930) shows; it has been given a new lease of life by the mid-nineteenth century authorisation of hymns in the Church of Scotland.

---

[1] See Millar Patrick, *Four Centuries of Scottish Psalmody* (O.U.P., 1949), pp. 151 f. and 181 ff.
[2] Millar Patrick, *op. cit.*, p. 185, prints in full the melody of CLIFFORD, one of these Methodistical tunes. By the standards of contemporary Methodism in England, it is magnificent; but the effect of this style on the kirks may be imagined.

In general, then, we may comment on the Methodist style that it indicates a flight from reason and judgment. Its florid melodies, supported by minimal harmonic and contrapuntal movement, tend to become irresponsible. Let it be observed how, from end to end of these tunes, we find nothing so harmonically arresting as the cadences of BRISTOL (*E.H.* 6) or LINCOLN (*E.H.* 140), and the point is proved. Tonic and dominant had come to stay, and we have not by means heard the last of them, or of the Methodist style, by the year 1800.

14

THE EIGHTEENTH AND NINETEENTH CENTURIES IN GERMANY

THE last age of Lutheran hymnody need not detain us long. We are prepared for what we shall find. This chapter will trace its development from 1715 to 1855 and add a brief note on certain modern developments.

It is largely a story of decline. Primitive idiom in rhythm and mode has now finally given way to the bar-line and the major-minor key-system. As a result, everything will hang on the persuasiveness and coherence of the melody. This presented an almost insuperable problem to the chorale-composer. The new musical orthodoxy, based on dance-measures and the four-bar group, consorts ill with the wayward metre of some of the great German hymns. Moreover, while a composer of the stature of Mozart can pack a symphonic movement with rhythmic interest, setting up new tension between the four-bar unit and the rhythm of his phrases (as he does in the minuet of his fortieth Symphony), there is not much scope for this in the restricted form of the hymn tune. On the other hand, we do find here and there a chorale wrongly and misleadingly barred, and when we find it we rejoice in the persistence of the old style of unsymmetrical rhythm.

We take up the tale at 1715, in which year Christian Frederick Witt (c. 1660–1716), Kapellmeister at Gotha, published *Psalmodia Sacra*. His STUTTGART (*E.H.* 40)[1] is typical of the solid and unpretentious idiom he affected. GLÄUBIGES HERZE (Ex. 124) shows his handling of a more complex metre, and already we have an example of bar-lines arbitrarily and misleadingly placed. There is in Witt the ghost of Crüger but no more substantial influence than that.

Johann Ludwig Steiner (1688–1761), 'Stadttrompeter und Gesang-lehre'—state-trumpeter and music teacher at Zurich, affects a more hearty style. We have GOTT WILLS MACHEN unaltered at *E.H.* 253. GOTT DES HIMMELS (Ex. 125), his replacement of Albert's own tune (*E.H.* 132) is another very simple tune in the modern, square style, economical but not musically profound.

It begins to look as if the German chorale may have to choose between being dull and being vulgar. Cornelius Dretzel (1698–1731)

---

[1]   The tune is here given in Gauntlett's melodic arrangement (see *S.P.D.* at 84 for the original).

makes, in his collection of 1731, a brave effort to defer the dilemma. His WELT ADE, a good solid chorale, has been adapted to make our DRETZEL (*E.H.* 281), and his DER DU BIST DREI IN EINIG-KEIT survives, altered from triple to duple rhythm, at *H.A.M.* 36. Both these are sound tunes. WOHL MIR, JESUS (Ex. 126) is another example of his plain but purposeful style, and ACH GOTT, VERLASS MICH NICHT (Ex. 127) has the genuine power of the classical chorale; it is very nearly the last of the great German tunes, so we must make the most of it.

Johann Balthazar König (1691–1758), of Frankfort, produced an ambitious book in 1738 containing 361 new tunes. One of these is the delightful original of FRANCONIA (*E.H.* 370).[1] We quote WAS WILLST DU DICH at Ex. 128 to show in what difficulty a reason-able melodist of this period finds himself when faced with a hymn in one of the old complicated metres; König copes fairly well, but what could not a Walther or a Reinigius have done with this?[2]

Thommen's *Erbaulicher Musikalischer Christen-Schatz* (1745) contains the original of BATTY (*E.H.* 105), a simple tune originating in the Moravian community at Herrnhut.[3] J. B. Reimann (1702–49), of Hirschberg) who gives us O JESU (*E.H.* 406) is softer in idiom and altogether more vulnerable. THRÄNET, IHR AUGEN (Ex. 129) is a characteristic tune of his, in a metre common in secular songs of the age. The tune itself suggests a folk-song, with its insistent melodic figure beginning so many bars with repeated notes. Another tune with almost certainly secular origins, and in the same metre, is WAS LEBET, WAS SCHWEBET (*E.H.* 42),[4] from a MS collection made by J. Reinhardt, at Üttingen, in 1754.

In UN DU ALLEIN and SO JEMAND SPRICHT (Exx. 130, 131) we have a continuation of the lyrical style of Freylinghausen and Bach. J. F. Doles[5] was a successor of Bach at the Thomaskirche, at Leipzig; C. P. E. Bach was of his school. Both these tunes have great merit as instrumental or operatic exercises; but their style dies out fairly soon with the passing of the leisured and courtly forms of

---

[1]   See *S.P.D.* at 455, or *C.C.P.* at 206 for the original (Zahn 2207).

[2]   König is the principal intermediary between ZEUCH MEINEM GEIST (Ex. 92) and ST. GREGORY (*E.H.* 49).

[3]   See Zahn at No. 1304.

[4]   This tune has an interesting history. If the *E.H.* version be compared with that at *A.M.(S)* 746, it will be found that the tune has been turned from the authentic to the plagal position (for this terminology, recall pp. 33 ff). This is just what would happen if a singer found he had started his tune too high and had to transpose its third phrase down an octave, compensating this by a leap upwards when the notes fell once more within his range. This is the strongest evidence for its secular origin. Probably, the 'authentic' (*E.H.*) version came first. Both are written down by Reinhardt. I can recall no other example of a tune being tonally turned 'sides to middle' in this fashion, but the process is a natural one.

[5]   DA CHRISTUS GEBOREN WAR (*E.H.* 287) is in Doles' book, but is probably not of his composition (see Zahn).

sacred music consequent upon the social and religious disturbances of the middle eighteenth century.

We may mention Johann Christoph Kuhnau (1735–1805), of Berlin, better known in works of larger dimensions, as a characteristic editor and composer of the next generation. He has passed on to us a fine tune by J. F. Rötscher (EXODUS, *A.M.* 501/605) from his edition of 1790. He, like König of the earlier generation, is also responsible for the simplifying of several tunes which have passed in their later form into English use; one of these is BATTY (*E.H.* 105) which we now sing almost exactly in Kuhnau's form.

Christian Gregor (1723–1801) is the most distinguished musician of the newly-revived Moravian movement; but he is a cautious musician whose tunes do not greatly advance the story.

The next example, WIE SCHNELL VERFLIESSEN (Ex. 132), comes from Switzerland. Johann Heinrich Egli is a product, like Steiner, of Zwinglian Switzerland, and like Steiner he affects a very popular idiom. This tune is a good sample, with its amiable and unchallenging idiom. Switzerland, drawing freely on popular styles, produced some notably trivial styles in chorale-composition. One of the very few strong tunes from Switzerland in the eighteenth century is that which we know as LUCERNE (*C.P.* 8); but even this has its moment of indecision just after the half-way point.

J. A. P. Schultz (1747–1800) is best known to us as the composer of WIR PFLÜGEN (*E.H.* 293); this is not strictly a chorale but a semi-secular song in Germany, and is regarded as a hymn tune only in this country. But he wrote or adapted many tunes, of which the most celebrated is DER MOND IST AUFGEGANGEN (Ex. 133). Almost equally popular in present-day Germany is IHR KINDEL-EIN KOMMET (Ex. 134); but this tune seems to have a close affinity with WO FINDET DIE SEELE (Ex. 135), which is marked in modern collections 'Irische Melodie',[1] and which is undoubtedly a German form of 'Home, sweet home'. This melody, in its German form, is typical of the easy-going music that speedily commended itself to congregations at this time.

It is, perhaps, in Christmann and Knecht's *Vollstandige Sammlung . . . Christenmelodien* (1799) that the gates are thrown wide to the popular idiom. We know Justin Heinrich Knecht (1752–1817) for the tunes we now call KNECHT (*E.H.* 452) and VIENNA (*E.H.* 500).[2] He contributed ninety-six other tunes to the 1799 book, and their general style is not unfairly represented by SCHMAL IST DER

---

[1] Deutsche Choralbuch, ed. R. Mauersburger, undated (about 1936), No. 206, where the ascription is 'Irische Melodie, Tübingen um 1834'.
[2] Originally, phrase 3, *n.* 2 is flattened.

PFAD (Ex. 136). STARK UNS, MITTLER (Ex. 137) is perhaps worse than his average, but not the worst of which he was capable. His partner, J. F. Christmann (who shares both of his dates) is little better (see PREIS DEM TODESÜBERWINDER (Ex. 138)). A not dissimilar idiom is that of H. G. Nägeli (Ex. 139), and of HARRE MEINE SEELE (Ex. 142), by the popular evangelist, César Malan, which is as popular in Germany as in France, the country of its origin. The shameless romanticism of Tcherlitzky (Ex. 141) and Bortniansky (WELLS, *C.P.* 382),[1] two Russian-descended composers whose music swiftly became popular in Lutheran circles, completes the tale.

We have here a close parallel to what happened in Methodist England. Germany had no Wesley, and the Lutheran tunes of the period do not indulge in endless repetitions of the words. But the cleaving to secular romantic music is the same; in the end, for Handel we simply substitute Weber. The tonic-dominant stagnation of the bass, the emphasis on seductive melody, are just the qualities in later Methodist music against which Wesley wrote so sternly. The composers and editors who let loose this music on their congregations were taking a line of universal concession and complaisance, and they infected Lutheran hymnody with a conventional romantic idiom from which it needed, literally and historically, the fulminations of Karl Barth and the Nazi persecution to separate it.

But, as in England, the more sober style is not quite lost. Johann Christoph Kittel (1732–1809) left a good collection of whose contents GROSSE PROPHETE (QUEDLINBURG, *E.H.* 245) is an adequate sample. Georg Peter Weimar (1734–1800) left a posthumous collection, published in 1803, which we remember for ALLGÜTIGER, MEIN PREISGESANG (*A.M.* 276/611). AUCH JETZT MACH GOTT (*E.H.* 550), comes from the same period and is in the same quiet style.

But, perhaps, the most important composer since König was Johann Gottfried Schicht (1753–1823). It was an ambitious gesture to publish in 1819 a book containing 191 new tunes of his own composition; and it was inevitable that there should be a wearisome repetitiveness of style and phrase from one to the other. But we may fairly judge ZU MEINEM HERREN (*E.H.* 119)[2] and SO HOFF ICH DENN (ASCENDIT DEUS, *C.P.* 427),[3] tunes of real beauty, and ICH KAM AUS MEINE MUTTER (MANNA, *A.M.* 314/389)

---

[1] See *C.C.P.* at this number for the original. The adaptation preserves most of its essential character.
[2] Originally, 11.10 thrice, the first pair of phrases repeated.
[3] Originally, 8.8.7.8.8.7.

is not far behind. Schicht's weakness was not open vulgarity but rather a kind of listlessness—no less a vice, but at least something of a change from Knecht and Nägeli. To show that English books do not contain his last word, we quote his two magnificent settings of WAS SOLL ICH, LIEBSTER KIND (Ex. 140 (a) and (b)).

With Conrad Kocher (1786–1872) we enter on the last stage of the story of Lutheran hymnody as we are telling it; it is a stage of reaction, mild in Kocher but more emphatic in his younger contemporaries, against romantic excesses. Kocher is normally remote in his manner, without danger of excessive passion. DIX (*E.H.* 39) is a recension of his TREUER HEILAND, which may be read in the original version at *Songs of Syon* 57; URQUELL ALLER SEELIGKEITEN (*E.H.* 640) and IN ALLEN MEINEN THATEN (*E.H.* 321) are from a later collection of his. The atmosphere here is cooler, but by no means bracing. See also Ex. 143.

Friedrich Filitz (1804–76) of Berlin left three tunes in his 1847 book that have become well known here. WEM IN LEIDEN-STAGEN we sing as he wrote it (CASWALL, *E.H.* 315)—it could hardly be simplified further. MORGENGLANTZ (CAPETOWN, *E.H.* 501) we sing in Monk's version, which only alters his last three minims[1] to five minims in order to accommodate a longer line. Our abominable but popular MANNHEIM (*E.H.* 426) is an adaptation by Lowell Mason of the more ambitious and rather impressive tune AUF, AUF, WEIL DER TAG ERSCHIENEN (Ex. 144). Filitz cuts to the bone all expenditure on inessentials—simple, syllabic and sometimes monstrous dull, he thus avoids most of the dangers of his time.

Two great hymnologists may properly close the story for us. Friedrich Layriz (1808–59), theologian and musician, did for Germany what G. R. Woodward at a later stage did for this country. He collected, and reproduced in their ancient versions, the best melodies he could find in the whole Lutheran repertoire, usually reharmonising them for four-part singing. He adds little new material, and the austere style of the new tunes he contributes can be gathered from INS FELD GEH' (*E.H.* 440) and MEINE HÖFFNUNG (Ex. 145).

Johannes Zahn is, in this field, immortalised by his monumental catalogue of Lutheran melodies, containing 8,806 different tunes, published periodically from 1888 to 1893. As a composer he was even less prolific than Layriz, but GOTTLOB, NUN IST DIE NACHT VERSCHWUNDEN (Ex. 146), with its graceful return to the primitive rhythmic and slightly florid idiom brings the tale neatly to a close.

---

[1] In the original, of course, crochets.

By way of epilogue, we may briefly deal with the developments of the last hundred years. The work of later nineteenth century composers which may occasionally be found in modern Lutheran books is sometimes corrupt, sometimes struggling towards a cleaner style. Paul Teichfischer (b. 1863) of Erfurt, Johannes Jehle (b. 1881) of Wurtemburg, and Johannes Wullschlegel (b. 1849) of Basel are perhaps the best of them. The reader who wishes yet to be convinced that the chorale has not lost its power to shock us, and that nothing new can happen in its development, is invited to look at the astounding tunes of Pastor Friedrich Mergner (1818–91) of Erlangen; they are scattered over the pages of Zahn, and constitute the most remarkable excursion into the romantic idiom to be found anywhere in the literature.

But although it might seem that the only answer in Lutheran hymnody to the corruptions of 1750–1825 was a negative and antiquarian one, there are signs at the present time that all is not lost. Lutheran congregations are being gradually weaned from the decadent idiom by the younger pastors; and the tiny hymn book, *Wehr und Waffen* ('Defence and Armour'), a paper-bound volume of forty-eight pages published under the threat of Nazi persecution some time after 1933, bravely challenges the supine conventions of past generations in its new tunes. It is proper that we should do honour to the heroic Bishop of Berlin, Dr Martin Dibelius, in quoting as our last Example one of the tunes he contributed to this book, HIER IST GEDULD UND GLAUBE, Ex. 147 for a hymn of his own. Here we have more than a reminiscence, possibly a genuine revival, of the folk song of fighting Lutheranism; more than an echo, perhaps a living return, of the voice of Löwenstern and Crüger. But the stream is necessarily a narrow trickle as yet, and present distresses have gone far to choke it out of existence in Germany. It is flowing freely, however, in Sweden, and it is impossible to believe that the immortal voices of the Lutheran chorale-composers have been silenced for good by the pressures either of nineteenth century vulgarity or of twentieth-century brutality.

15

THE EARLIER NINETEENTH CENTURY, 1801–61

THE nineteenth century in England is sharply divided into two parts by the publication in 1861 of the first music edition of *Hymns Ancient and Modern*. The earlier of these two parts is not, on the whole, a fertile field for this study, but it is punctuated by two dates of the greatest importance; one is 1821, the year in which, after great controversy in which James Montgomery and Thomas Cotterill, vicar of St Paul's, Sheffield, were actively engaged, Archbishop Vernon Harcourt, of York, caused the authorisation of hymns in the liturgy of the Church of England; the other is 1833, the year in which John Keble's Assize Sermon at Oxford inaugurated the Oxford Movement. But the full effect of both these momentous events is not felt until the second half of the century. In the first half we continue the story which we broke off at the turn of the century in Chapter 13.

We shall find three important new forces at work in this period. The first is the rise of the publishing house of Novello, founded in 1811 by Vincent Novello, and followed by a 'boom' in music publishing which made hymn books easier to publish and to obtain for whole congregations. The second was the rise, under such leaders as Joseph Mainzer (1801–51) and John Hullah (1812–84) of singing classes in England, and the choir-movement in Scotland, to which reference was made at the end of Chapter 13. The third force is a rising sophistication of public taste, which called for, and was provided with, hymn tunes in the romantic idiom of Weber and later of Mendelssohn rather than in the classical virtuoso-idiom of Handel. The consequence of this was closer attention to the possibilities of harmony for the sake of its sensational effects, at the expense of florid melody and, of course, to be distinguished from the contrapuntal application of harmony which was the distinguishing feature of Bach's technique with chorales.

The turn of the century left the English churches with a rich treasury of music in contemporary idioms, the psalm-tunes of the eighteenth century on the one hand and the Methodist tunes on the other. Both traditions continue, but during the new century they tend to become merged, the Methodist style becoming more restrained, except in strictly revivalistic contexts, and the Anglican style becoming more free. The tension by the end of the century is not between the psalm-tune style and the Methodist style, but between those, of every denomination (but notably of the Anglican) who were content with the new Victorian idiom and those who reacted violently against it.

The year 1802 saw the publication of two important sources, Edward Miller's *Sacred Music*, the last of his three important books, and Samuel Stanley's *Twenty-four tunes*. Miller in his three books gave us our present version of RICHMOND (*E.H.* 375), something like our present version of ROCKINGHAM (*E.H.* 107)[1] and the first printing as a hymn tune of AUSTRIA (*E.H.* 393). Stanley, precentor of Carr's Lane Independent Chapel and innkeeper of Birmingham, gave us SIMEON (*E.H.* 320), WARWICK (*S.P.* 513) and CALVARY (*E.H.* 530).

About this time we may date the composition of STOCKTON (*E.H.* 82), an admirable psalm-tune not printed in its original version before *E.H.* (1906), but popularised in an altered version by Dykes from the 1868 *A.M.* Other isolated tunes of excellent quality from the period are MELLING and RELIEF (*E.H.* 373, 497) from Fawcett's *A New Set of Sacred Music* (1822), Reinagle's ST PETER (*E.H.* 405) from a small collection of his own, dated 1830, and two tunes by William Horsley (1779–1858), BELGRAVE, from a collection of 1817 (*E.H.* 511), and HORSLEY from a later one of 1844 (*E.H.* 106). All these are excellent in their own kind, whether using the free idiom of the eighteenth century psalm-tune or a new-found reticence.

The Methodist tradition continued, and issued during this period in a large number of tunes which are in present-day Methodist circles a good deal more popular than either the classics of the 'Foundery' era or the wild tunes of the later eighteenth century. Examples may be found in the current *Methodist Hymn Book*—SAGINA (*c.* 1800), for instance (No. 371), JOB (*c.* 1801, *Additional Tune* 14), LYNGHAM (*c.* 1820, *A.T.*[2] 8) and DIADEM (*c.* 1840, *A.T.* 6). These, so commonly referred to as 'old Methodist tunes' are, in fact, the last examples of the old Methodist idiom—repetitive, florid, melodically seductive and harmonically trivial.

Two or three important collections of 1830–50 will provide what evidence we need of the development of public taste. The greatest influence of all was, no doubt, that of *The Psalmist*, edited by Vincent Novello (1781–1861), which was published in four volumes, each

---

[1] The original of this is a tune called TUNBRIDGE in fives and elevens (for Wesley's 'All ye that pass by'), published in 1786 (see *C.C.P.* at 131.)

[2] 'Additional Tunes' grouped in an Appendix at the end of the book.

containing a hundred tunes, between 1835 and 1843. Its two outstanding legacies to present day hymnody are Turle's WESTMINSTER (*E.H.* 441), there called BIRMINGHAM, and the arrangement of the Alleluias at the end of Purcell's 'O God, thou art my God' which it called BELVILLE but which we now know as WESTMINSTER ABBEY (*A.M.(R)* 620).

The book was a commercial venture in the new style, and had great success. It was preceded by a long Preface which set out the history of church music and the principles to which it should conform. This set the standard for those didactic and hortatory prefaces which always appear in books of this time, replacing those instructional ones, setting forth the rudiments of music, which grace their eighteenth century predecessors. Here is a brief quotation from it:

> Yet, with regard to singing as a part of the worship of God ... there has for some years prevailed such a disregard of the nature and design of that sacred service, as must excite astonishment and regret in the minds of those who can appreciate it aright. In the Churches there exists a lamentable indifference to its performance as a duty ... On the other hand, the Wesleyans and Dissenters, if not chargeable with *indifference* to its performance, have too generally degraded its quality, by the admission of light and trivial music ... To rescue this *heavenly* part of public worship, ... to recall and induce a relish for the chaste and dignified style of our ancient Psalmody: to invest that Psalmody with such additional attractions as are derivables from *Modern* Harmony, without injuring its essential qualities; and to introduce to more general notice the works of Modern Composers of established reputation ... are the principal designs of the present publication.

Here was a laudable object weightily set forth. It was unfortunate that there was yet no new musical vocabulary available that would enable that object to be more impressively achieved than it was in *The Psalmist*. With ancient tunes the editor is compromising, avoiding the more austere, and amending the more popular much less violently than did the Greens in 1715. As for modern tunes, apart from Turle's WESTMINSTER, he found nothing that has made any mark. TREVILYAN, a composition of his own (Ex. 148) is a happy example of his amiable style, well to be seen in several anthems of his that are still in use. His ALBANO (*E.H.* 327), by which he is today remembered, did not appear in *The Psalmist*. As for *Modern Harmony*, PORTLAND (Ex. 151) affords some notion of the way in which popular taste was veering—its harmony is here and there academically faulty, but there is no mistaking its seductive appeal.

The general style of the book is more restrained than this, and its new tunes are distinguished neither for strength nor for wild vulgarity. There is no doubt that the large number of repeating tunes that are here preserved are kept for the comfort of the older generation;

Novello says so in his Preface.[1] A number of German chorales are experimentally introduced, often in bowdlerised versions. The PASSION CHORALE appears in D.C.M., NUN DANKET in 7.6.7.6.D, SCHMUCKE DICH in 9.6.9.6.D. But (all honour to him), Novello includes NICHT SO TRAURIG (*E.H.* 100) and ICH HALTE (*E.H.* 644) in virtually their original forms.

Another book of similar, but less elevated style is the *Union Tune Book* (2nd edition 1842). This is the first tune book of the newly-formed Sunday School Union, and its chief legacy is the tunes of Thomas Clark (1775–1859), of which WARSAW (*E.H.* 386) and CREDITON (*E.H* 206) still remain in standard books. Clark was, as the former of these suggests, a practitioner of the florid idiom, and the book makes, apparently, less demands on that public taste which its Preface seeks to elevate than did *The Psalmist*.

The *Comprehensive Tune Book* of 1846 is of some interest as being an early effort of that indefatigable editor and composer, H. J. Gauntlett (1805–76). Once again we have a high-minded Preface:

> The compromise between popular feeling and a deeper sense of what is ours and right has been considered the best course . . . Strength, not delicacy—feature, not grace, has been the endeavour.

This book adopts the same general style as *The Psalmist*. It includes a group of ancient plainsong tunes, distorted of course, but remarkable for their appearance at all; it has the first common-time appearance of WINCHESTER NEW (*E.H.* 9), though this is not the version now used. It contains EIN' FESTE BURG in 888.888, and revives Gibbons's SONG 1, adding a syllable to each of its last lines to accommodate the metre of the Old 50th Psalm. It has much of the restraint of *The Psalmist*, and does not disdain long initials in some psalm-tunes; but it gives ground here and there, as in the first (and we suspect without regret the last) appearance of the anonymous JUDGMENT (Ex. 152).

Similar techniques may be found in Gauntlett's *The Hallelujah* (1849) and Hullah's *The Psalter* (1843). The story that all these books tell is of an attempt to elevate popular taste, to create interest in hymn-singing in home, church and school, and to restore some consciousness of the rich heritage of hymnody in English and in German history. They are all, it will be observed, *tune*-books. They do not contain the words, or not more than the opening verse, of hymns. The tunes are marked for use with certain hymns; but the era of the 'proper tune' and of the liturgical hymn book has not yet come. That is material for the next chapter.

---

[1] Page ix, col. 1.

For other respectable tunes of this period see *E.H.* 274 (i), 343 and 429, and for a very late tune in the homophonic 'Methodist' style, DISMISSAL, 523. This style was, and a debasement of it continued to be, perpetuated in the music of Sunday School Anniversaries, especially in nonconformist circles in the Midlands and North of England; DISMISSAL and DIADEM both come from this context.

Popular Classics

During the earlier years of the nineteenth century we pass the opening of a curious by-way in hymnody which has turned out to be a blind-alley, but which makes a not uninteresting field for exploration. The adaptation of instrumental classics for use as hymn tunes, which became a popular fashion, may be said to begin with *Sacred Melodies* (1812 and 1815), by William Gardiner, a Leicester stocking-manufacturer who was also a cultivated musician. His book contained a number of tunes from the eighteenth century classics adapted for use with hymns. He also compiled an oratorio, *Judah*, by setting English words to music adapted from Haydn, Mozart and Beethoven.

Few of Gardiner's adaptations have survived. FULDA or WALTON (*C.P.* 101), from a melody in Mozart,[1] ST POLYCARP (*C.P.* 268), from Pleyel,[2] and BELMONT (*C.P.* 671) also found as a popular song called 'The Ratcatcher's Daughter', all originate in tunes in Gardiner.

Just as the popularity of instrumental music for concert use (as distinct from chamber music for domestic use) grew naturally out of the development of oratorio and opera; so this practice of using instrumental tunes for hymns is an obvious extension of that of using melodies from *The Messiah*. But it is an illegitimate extension, because while you may reasonably adapt a song of one form to form a song of another form, the adaptation of instrumental music for vocal use is in practice fraught with danger. For one thing, instrumental intervals are not necessarily good for the voice; for another, instrumental music is increasingly at this date written in long paragraphs of some rhythmic complexity which need drastic pruning to be suited to hymn metres; and for a third, the instrumental movement is designed for concert performance, not for the hack-work of the hymn tune.

That last point has implications far beyond the immediate concern of William Gardiner. But in and just after his day we find a good deal of this adaptation of the classics, and further adaptations from

---

[1] See *C.C.P.* at 101. The tune is often erroneously attributed to Beethoven.
[2] This comes from Gardiner via S. S. Wesley and the *Bristol Tune Book*; (see *C.C.P.* at 268).

secular opera. Here is a list, not exhaustive, of adaptations of this kind:

From *The Psalmist* (1835–43): *Survives at*

ALSACE (250) arr. Gauntlett from Beethoven, Symphony No. 2, 2nd movement. *Cong. Hy.*[1] 97

NEAPOLIS (261) arr. Goss from Haydn, Symphony No. 88 in G, 2nd movement. *Cong. Hy.* 492

BONCHURCH (390) arr. Novello from Beethoven, Septet Op. 20, Variation-theme *Cong. Hy.* 314

EMMAUS (271) arr. Hawkins from Beethoven, *Die Ehre Gottes*, Op. 48, No. 4 (still heard as an anthem: ' The heavens proclaim Him'). *Cong. Hy.* 898

EPHESUS (273) arr. Gauntlett from a Mass by Cherubini.

HUNGARY (364) arr. Novello from Haydn, 'With Verdure clad' (*The Creation*)

NEWCASTLE (370) arr. Novello from Handel's *Berenice* Minuet.

GUERNSEY (386) arr. Novello from the Beethoven, piano-sonata in G, Op. 79, Minuet.

PLUMSTEAD (372) arr. Novello from Handel, 'Dead March' in 'Saul'. (This was used as early as Williams' *Psalmodia Evangelica*, 1789.)

BAUN (282) from Beethoven (see Ex. 150).

From other sources:

EMMANUEL, from Beethoven's Quartet for piano and wind instruments, Op. 16, Scherzo. *Cong. Hy.* 234

SARDIS, from Beethoven, Romance in G for violin and orchestra, Op. 40. *Cong. Hy.* 116

CANONBURY, from Schumann's Nachtstücke in F. *Cong. Hy.* 591

BURGUNDY, from the theme of Handel's Variations in E ('The Harmonious Blacksmith', ascribed in the *Comprehensive Tune Book* to Clément Marot, 1550!)

PEACE IN SORROW, arr. Walford Davies from Beethoven, violin concerto, slow movement. *Students' Hymnal* (Hymns of the Kingdom) (1923), 185

THAXTED, arr. (presumably by the composer) from Holst's theme 'Jupiter' in *The Planets*. *S.P.* 319

---

[1] *Congregational Hymnary* (undated, *c.* 1916).

A vesper tune, 'Lord, keep us safe this night', still popular in non-conformist circles, may be traced to the variation theme in Beethoven's *Sonata Appasionata*, Op. 57.

From sacred vocal works we have new arrangements from Handel —SAMSON (*C.P.* 489), SOLOMON (*E.H.* 80) and BRUNSWICK (*E.H.* 555), and a tune arranged (possibly by Gauntlett) in the *Congregational Psalmist* (1858), from Schubert's *Deutsche Messe*[1] (1827) (*C.P.* 758). Secular vocal works were raided for NORWOOD (Ex. 149), a very daring experiment!—and HYMN TO JOY, which Walford Davies arranged from the familiar theme in Beethoven's *Choral Symphony* (*Fellowship Hymn Book*, 1933, 139).

The merit of these arrangements is solely to be assessed by their success as hymn tunes. Nearly all of them are impossible; one or two are grotesque. On the other hand, FARRANT (*E.H.* 339) from the sixteenth-century anthem, 'Lord, for thy tender mercies' sake', not nowadays attributed to Farrant, is as legitimate as WINCHESTER OLD from Tye's *Acts*. Nowadays, so much more respect is paid to the *ipsissima verba* of composers, and so much wider are the opportunities for hearing them, that adaptations of this kind are no longer needed and are thought to be in questionable taste. But their frequent appearance during the days of *The Psalmist* indicates the influence which concert-music was beginning to have on hymnody. This is, however, only the beginning of that story. The influence of the *style* of concert music on the *style* of hymnody is the chief subject of the next chapter.

---

[1] Deutsch's Catalogue (1951), No. 872.

16

THE OXFORD MOVEMENT AND HYMNODY

BISHOP Horsley, of Rochester, wrote in 1800 that the religious condition of the country was marked by the 'vicious ignorance' of the poor and the 'presumptuous apostasy' of the wealthy. This omits, of course, the great awakening in individual consciences produced by Methodism, and the upsurge of missionary activity in the last years of the century. But, none the less, it was well written, for that great part of the Church of England which was not yet infected by Methodist uplift and, in consequence, the greater part of England's population even then suffering the first effects of the Industrial Revolution, was indeed being robbed of its faith by the example of an idle priesthood and of a socially inarticulate church organisation. The ordinary parish priest was able to talk intelligently neither about the necessity of Sacraments nor about the French Revolution.

As the nineteenth century advanced it became clear to the minds of certain faithful Anglicans that the country would, under the rising pressure of the new industrial population and the revolution in social thinking which had begun to spread from the Continent, go either pagan or Methodist. This was the root cause of the Oxford Movement, and that Movement was the dominating force in the story of church music during the later nineteenth century.

The text books provide all that is necessary of the history of the Oxford Movement.[1] It was born of the conviction that the Church of England must re-think and re-assert its authority as the repository of Christian doctrine, the keeper of the public conscience, and the chosen channel of the Gospel to the new England. The marks of its work are found in a new inspection, appreciation, and interpretation of history, particularly as it affected the Anglican church; a revised attitude, consequent on that, of reserve towards the Reformers of the sixteenth-century and of respect for mediaeval (and, indeed, for contemporary) Rome; a revived interest in Christian doctrine, especially the doctrines of the Church, the Sacraments and the Ministry; and a new interest in liturgy accompanied by close attention to historic details and a critical view of the Book of Common Prayer.

---

[1] See, especially, L. Elliott-Binns's brilliant study, *Religion in the Victorian Era* (Lutterworth Press, 1936).

All this is carefully argued and elaborated in the *Tracts for the Times*. Two things must at once be said about it. One is that its history (at that date when the study of history in the modern sense was still a new technique) was considerably infected by romance; that there was as much of Sir Walter Scott as of St Thomas Aquinas in the new cult of the Middle Ages. The other is that the impact made upon the common man by the outward symptoms of the Movement had nothing to do with his reason (and therefore nothing to do with the Tracts) and everything to do with his imagination. Dispossessed, bewildered, discontented and in a measure homeless, the industrial peasantry of England looked to religion for shelter and colour. These were provided in one way by the Sankey revivals, in another by that new spirit in the Church, under which public worship became in a new way rhythmical and ceremonious, and under which the Church, enjoining upon its ministers personal holiness and even asceticism, invested them with a new authority expressed in their colourful vestments, their new title of 'Father', and their use of the Confessional. All this took some time to work its way into the consciousness of the industrial population, and has never commended itself to the landed countrymen, but its effects in Church-extension and mission work on the one hand, and in appealing to the reason and the imagination of the highly-educated on the other, have been notable and lasting. At the present time, the work of the Oxford Movement persists on the one hand in the popular hymnody of the *Mirfield Mission Hymnal*, and on the other in the rich but ordered praise prescribed by the *English Hymnal*.

In hymnody the sympathisers with the Oxford Movement set themselves to recover the lost treasures of the past by translating hymns from Latin and Greek, to attend to the needs of the liturgy, and to provide a hymnal companion to the liturgy which should combine judicious and dignified restraint with attractive variety of styles. In music, the effects were the same—to extend the repertory of the singing congregation over the heritage of Germany and Geneva and ancient English psalmody, and to resist firmly any incursion of the florid style associated with everything in eighteenth century English piety that the Oxford Movement found most offensive. For the hearty music of Methodism the hymnal editors substituted the serenity of plainsong.

All this is excellently epitomised in *Hymns Ancient and Modern*. That book, whose success is unique in the history of hymnody, had its way prepared by certain interesting experiments.

116

A pioneer in the new archaism was W. H. Havergal (1793–1870), who produced in 1844 a reprint, with a learned Preface, of *Ravenscroft*, and in 1847 his *Old Church Psalmody*, an anthology of tunes from many sources adapted for the needs of English hymns. In the Ravenscroft edition he is faithful to the originals; in the later book he does not hesitate to adapt German chorales to English metres. And since one of the symptoms of that restraint and impersonality which the Oxford Movement sought to impose upon public worship was the preference of common to triple time, Havergal naturally took his adaptations from those late versions of chorales which had already abolished the rhythmic freedom of their early forms. And so, we have from Havergal, FRANCONIA (*E.H.* 370), NARENZA (*E.H.* 518), and WINCHESTER NEW (*E.H.* 9, but not the harmony). Richard Redhead (1804–76) published in 1853 a similar anthology, *Ancient Hymns and Other Church Melodies*, in which the adaptations are even more drastic. Havergal and Redhead were both trivial as composers, Havergal surviving only in CONSECRATION (*A.M.*(*R*) 361), and Redhead in one serviceable tune, REDHEAD 46 (*E.H.* 372) and a few other holy terrors (*E.H.* 477, 513, *Appx.* 29).

An example of the class of book which sought to accommodate the new liturgical interest is Helmore's *Hymnal Noted*. The full music edition of this book was published in 1852, and is devoted entirely to Latin hymns, translated by various hands and set to arrangements of their plainsong tunes. The tunes are harmonised on four-part principles, a chord for each note, with restrained use of tonal discords like the dominant seventh. This style is now unfashionable, but for its time it was well applied. When he deals with genuine plainsong tunes, Helmore is not unreliable; but he understandably misses the rhythmical import of such dance-like tunes as DIVINUM MYSTERIUM.[1] And, in one case, it seems that he actually composed a quasi-plainsong tune, VENI IMMANUEL (*E.H.* 8).[2] Helmore undoubtedly led the way in which those followed who further, and according to better lights, probed the treasuries of plainsong and *Piae Cantiones*.

---

[1] Compare Helmore's version of the melody at *A.M.*(*S*) 56 with the version at *A.M.*(*R*) 58 or *E.H.* 613.

[2] The original of this has never been discovered even at the source Helmore mentioned. The history of the tune provides an entertaining study in progressive musical tastes. In *The Hymnal Noted*, it appears in slightly irregular rhythm with conventional pauses of one beat at the end of each line. In *A & M* (1861 and 1868), it is given in square rhythm with three beats on each final note *except* that of the fifth line, which is a plain minim. The 1868 edition adds a modern (and terrible) tune. The 1875 edition adds, for symmetry, the notorious three-beat pause at the end of the fifth line. *E.H.* in 1906 abolished this and the pause at the end of the first line, harmonising freely but still on the chord-for-note principle. The 1933 edition of *E.H.* has a very free harmonisation by Dr J. H. Arnold in the style he uses for genuine plainsong—two or three chords per line. *Congregational Praise* has imitated this. So we now have at the same time the conviction that this is not a plainsong tune, and the treatment of it strictly as though it were, whereas in its own day it was thought of as plainsong and harmonised as a conventional hymn tune.

But observe one consequence of the providential election of 1861 as the date for *Hymns A & M*. All secrets but one had now been laid bare. That one was the technique of transcribing German and Genevan tunes in their ancient rhythms and metres, and providing new English hymns and translations to fit them. This was virtually begun by Catherine Winkworth (1829–78) in her *Chorale-Book for England* (1863), with harmony by Sterndale Bennett and Otto Goldschmidt.[1] The successors of this book were the *Yattendon Hymnal* (1899), by Robert Bridges, and G. R. Woodward's *Songs of Syon* (1904 and 1910). But this was a specialised technique, making heavy demands on the singer. No doubt if it had been in existence in the 1850's on any scale it would have been applied in *Hymns A & M;* but this would have detracted from the popularity of that book.

A & M, therefore, adopted a policy of compromise, balance of power, and annexation characteristic of the public life of Victorian England. It was a short book—273 hymns only. It provided hymns for the liturgy of the Book of Common Prayer and took note also of Saints' Days and the Offices of Prime, Sext, Terce, and None. It classified its hymns in a new way, dividing them into seasonal and 'general' hymns, thus defying the theological convention of the Wesleys. It applied—we shall later see with what resounding success—the principle of the 'proper tune'. And by the judicious inclusion of the word 'Ancient' in its title, which covered its many translations from Greek and Latin, it appealed to the romantic sense of history which was associated with this new English piety.

The history of its compilation is well set out in Frere's *Introduction*. Its bibliography we had better rehearse here for history's sake.

1859: A trial book of 160 hymns, words only.

1860: First complete edition, words only.

1861: First full music edition, 273 hymns.

1868: Supplement of 113 hymns added, the former part reset with additional tunes but not renumbered; 386 hymns in two series.

1875: First revision: 473 hymns in a single series.

1889: Supplement of 165 hymns added to 1875 edition; 638 hymns in two series.

---

[1] Our familiar version of HAST DU DENN, JESU (*E.H.* 536) is literally transcribed from this book. So is O DER ALLES (*E.H.* 382). Each provides an example of the harmony of one of the editors, and it is impossible to judge which of them, here and elsewhere, is the more highly to be praised for his sensitive work.

1904: Second complete revision, 643 hymns in one series. This was the basis of Frere's Historical Edition of 1909.

1916: Second Supplement separately published for use with 1889 edition, numbered from 639 to 779.

1922: Complete edition of 1889 plus Second Supplement, the whole reset with additional tunes in the earlier parts, but omitting nothing from the 1889 edition; 779 hymns in three series.

1939: Shortened edition, printing full 493 of the 1922 hymns under their old numbers, mentioning the remainder by reference only, and adding some new tunes in all parts.

1950: Third complete revision, 636 hymns in one series.

The musical editors[1] were: W. H. Monk from the beginning to 1889, the year of his death, C. Steggall until 1903, the year of his death; B. Luard Selby (1853–1918) saw the 1904 edition through the Press; and Sir Sydney Nicholson for the remaining editions, until his death in 1947, when his work was taken over by Dr John Dykes Bower of St Paul's Cathedral, and Mr Gerald H. Knight, Warden of the Royal School of Church Music and (until 1952) Organist of Canterbury Cathedral.

Hymns A & M became nothing less than a national institution. It is the only hymn book about which jokes are consistently made, the only one whose name the ordinary unchurched Christian may be expected to know.[2] In one direction especially it became, more than any of its numerous contemporaries and imitators, a standard book of English praise. It arranged marriages between certain hymns and their tunes which have been regarded in many cases as indissoluble for a century since. This it did either by finding older and hitherto unattached partners or in a few cases by divorcing existing marriages; and, of course, its editors provided some new tunes which have become universally popular.

---

[1] I am conscious that the term 'musical editor' is here used inaccurately. There are no editors in this book. Its oversight is divided between 'proprietors' and 'assessors', and those whom we have called musical editors are really 'assessors for music'; they are the leaders of the small groups called in by the Proprietors to prepare the music for the various editions. It may here be added, to correct a popular error, that *Hymns A & M* is not the 'official hymn book' of the Church of England. It is a private venture. That Church has never had an 'official hymn book'.

[2] The reader may care to consult my book, *Hymns and Human Life* (John Murray, 1952), for some comments on this fact. It might be added, for those who are impressed by statistics that over 100 million copies of the various editions have been sold in ninety years, and that the 'failure' of 1904 sold 2½ million within a year of publication (see Clowes, *A Family Business*, 1953).

Here are some collocations between hymns and *new* tunes in the 1861 edition which are still virtually sacrosanct:

'Abide with me'	EVENTIDE (Monk)	*E.H.* 363
'Sweet Saviour, bless us'	ST MATTHIAS (Monk)	—
'Hark, a thrilling voice'	MERTON (Monk)	*E.H.* 5
'O come and mourn'	ST CROSS (Dykes)	*E.H.* 111
'Holy, Holy, Holy'	NICAEA (Dykes)	*E.H.* 162
'Our blest Redeemer'	ST CUTHBERT (Dykes)	
		E.H. Appx. 31
'Eternal Father, strong to save'	MELITA (Dykes)	*E.H.* 540
'Jerusalem the golden'	EWING (Ewing)	*E.H.* 412

Here are a few of the many marriages between adapted German tunes and new or old hymns:

'Christ, whose glory fills the skies'	RATISBON	—
'As with gladness'	DIX	*E.H.* 39
'Hail to the Lord's Anointed'	CRÜGER[1]	*E.H.* 45
'The strife is o'er'	VICTORY	*E.H.* 625
'Lord, thy word abideth'	RAVENSHAW	*E.H.* 436
'Blest are the pure in heart'	FRANCONIA	*E.H.* 370
'Ye servants of the Lord'	NARENZA	*E.H.* 518

The following are marriages between already mature tunes and hymns new or old:

'New every morning'	MELCOMBE	*E.H.* 260
'All glory, laud and honour'	ST THEODULPH	*E.H.* 622
'While shepherds watched'	WINCHESTER OLD	*E.H.* 30
'Forty days and forty nights'	HEINLEIN	*E.H.* 73
'God moves in a mysterious way'	LONDON NEW	*E.H.* 394
'O God, our help in ages past'	ST ANNE	*E.H.* 450

And here are some marriages resulting from divorces of previous partnerships:

ST GEORGE'S, WINDSOR	(Old partner) 'Hark the song of jubilee'
	(New) 'Come, ye thankful people' *E.H.* 289
ST PETER	(Old) Psalm xviii, New Version
	(New) 'How sweet the name of Jesus sounds' *E.H.* 405
'JESU DULCIS MEMORIA' (plainsong)	(Old) Christ redemptor omnium (as *E.H.* 14)
	(New) Jesu, the very thought is sweet.

---

[1] Arranged by Monk from Crüger's VON GOTT WILL ICH NICHT LASSEN (1640), for which see Zahn 5266; *S.P.D.* at 87, *C.C.P.* at 326. For once Monk's version is a clear improvement.

Some of these marriages have been disturbed by divorce-proceedings recently, but in none of them has public opinion yet been satisfied by the evidence. The lists could be lengthened, but what we set down here is enough to show the responsibility which *A & M* bears for hymns which, with their tunes, have become 'national institutions'. The process was continued in 1868 with 'Praise to the Holiest'. 'Through all the changing scenes of life' and many more.[1]

Hymns A & M, then, was the most popular fruit of the Oxford Movement, and was itself a more potent force than anything else in extending the basic principles of that Movement through the churches.

Now, in considering some of the composers of this era, we must turn to another side of the picture. We must, in fact, face the vexatious and controversial problem of the Victorian Bad Tune.

---

[1] For an excellent account of the hymn books inspired by the Oxford Movement (see two articles by the Rev. C. E. Pocknee, 'Hymnody since the Oxford Movement' in the *Bulletin* of the Hymn Society, Vol. III, Nos. 2–3, Spring and Summer, 1952).

17

VICTORIAN COMPOSERS

JOHN BACCHUS DYKES (1823–76) is not the ablest nor the eldest of the Victorian group of hymn tune composers; but he was easily the most successful in capturing the popular imagination, and he is, to all who are interested in hymns, the 'typical Victorian composer'. I propose, therefore, to explore the implications of modern criticism of the Victorians by giving a good deal of attention to him and to a younger contemporary of his, Sir Arthur Sullivan. The others whom I shall mention will then fit into the picture and need less detailed treatment.

Dykes's success was bound up with, and parallel to, the success of *Hymns A & M* itself. He has seven tunes in its 1861 edition,[1] twenty-four in the 1868, fifty-six in the 1875 edition. One in every eight hymns in the 1875 book goes to a tune by Dykes. Of modern standard books, *E.H.* has eleven of his tunes, the *Methodist Hymn Book* and the *Church Hymnary*, twenty-six each; the 1950 *A & M*, thirty-one; *Congregational Praise*, seventeen; *Songs of Praise* and the *B.B.C. Hymn Book*, five each; the *Hymnary of Canada*, twenty-four; the *Episcopal Hymnal* (1940) of the U.S.A., twenty.

This gives some indication of the degree to which modern editors of popular taste regard Dykes as indispensable.

Now, Dykes has been widely criticised. A keen critic recently summed up his idiom in the words 'self-satisfied and unctuous optimism'.[2] The words imply a decadence of that confidence and faith in success which are the marks of the Victorian age at its best.[3] And his defects can be summarised under a single head—the flight from reason, and from the tensions and controversies to which reason leads, which is the mark of Victorian England at its worst. This may be musically translated in terms of harmony and melody.

What, let us ask, is to be said against his almost perfect melody, DOMINUS REGIT ME (*A.M.* 197)? One thing only—a regret for the stagnant bass in the last line. But if anyone tries to reharmonise the tune, he will soon be persuaded that no other satisfactory bass is possible under the melody. The melody demanded that bass and no

---

[1] All but one are in *E.H.*: NICAEA (162), ST CROSS (111), ST CUTHBERT (Appx. 31), HOLLINGSIDE (414), HORBURY (444), MELITA (540). There remains DIES IRAE (*A.M.(S)* 398).
[2] C. H. Philips, *The Singing Church* (Faber, 1947), p. 157.
[3] The reader may care to read chapter VIII in my book, *The Church and Music* (Duckworth, 1950), on the temper of Victorian religious music.

other; it demanded, that is to say, that the reasonable principle in music, the counterpoint of bass and melody, should be suspended at this point. Compare the magnificent tension of bass and melody right to the end in, say, HANOVER (*E.H.* 466). BEATITUDO (*A.M.* 438/528) is in the same case exactly. In other places we have the same symptom inverted; in GERONTIUS (*A.M.* 172/185), MELITA (*A.M.* 370/487), ST DROSTANE (*A.M.* 99) we have melodies with powerful openings that degenerate as they proceed, demanding what distraction the inner parts can provide. In yet other cases we have tunes that fail from the start and become increasingly hysterical in their vain efforts to provide some sort of musical interest, like SANCTUARY (*A.M.*(*S*) 436) and VOX ANGELICA (*A.M.*(*S*) 223), or tunes that unsuccessfully employ modulation, as a refuge from the necessity of working out their implications within their home key, like OLIVET (*A.M.* 149) and CHARITY (*A.M.*(*S*) 367).

Whenever Dykes is weak, it is always here, in his reasonable principle. When he is vulgar it is always because he renounces the discipline of modesty which is the secret of good hymn-tune writing. When he is 'unctuous' or 'sentimental' it is because his superficial effects are achieved not in consequence of but as a refuge from the tension of his musical argument.

The tendency of Dykes to be too dramatic and pictorial for our taste is derived from the same principle. He can handle the rhetoric of music better than its argument. His sensitiveness to words produces, time and again, a really arresting first line, as in 'Praise to the Holiest' and 'Ride on'; sometimes he deliberately suspends melody and employs the device of rhythmically repeated notes, so characteristic of certain obsessive passages in Beethoven and Chopin, to impart a dark colour to a tune like ST AELRED (*E.H. Appx.* 62) or ST ANDREW OF CRETE (*A.M.* 91). Sometimes, as in that last tune or VOX DILECTI (*A.M.* 257/351) he uses a two-movement form for the sake of contrast in the verses, but, of course, he normally overdoes it. And then again, the obsessive single note becomes a rhetorical habit, as in RIVAULX (*A.M.* 164), and the sensitive, slowing, friendly melody degenerates into a mere reminiscence of the cushioned ease of the *salon*, as in ST AGNES (*E.H. Appx.* 55).

All this is illustrated in Ex. 153. There the reader will find a number of examples of ways in which Dykes sought to evade the discipline of congregational psalmody. But the vital point is, not that Dykes was in this or that way a defective musician, still less that he was a bold experimenter, but that he was writing in the conventional idiom of the time for conventional church-goers; that, moreover, when they had had a little of him in 1861 they demanded more and more. The quality of his 1861 tunes is, as a whole (except the ghoulish DIES IRAE, which is an anthem rather than a hymn) chaste compared with that of his later work. It was, to cut a long story short, not so much Dykes who was at fault, as Lady Lufton at Framley and Archdeacon Grantley at Plumstead Episcopi, who took such pleasure in these musical evidences of security and ease, in hearing the choirboys enunciate these mellifluous melodies, in thus being reassured that their duties as clergy and people were confined to preserving the present state of things rather than to prophesying and preaching to dying men. Of that diagnosis of Dykes's success and of his degeneracy I am in no doubt; the conclusion is reinforced by the fact, not usually stated as plainly as it might be, that among Victorians, Dykes is a man of great moderation and musical sense. He is sometimes vulgar, but others than he were chosen to plumb the depths; he is more reliably friendly than any, but in no direction does he run to the excesses which we see in his later imitators. And with it all he has a congregational and choral sense which are entirely to his credit.

The other composer at whom we ought to look closely is Sir Arthur Sullivan (1841–1900). He is not of the founders of *Hymns A & M* because he was born too late. Most of his hymn tunes are comparatively early works, appearing in *The Hymnary* (1872), and *Church Hymns* (1874). They are not evidence of the musical effect of the Oxford Movement or for the style of *Hymns A & M*, a book which has never much patronised him. But their value for this study is in the poignant evidence they give of the disastrous rubbish which a musician of outstanding gifts thought appropriate for church use.

It is necessary, though disagreeable, to record that Sullivan (so far as we can ascertain) wrote hardly a tune that is not virtually intolerable for modern singing. Exceptions are perhaps ST GERTRUDE (*E.H.* 643) which is an irreplaceable setting for its words, 'Onward Christian soldiers', and SAMUEL (*C.P.* 455), a tune of real modesty for 'Hushed was the evening hymn'.[1] The outstanding vices of his tunes are two—either secular and vulgar rhythm, as in ANGEL VOICES (Ex. 156) and 'Brightly gleams our banner' (*Cong. Hy.* 683), or—mark this—woefully defective melody, as in the series of examples at Exx. 156–8.

Can it be believed that this man, in another sphere the greatest master of melody that England produced in a hundred years, is to be chiefly criticised as incapable of writing a *tune?* But it is so—Exx. 156

---

[1] NOEL (*E.H.* 26) is an extension of the folk song, EARDISLEY (*E.H.* 601). Where did he hear it?

and 157 say so categorically. Sullivan was an English heir of Schubert. In 1866, he had helped Sir George Grove in the discovery of *Rosamunde*. He was soaked in Schubert, and Schubert often sings to us in the Savoy Operas. Moreover, as examples of delicate and subtle musical artistry the Savoy Operas leave us with nothing but admiration. Yet, not only in his hymn tunes, but all the way through his volumes of church music from the first page to the last, Sullivan shows himself ponderous, inept, vacillating between appalling vulgarity and glum monotony.

The clue, of course, is 'The Lost Chord'. Religious music, for which all his admirers pressed him to abandon the theatre, meant that to him—the abandonment of his gift of melody. He could not be a 'joculator Dei'—the religious temper of the time was all against it, and his conviction that there was no point at which religion and the theatre could meet each other (a conviction reaffirmed by every churchman of his acquaintance) made possible this tragic division in his mind. Here again, I see no explanation of a phenomenon which makes the tragedy of Dykes appear almost hilarious by comparison but this, but that the fundamental security and complacency of Victorian churchmanship, defensive against those disruptive social forces which it had not the wit or the courage to baptize, killed Sullivan, as a church musician, stone dead.

S. S. WESLEY (1810–76) is the ablest church musician of the group; he is designated by the late E. H. Fellowes 'the greatest English church musician between Purcell and Stanford'.[1] His hymn tunes are collected in his anthology, *The European Psalmist* (1872); this has 131 tunes of his own composition, together with a large number of arrangements by him of older tunes. We find contributions of his in *The Psalmist* (1835–43); only one has survived, PHILADELPHIA (*C.P.* 579). HAREWOOD (*A.M.* 239/243) was composed in 1839. Both show a sturdiness which typifies his first approach to the form. Later he developed, on the one hand, the sheer artistry of HEREFORD (*A.M.* 698/329), CORNWALL (*A.M.* 195) and WIGAN (*A.M.*(*R*) 212), and on the other an experimental idiom which grew increasingly impatient of convention and is to be found in many of his tunes preserved in the *Oxford Hymn Book* (1908). Of particular interest are his defiance of the convention that places the melodic climax nearer the end than the beginning of a tune (*O.H.B.* 2, 41, 190, 211, 249, 317 and ALLELUIA (*A.M.* 316/399)) and his experiments with tonality, of which SERAPHIM (*A.M.*(*S*) 550), GWEEDORE (*A.M.*(*R*) 393) and KENSINGTON (*O.H.B.* 299), all wrenching their melodies at some

---

[1] Fellowes, *English Cathedral Music* (1941), p. 205.

point for the sake of a harmonic quick-change, are adequate examples.

As examples of his profundity of musical sense we may quote ATONEMENT (*O.H.B.* 127) and, most remarkable of all his tunes, ORISONS (*C.P.* 622). This latter tune he wrote twice over, the other version being available at Ex. 154. It is pure tone-painting, relying entirely, in a manner quite foreign to the hymn tune idiom, on the juxtaposition of chords. It is worth prolonged study, which should not disregard his use of, and his abstention from, the dominant seventh. It was this aspect of his genius which made him seek out and so magnificently harmonise the eighteenth century tune ELTHAM (Ex. 106b).

Many of his experiments either carry the tune out of the proper sphere of congregational hymnody or wreck the music altogether. But of his far-reaching and alert musicianship there can be no doubt. It is little hinted at in the tune by which we know him best AURELIA (*E.H.* 489), but that and HORNSEY (*E.H. Appx.* 28), ST MICHAEL (*E.H.* 244) and HAWARDEN (*E.H.* 496) show that he was able to come out of the organ-loft into the congregation's pews when necessary.[1]

H. J. GAUNTLETT (1805–76) is the senior and most prolific of the Victorians. He is said to have written ten thousand hymn tunes; and certainly his material is in the main beaten out thin enough to make that possible. Gauntlett was very rarely vulgar or sensational; he was very frequently dull. He neither blusters like Wesley, sobs like Sullivan or croons like Dykes. At his best he is a true and inspired master of the commonplace, and a large number of the best known tunes in our modern repertory are his; they can be identified by their hymns, 'Once in royal David's city', 'Oft in danger, oft in woe', 'Jesus lives!', 'Brief life is here our portion'; and we can add ST FULBERT (*E.H.* 139), ST GEORGE (*A.M.* 180/198), LAUDATE DOMINUM (*A.M.* 308/376), and many more. The secret of this is that while Dykes ministered to the parish church, and Wesley to the cathedral, Gauntlett spent his best years at Union Chapel, Islington, with Dr Henry Allon, who had inaugurated the psalmody-class, and who had raised congregational singing there to the best that hearty and strident nonconformity had compassed for many long years. Much of Gauntlett's work can be found in *The Congregational Psalmist* (first edition 1858, last edition 1886) which was compiled for that church, and which abounds in strong, bright tunes and simple congregational anthems on a broad scale and on low musical voltage. This essentially congregational idiom is never far from Gauntlett's

---

1 An unusually wide selection from S. S. Wesley appears in *Moravian Liturgy and Hymns* (1914).

work, which is often trite, usually key-tied, rarely imaginative, but always singable. Here and there he deviates from this beaten track. His astounding ST BARNABAS survives at *A.M.(S)* 413—one of the few hymns in existence containing *staccato* marks over the melody; and, on the other hand, we should be sorry to forget, as the editors seem to have done, that he could write anything as beautiful as ST THOMAS (Ex. 155) or as dignified as ST MAGNUS (*C.P.* 452). But it is undoubtedly IRBY (*E.H.* 605) that makes him immortal.

The other Victorians do not take us beyond the boundaries marked out by these four. HENRY SMART (1813–79) wrote sparingly, and gave us excellent material in a strong, reticent manner. REGENT SQUARE (*E.H.* 431) is no doubt his best and most celebrated tune, but BETHANY (*C.P.* 558), REX GLORIAE (*E.H.* 616) and HEATHLANDS (*E.H.* 395) are admirable. EVERTON (*E.H. Appx.* 27) is less weighty. TRISAGION (*A.M.* 423/288), ST LEONARD (*A.M.* 278/443), and in a quiet way MISERICORDIA (*A.M.* 255/349) are all commendable, and even PILGRIMS (*A.M.* 223/354), associated though it is with a hymn that symbolises with searching faithfulness the fugitive and sentimental in Victorian piety, is in its own right an agreeable tune. Smart in larger forms is dominated by conventionality[1] but his hymn tunes are admirably free from fuss.

CHARLES STEGGALL (1826–93), who had much to do with the 1904 *A & M*, and who committed certain indiscretions in larger forms, was very safe in hymn tunes. CHRIST CHURCH (*E.H.* 411) is one of the outstanding tunes of its age. Excellent also is ST LAWRENCE (*H.A.M.* 629), and sound, though less impressive, ST EDMUND (*E.H.* 47).

E. J. HOPKINS (1818–1901), one of the most sought-after editors of his time, was more prolific and less reliable. ST HUGH (*A.M.* 247/317), ELLERS (*E.H. Appx.* 38) and ST RAPHAEL (*E.H.* 75) are his best known, but they lack distinction.

Havergal and Redhead have already been dealt with. W. H. MONK (1823–89), first music-editor of *Hymns A & M*, kept a very fair standard. Beside those tunes of his mentioned on page 120 above, there are ASCENSION (*A.M.* 147), ST ETHELWALD (*E.H.* 479), ALL THINGS BRIGHT AND BEAUTIFUL (*A.M.* 573/442) and ST CONSTANTINE (*E.H. Appx.* 53), none of which is without a good point well made. One of his most beautiful tunes (with a beautiful hymn) is WALTHAM (*A.M.* 528/324), and one of his strongest, EVELYNS (*A.M.* 306/225). *E.H. Appx.* 10 and 15 are more commonplace. To Monk, also, we owe the arrangements from older tunes

---

[1] Fellowes, *op. cit.*, p. 215.

which we now call CRÜGER (*E.H.* 45), VICTORY (*E.H.* 625) and WURTEMBURG (*E.H. Appx.* 12).

The Reverend Sir Frederick OUSELEY (1825–89), the pioneer of the serious revival in Cathedral music for which his foundation, St Michael's, Tenbury, still stands, had a rare gift for melody which is seen at its best in the lovely tune CONTEMPLATION (*A.M.* 517/177). Less distinguished, but of solid merit, are HEREFORD (*A.M.* 88), ST GABRIEL (*A.M.* 19) and CHRISTCHURCH (*E.H.* 460).

ARTHUR HENRY BROWN (1830–1926) was a prolific composer of the better sort. ST ANATOLIUS (*E.H. Appx.* 40) and SAFFRON WALDEN (*E.H.* 117) are among his best tunes.

Joseph BARNBY (1838–96) leaves us several tunes that exemplify the less endearing aspects of Victorianism. He is purely inspired, we think, only once, in LONGWOOD (*C.P.* 514), a simple, diatonic, unpretentious and thoroughly lovable tune. CANTATE DOMINO (*E.H.* 48) is conventional and inoffensive. O PERFECT LOVE (*C.P.* 675), CLOISTERS (*A.M.* 214/253), FOR ALL THE SAINTS or ST PHILIP (*E.H. Appx.* 23) and ST CHRYSOSTOM (*E.H. Appx.* 19) are in various ways regrettable. Barnby could write a good Anglican chant, and a good drawing-room ballad. Close examination of his LAUDES DOMINI (*A.M.* 303/223) will not fail to reveal that its harmonic structure is virtually the same as that of 'Sweet and Low'.

Philip ARMES (1838–1909) with GALILEE (*A.M.* 220), Sir John GOSS with PRAISE MY SOUL (*E.H.* 470), Archbishop MAC-LAGAN (1826–1910) with BREAD OF HEAVEN (*E.H. Appx.* 43), G. M. GARRETT (1834–97) with BEULAH (*A.M.* 536/32); Sir George ELVEY (1816–93) with DIADEMATA (*A.M.* 304/224) and ALFORD or ST GEORGE'S WINDSOR (*E.H.* 289), and Sir George Martin (1844/1916) with ST HELEN (*A.M.* 555/400); C. C. Scholefield (ST CLEMENT *E.H. Appx.* 16), Bishop Jenner (QUAM DILECTA *E.H.* 508) and Sir Francis Champneys (ST JEROME *C.P.* 606)—all these confirm the view that at its best Victorian hymnody had a great and enviable confidence. Sir John STAINER, sometimes capable of real beauty (ST PAUL, (*A.M.* 185/200) and VESPER, (*A.M.* 22)), sometimes of abysmal bathos (REST (*A.M.* 428/572) and AUCTOR VITAE, (*A.M.* 319/402)), sometimes roundly and genially popular (LOVE DIVINE, (*A.M.* 520/205) and SCIENTIA SALUTIS (*A.M.*(*R*) 604)), tries all the stops of the Victorian organ and is best pleased when his wandering fingers lead him into the mediant minor. Stainer's musicianly modesty, which makes him almost apologise for his hymn tunes, may be seen in the Preface to his collected *Hymn Tunes* (1901). Among his contemporaries, he stands high. He was quite incapable of anything so flaccid in melody and harmony as, for example, E. H. Thorne's ST ANDREW (*A.M.* 403/ 533), one of the very worst examples of the period.

For other Victorian tunes by various composers, see the following in *E.H.*, which on the above principles we may tentatively classify: (Good): *Appx.* 32, 33, 42, 48, 57, 63, 64, 67; (Non-committal or poor): 169, 422, *Appx.* 9, 17, 20, 25, 34, 36, 41, 44, 50, 52, 61, 65; (Astounding): 361, *Appx.* 18, 51, 70, 71, 72.

18

EVANGELICAL AND NONCONFORMIST CONTEMPORARIES OF HYMNS ANCIENT AND MODERN

IN the field of hymnody not covered by Hymns Ancient and Modern we may expect to find some reaction against the principles for which it stood. Within the Church of England this is largely what we do find. In books like *The Hymnary* and *The Hymnal Companion*, and *Church Hymns* and *The Church Hymnal for the Christian Year*, designed to satisfy those who reacted less unfavourably than the Oxford Movement leaders to Wesleyan and Lutheran piety, we have music of so depressing a standard that the present author, for one, declines to dwell on it. Suffice it to say that, while adding nothing new to the picture we have so far sketched from the *A & M* side, these books managed so to litter the scene with mediocre and unmeritable music that the Victorians have been painted blacker than they really are by those who have a legitimate grievance against this shameless debasement of the hymnodic coin. No great composer of the period (if we except the unhappy Sullivan) has his first or chief source in these books; and the work of those who do have it had better be studied in the sources by those who have a taste for self-mortification.

The same may broadly be said of the many local tune-books which appeared, the *Leeds Tune Book*, the *London Tune Book*, the *Bradford Tune Book*, the *Bristol Tune Book*. The less felicitous pages of *Congregational Praise* provide the kind of tune in which these books delighted—NEWCASTLE (21), OMBERSLEY (23), MARYTON (415), EVENING HYMN (624), and so forth.

Victorian nonconformity, however, although its musical history is almost uniformly pathetic, suffered a remarkable liturgical revival during the nineteenth century. Indeed, if that revival be taken along with the later theological, sacramental, and historical revivals to be noted in all the greater denominations during the present century, the conclusion is inevitable that they have gone through something very like an Oxford Movement spread over a century.

The pioneer of the liturgical revival was a Congregationalist, the Reverend Thomas Binney (1798–1874), one of the greatest of romantic preachers of his time. In tract, speech and book he pleaded eloquently for an enrichment by poetry and music of the aridity of nonconformist worship. At the King's Weigh House Chapel, where he was minister for forty years, he inaugurated the singing of prose psalms in nonconformity. There was so much of romance and so comparatively little of theological backing in what he said and did that his aims bore little fruit in his lifetime. But they received impetus from a different direction in the founding of the psalmody-classes at Islington, in 1848, and at Carr's Lane, Birmingham, a year or two later, which encouraged choral singing by the whole congregation, and directed attention in a new way upon hymns and their music.

But here again, the movement was one of enthusiasm rather than of principle, and it opened the way for a great effusion of platitudinous, mediocre music, either hearty or lachrymose, which did not do much to kindle or to satisfy the finer sensibilities. As a result, the tune-books of nonconformity are no great source for good music, and do not advance this story very far. Exx. 159 and 160 summarise the debasement of hymnody in this period, for which these sources were as much to blame as the evangelical anglican sources. Hymn books were issued in all the denominations on the 'proper tune' principle— *Wesley's Hymns* (1877), the *Congregational Church Hymnal* (1887), the *Baptist Church Hymnal* (*c*. 1900) and, for Scotland, the *Church Hymnary* (1898). These contain a good deal of ancient material that they would not have had if *A & M* had not led the way; but their own contributions are distinguished only for their singular and monotonous feebleness. *The Congregational Psalmist* in its 1886 edition, which grew out of the great musical tradition at Islington, alone shows any grasp of the sweep and range of the hymnological treasury. *The Bristol Tune Book* (1863, 1876, 1881) is a characteristic collection of the time, used by Baptists and Congregationalists, renouncing the 'old Methodist' idiom, but replacing it with an idiom of the utmost complacency.

However closely these books be studied, not much evidence will be found that demands closer consideration of them here. Far more important, far more interesting and disturbing, is the emergence in this later period of what we may compendiously call the Sankey and Moody idiom.

I have written elsewhere upon what I hold to be the social and spiritual significance of this development.[1] It will be sufficient to say much less here than I wrote there.

We have already noticed in passing the dispossession and depression of the English industrial peasantry; our context there was the

---

[1] *The Church and Music* (Duckworth), Chapter VIII. For a documented history of the early revivals of 1859 in America and in this country see Edwin Orr, *The Second Evangelical Awakening* (Marshall, Morgan and Scott, 1949).

efforts of the Oxford Movement to provide them with a home in the church. Christian Socialism under Maurice and Kingsley has, as it happens, no part in our present story because though it gave us some hymns it did not give us any music. But the Revivals of Sankey and his friends and followers achieved their great success because their aim and strategy were directed to the same end. Their hymns are the folk-song of their piety, and their colourful tawdriness are just the qualities that provided an invitation to the peasantry of England to turn aside from their desperate insecurity and find rest in the Faith.

Although this music is written in a crude idiom, it has a certain distinctive diction that separates it from the music of some of Sankey's later imitators. That idiom is essentially melodic. The tunes are simple melodies with choruses that rely not on harmonic colour but on a bass confined often to the three primary chords—tonic, dominant, and subdominant. (See HOLD THE FORT, *E.H.* 570, SAFE IN THE ARMS, *E.H.* 580, and THERE WERE NINETY AND NINE, *E.H.* 584). This is the folk-song of the music-hall; widely different from the folk-song of agricultural England, which was at this time a mere curiosity. The tunes lack all contrapuntal interest, and contain the least possible of intellectual challenge. Rhythmically they are as crude as the music of backwoodsmen, relying on the endless repetition of memorable rhythmic units. The first beat of the bar is always rhythmically emphatic and always carries a chord of structural significance to the tune. In short, every tension, rhythmic, melodic, contrapuntal, has gone. The result is a regimented and artificial diction far removed from artistic vitality and corresponding to the essentially static quality of the Revivalistic message.

The revivalistic idiom is, in my judgment, an artificial idiom coined for a special purpose. Its use outside that context—its use, that is, otherwise than for the purpose of reclaiming the genuinely illiterate and spiritually maimed to some grasp of the Faith—is entirely to be deplored.

Unhappily, and almost incredibly, even this idiom has suffered a certain debasement. The 'vintage' tunes of Sankey himself (*E.H.* 570, 580, 584) have at least that humble simplicity that comes from the removal of tensions; they may be too simple, but they are at least honestly simple. More pretentious rhythmic forms and the positive seductions of chromatic harmony have, in later years, made matters much worse. The chromaticism of certain entries in the *Mirfield Mission Hymn Book* is no part of the classical idiom of Sankey. Nor is the complexity of part-writing and the high-powered jazz-idiom of the modern revivalistic song from America which is becoming very popular here at present. Neither Sankey nor Moody nor any of their hymns can be accused, as can some of their imitators, of pretentiousness or flamboyance. These qualities are seen at their rankest in another source altogether, to which we shall come in its place.[1]

It seems clear then, that the best in Victorian music expresses the confidence and sureness of that age in England; but that all the way the music is in danger of yielding to the essentially fugitive nature of Victorian piety. The weakness of Dykes is in that he is really running away from the challenge of reality. The pathos of Sankey is that he deliberately invites his people through music to run away from a challenge that has proved too much for their artificially weakened spiritual constitution. The answers to this *impasse* appear in the works of the composers to whom we now turn.

---

[1] Chapter 21.

19

THE MUSICAL REAWAKENING, 1890–1906

THE debased coinage of Victorian hymnody needed a new mint. The revival of hymnody which we have recently witnessed is chiefly to be ascribed to the fact that this need was recognised by certain musicians altogether more eminent, weighty in authority, and versatile in talent than Dykes, Barnby, Gauntlett or Goss. The two outstanding musicians of the Victorian era, Wesley and Sullivan, failed in their own time the one through his impatience and the other through his divided mind. What we now have is the spectacle of Parry, Stanford, Harwood and Walford Davies on the one hand, and on the other, Vaughan Williams, making what answer they can to the question. How can hymnody be redeemed from its debasement? The first group said, in effect, 'We will show how the familiar idiom of our century, competently and imaginatively handled, can produce vital music yet'; their work is exemplified in the 1904 edition of *Hymns A & M*, the *Oxford Hymn Book*, and some of the more enterprising noncomformist books. Dr Vaughan Williams said, in effect, 'Radical revolution is required, and we shall substitute for the narrow canons of Victorian church music that freedom which will be gained from reverently studying and using the music of the whole treasury of three hundred years; and, especially, we shall substitute for the secular idiom of the nineteenth century, the secular idiom of the sixteenth; away with "Daisy, Daisy", and let the floor be given to "Greensleeves" '.

Subsequent history shows that the first group, left to themselves, were incapable of achieving their aim; that only because of the severe and drastic action of Vaughan Williams, preceded by a few devoted specialists, was it possible to achieve a new idiom which is neither sentimental nor pedagogic. In a word, the 1904 revision of *Hymns A & M* was a failure; not until *English Hymnal*, followed by *Songs of Praise*, had made its clean sweep and a generation had been brought up on their austere canons, could *A & M* appear in a new and successful revision in 1950 without losing either its essential popular quality or its musical integrity.

Consider the work of these eminent composers who were the architects of the orthodox revival, and the history will unfold itself.

Sir HUBERT PARRY (1848–1918) is the senior and the most effective. His output of hymn tunes is small; he wrote less than twenty tunes. He was a master of melody like Sullivan, but unlike Sullivan, primarily schooled and inspired in the tradition of English church music. No controversy about its words can obscure the fact that JERUSALEM is a magnificently-contrived melody. Neither this nor REPTON (*E.H.* 383) can be called hymn tunes in the strict sense, but both show his masterly grasp of melodic architecture. His finest hymn tunes, LAUDATE DOMINUM (*A.M.* 308/376), originally part of an anthem, and INTERCESSOR (*A.M.* 648/115) are models of strength and grace. RUSTINGTON (*A.M.* 274/292) is almost as good. Kenneth Finlay worthily sums him up thus:

> 'Technically, Parry's tunes are outstanding. They are scholarly and free from all unhealthy sentimentality . . . Not every composer of his stature can resist the impulse to use an unexpected turn of melody or harmony, just the sort of thing to make the worshipper hesitate and wonder what is coming next.'[1]

He shares with his Victorian elders the danger of becoming commonplace; but at his best he achieves greatness.

Sir CHARLES STANFORD (1852–1924) is Parry's extreme opposite. It is doubtful whether he was ever commonplace, but he never wrote a congregationally successful tune. His most enduring contributions were his arrangements of ST COLUMBA (*A.M.* 13/16) and ST PATRICK'S BREASTPLATE (*A.M.* 655/162), both in the 1904 *A.M.* ENGELBERG (*A.M.* 437/527) has had some success as a Festival piece, but it is more nearly an anthem than a hymn. AIREDALE (*A.M.* 520/205), GERONIMO (*A.M.* 639/46) and JOLDWYNDS (*H.A.M.* 28, *S.P.* 56) are intriguing but not congregational, and ALVERSTONE (*H.A.M.* 337) and OCKLEY (*H.A.M.* 520) are full of Irish perversity and inconsequence. The nearest he comes to dulness is BLACKROCK (*H.A.M.* 325), which is a failure from every point of view.

Parry's remedy for Victorian bathos had been the 'big tune'. Stanford's was 'more and more music in less and less space'. In longer forms Stanford is great—he masters afresh the long paragraph of musical argument in his service-settings; but his was not the hymn-technique.

BASIL HARWOOD (1859–1949) owes something to Wesley and a good deal to Stanford. His vocabulary is wide, and his capacity for perverse complexity almost limitless. THORNBURY (*E.H.* 545) and LUCKINGTON (*A.M.* 548/375) are now great successes, the latter deservedly so. The rest of his work may be examined in the *Oxford*

---

[1] Article on Parry in the *Bulletin* of the Hymn Society, Vol. I, No. 33 (1948).

Hymn Book (1908). He had a more developed appreciation of modal values than either Parry or Stanford; he was one of the first Englishmen to use that free style of plainsong-harmonisation that has been brought to its height by Dr E. T. Cook and Dr J. H. Arnold. His experience was that of the cathedral and collegiate chapel (Parry and Stanford were both university musicians). In consequence, he was little in touch with the ideals of congregational singing, and most of his tunes are really anthems. RAGLETH HILL (Ex. 161) is a good example of his tendency to elaborate inner parts and wayward melody. Like Stanford, he put more musical ingenuity into a hymn tune than its framework could stand.

Sir WALFORD DAVIES (1869–1941) is the least musically reliable of these four. A great choirmaster and radio-teacher, he was not a great composer in any form. The sources for his tunes are *Worship Song* (1905), *In Hoc Signo* (1916), and the 1922 edition of *A & M*. While his tunes are immeasurably more adventurous and richer than the common run of Victorians, his idiom was basically Victorian and conventional. His melodies are distinguished by an insistence, amounting to an obsession, upon one or two mannerisms. The most obvious is the rising sixth in the melody; but hardly less conspicuous is his filling out of the last chords of a tune into a number of subsidiary vocal parts—an organist's fault.[1]

Walford Davies makes some interesting experiments in free rhythm which take him beyond some of his contemporaries (Ex 162 and *E.H.* 454). But his style is too mannered to achieve more than an occasional exquisite moment. CHRISTMAS CAROL (*C.P.* 718) is perhaps his most successful tune.

In one achievement, however, which is the outcome of his surpassing gifts as a teacher, Walford Davies is unique. When he was Professor of Music in the University of Wales, he gathered his students together to make their own hymn book. This was *A Students' Hymnal* (1923).[2] Many of the tunes in this book (see Ex. 163) are the work of several students acting corporately. But every one of these tunes carried, so to say, if not the signature, at least the initials of the Professor somewhere in the picture. The best known of these is CHILDHOOD

---

[1] H. C. Colles, *Walford Davies* (1942), preserves this from some notes to an unpublished book by Walford Davies on organ-accompaniment: 'I substitute big chords at cadences for their 4-part harmonies, not increasing them suddenly but building up to them as triumphant climaxes. This ought to be embodied in organ technique by going systematically from 4 to 5 to 6 to 7 to 8 parts . . . I continually reinforce one particular part by some method or other: (a) by playing it in octaves; (b) by holding it in 2 or 3 octaves accompanied by shorter chords' (there is much of this in his hymn tunes—tenor of ten doubling treble) . . . 'The principles underlying two-part accompaniments . . . are controlled I think by two facts; the strength of contrary motion and the eternal beauty of similar motion in thirds and sixths'. GOD BE IN MY HEAD (*C.P.* 745) is an epitome of all this.

[2] Some of the hymns in this are in Welsh. The English section was published separately as *Hymns of the Kingdom* (1923).

(*E.H.* 227). Another is TREGYNON (Ex. 163), which has an odd history mentioned at the Example. CHRISTMAS (*C.P.* 640) is in the traditional vein, and appeared in our discussion on pages 57 ff. above.

Other composers of this school are Bishop T. B. Strong (1861–1944), who contributed several tunes of singular reflective beauty to the *Oxford Hymn Book* (see especially Nos. 176, 207 and 326), B. Luard Selby, Musical Editor of the 1904 *A & M*, who composed a number of tunes whose essential lack of sympathy and musical strategy epitomise the chief reasons for the failure of that book, and Charles Wood (1866–1926), who, to the great regret of any historian of the subject, wrote only a handful of hymn tunes. Wood's best known are RANGOON (*A.M.* 734/270) and CAMBRIDGE (*C.P.* 757), which is really an anthem. RECESSIONAL (*E.H.S.*[1] (1951) 753) is less successful, but he made a few interesting essays in the Irish modal idiom in the *Irish Church Hymnal* (1919), which are worth consulting (Nos. 350,[2] 352 and 353). His best contributions to hymnody are in his musical editorship of Woodward's *Songs of Syon* (which we are about to notice), and in his many anthem-arrangements of Genevan tunes, like 'God ominpotent reigneth' and 'How dazzling fair'.

The English Hymnal and its Antecedents

Liturgically and theologically, *E.H.* is the lineal descendant of *A & M*; but whereas the parent book had, largely through its music, become known to a constituency far beyond the strict sympathisers with Newman and Keble, *E.H.* set itself to develop the liturgical side of hymnody far beyond the point which *A & M* had reached. Allied with this were two contrasting forces whose origin in the nineteenth century is quite clear. On the one hand there was a more forthright expression of Romish devotion than *A & M* had dared to utter.[3] On the other hand, we have for the first time direct expressions of that Christian Socialism which had been in the 'sixties a powerful alternative to the Oxford Movement in answering the needs of the new age; this meant the inclusion of hymns like Kingsley's 'From thee all skill and science flow' and Scott Holland's 'Judge eternal', with several American hymns like 'City of God' and 'Thy kingdom come, on bended knee', which, though in common use among nonconformists under the influence of Garrett Horder's *Congregational*

---

[1]   *Hymnal for Scotland*, which is E.H. with a Scottish Appendix.

[2]   This, EMAIN MACHA, is in the 1926 edition of *Songs of Praise* (No. 373).

[3]   See this from the Preface to the 1907 edition of *E.H.*: 'At the request of the Bishops of London and Southwark, the editors issue this abridged edition of the *English Hymnal*, which it is hoped may be found useful by those who desire an alternative to the complete edition'. The 1907 edition omits Hymns 185, 195, 218, 213 and 350. A glance at these hymns, soon restored in later printings, shows what the Bishops objected to.

Hymns (1884) and *Worship Song* (1905), were now for the first time introduced to the Church of England.

These diverse aims, remarkably well fulfilled, together with that concern for home missions which brought in the section of revivalist hymns (567–84), made *E.H.* the most challenging and catholic book the Church of England had yet seen. Even if it had had no notable music it would still have been a notable collection of words for its period.

But it was in its music that *E.H.* had its most potent influence. Here we must go back a few years. Behind the robust figure of Dr Vaughan Williams, who with Dr Percy Dearmer (1867–1936), must take the credit for most of the influence of *E.H.*, stand the refined scholarship of Robert Bridges (1844–1930) and G. R. Woodward (1848–1934). Robert Bridges edited the *Yattendon Hymnal* in 1899. In every possible way it is typical of the unashamed and even aggressive championship of high culture which was characteristic of Bridges. Its full music edition is published only in a quarto edition,[1] the music written in open score and engraved in Walpergen type on exquisite paper. The music is edited by Harry Ellis Wooldridge (1845–1917), who adds to its rich store of Genevan and German tunes seven of his own, all in a very severe, and some in an overtly modal style (see *C.P.* 216, and several of his tunes in the *Oxford Hymn Book*).

But Bridges's principles are best expressed in his own words. He wrote a letter to the Church Music Society in 1911 which was reprinted as their Occasional Paper No. 2. Criticising current standards of church music, he wrote:

> It seems to me that the clergy are responsible. If they say that the hymns (words and music) which keep me away from the church draw others thither, and excite useful religious emotions . . . all I can urge is that they should hav at least *one* service a week where people like myself can attend without being moved to laughter.

He describes the modern hymn book (*A & M* and its kind) as an object which

> Fills the sensitiv worshipper with dismay so that there are persons who would rather not go inside a church than subject themselves to the trial.

We quote this, and recommend the reader to the whole letter and to the notes which Bridges adds to his hymn book, to demonstrate that Bridges here stands for that truculent and prejudiced purposefulness of mind which some felt (and rightly) to be the only force strong enough to break through the undergrowth of Victorian congregational stupor. This kind of utterance made it possible for

---

[1] Clarendon Press, 1899, *two guineas*.

Vaughan Williams's Preface to *E.H.* (a classic of the literature) to use milder forms of expression than it otherwise might have done.

Songs of Syon was a more ambitious venture. Woodward, its editor, was a priest of the Church of England of the extreme anglo-catholic school of devotion, and his book was a labour of love. He composed, in order to revive the original versions of the classics of hymnody, a large number of its 431 hymns, and although very few of his compositions have proved robust enough for popular use, the principle of reviving the classics came to stay. His first edition was published in 1904, just as the preparation of *E.H.* was beginning.

The truculence of Bridges and the rarefied genius of Woodward make a good background for *E.H.*; they throw into strong light the success with which *E.H.* managed, against great opposition from theological and from popular sources, to popularise their aims. Beginning with a Preface in which Dearmer boldly declares that this is a collection of 'the best hymns in the English language'—a broad and highly vulnerable statement even in 1906—and in which Vaughan Williams set it down that musical policy in hymns is 'a moral rather than a musical factor', *E.H.* represented the most important single historical event in modern English hymnody.

In restoring ancient versions and thus enlarging the congregational vocabulary, *E.H.* follows the example of the specialised books of 1899 and 1904, and of the *Chorale-Book for England* (1863). But it breaks new ground in introducing to hymnody a very large number of traditional English folk songs. The book has sometimes been heavily criticised for this policy; and most other books have treated the policy with reserve. *A & M*, even in 1950, has little to do with it. But when the 'English traditional melodies' of *E.H.* are examined through the index of sources in that book, we find an overwhelming majority of successful and delightful tunes, as simple as carols, as impersonal and adaptable as psalm-tunes. Many of them are now in common currency, and their fresh and naïve diction has almost impudently defied, and frequently defeated, the ponderous Victorian manner. If we are able to say in 1952 that in Sydney Nicholson, Eric Thiman, George Thalben Ball and W. K. Stanton there is a new flexibility and friendliness of idiom, we must add that this owes nearly everything to the enlargement of the vocabulary of public praise achieved by *E.H.* It may be said that some of these folk-songs have been mis-allied with their hymns. This is more true of *S.P.* and the later edition of *E.H.* than of the original *E.H.*, in which the folk-songs are chiefly associated with children's hymns, the more carol-like of saints' day hymns, and sacred ballads like 'I heard the voice of

Jesus say' or 'Jerusalem, my happy home'. A glance at CAPEL (488), LEW TRENCHARD (591), KING'S LYNN (562) and KINGS-FOLD (574) shows how rich was the new idiom; a quick look back at Ex. 160 shows what English hymnody was delivered from, and how necessary for our refreshment was the scholarship that unearthed these new tunes and the courage that published them.

Other directions in which *E.H.* enlarged the vocabulary of public praise were in introducing secular or non-liturgical music of other countries,[1] some of the simpler Bach chorale-versions,[2] and many of the Catholic 'Church Melodies'.[3]

The new tunes in *E.H.* are not numerous nor, with certain obvious exceptions, distinguished. The notable ones are Dr Vaughan Williams's SINE NOMINE (641), RANDOLPH (524) and DOWN AMPNEY (152), Arthur Somervell (1863–1937), WINDERMERE (522), KENDAL (566) and LANGDALE (590), Gustav Holst (1874–1934), CRANHAM (25) and SHEEN (310), Nicholas Gatty (1874–1946), TUGWOOD (146) and Walter Parratt (1841–1924), HUDDERS-FIELD (*Appx*. 37). Other tunes, interesting but not congregationally so popular, are Dunhill's BEATUS (650), John Ireland's EASTER-GATE (520), W. H. Bell's HAIL, HARBINGER (225) and CATHCART (546), and Hadow's SOUTH CERNEY (359). W. G. Whinfield's tunes at 409, 642 and *Appx*. 56, though not written for the book, were first given wide currency in it. On the whole, the new music is modestly and successfully handled.

Finally, let it not be overlooked that *E.H.*, for all its editor's critical attitude towards the Victorians, contains sixty-nine tunes by thirty English Victorians, only five of which were in 1906 relegated to the *Appendix* of Bad Tunes.

The influence and Successors of English Hymnal

The influence of *E.H.* in a general way has been profound. No later editors of any musical pretensions dared to ignore it. Its principles of criticism gradually became accepted among Anglicans and Non-conformists alike. Something like what *E.H.* did for Anglican hymnody was done by the Revised *Church Hymnary* (1930) and the *Methodist Hymn Book* (1933). Congregationalists and Baptists rejected these principles in that generation; but they have been boldly appropriated in *Congregational Praise* (1951). More particularly, a few collocations of hymn and tune originating with *E.H.* will show

---

[1] From Scotland, 290, 401; from Wales, 203, 268 and 423; from Italy, 150 and *Appx*. 49; from Switzerland, 243; from Holland, 145; from France, 318; from Germany, 338, 387, 392 and (in 1933), 371.

[2] See pp. 82-4 above.

[3] See pp. 155-7 below.

the influence of the book; comparatively little was left to be done after the great work of *A & M* in this field; but *E.H.* was not idle. Most of us accept the following nowadays:

NUN DANKET ALL'	For 'Jesus these eyes have never seen' (421).
ISTE CONFESSOR	For 'Lord of our life and God of our salvation' (435).
OLD 120th	For 'O Thou not made with hands' (464).

(these are in the *Congregational Hymnary, c.* 1916).

RICHMOND	For 'City of God' (375).
SONG 1	For 'Eternal Ruler of the ceaseless round' (384).
IRISH	For 'Thy kingdom come!' (504).

(these are in the Methodist and Presbyterian books).

GWALCHMAI	For 'King of glory' (424).
HERONGATE	For 'It is a thing most wonderful' (597).

(these are in the *Church Hymnary*, and the first in *A.M.(R)*).

UNIVERSITY for 'The God of love', AR HYD Y NOS for 'God that madest earth and heaven', BISHOPTHORPE for 'Immortal love', and BINCHESTER for 'Happy are they' are among the many collocations from *E.H.* taken over by the 1950 *A & M*. Many other new tunes for old hymns, like DOWN AMPNEY and SINE NOMINE[1] are now common property.[2]

But the direct successor of *E.H.* was *Songs of Praise* (first edition, 1926) enlarged and standard edition, 1932). Theologically more liberal than *E.H.*, it included much modern socialistic material at the expense of the liturgical material of *E.H.*

Musically, it is more adventurous and uncompromising. The new influences, pre-eminently those of Dr Martin Shaw and of his brother, Dr Geoffrey (1879–1943), are the influences of men who are primarily teachers. Martin Shaw, who has a large number of tunes in that book, shows a great vitality and versatility within the bounds of an essentially simple and innocent style.[3] His brother was more inclined to

---

[1] Note that the failure of *E.H.* copyrights to appear in *A & M* is a matter of law, not of taste.

[2] These comments on *E.H.* were written in 1952. Four years later the jubilee of its publication (Summer, 1956) was marked by an address by Dr Vaughan Williams to the Hymn Society at the Royal School of Church Music, the substance of which is preserved in a pamphlet, *The First Fifty Years*, published by the Oxford University Press. In the spring and summer, 1956, issues of the Hymn Society's *Bulletin* may be read articles on *E.H.* by the present writer and by Professor A. J. Hutchings of Durham.

[3] For Martin Shaw's versatility see (a) his assembly-songs, e.g. *S.P.* 196, 304, 327, (b) his popular hymns, *S.P.* 678, 396, 472, (c) his quiet style in *S.P.* 447, 543, 546 and *C.P.* 408, and (d) his occasional excursions into the unconventional, *E.H.* 205, 481, 548.

adventurous method.[1] *S.P.* has been the standard for school hymn books of the succeeding generation, being used in its original form or on one of many abridgements in the great majority of our state-schools today. Whereas the constituency of *E.H.* was primarily the anglo-catholic parish church, the later book was aimed primarily at (a) the school, and, in association with that (b) the congregation that accepted the principle of congregational practice, a technique in which Martin and Geoffrey Shaw were pioneers. The adventurous and *ex hypothesi* biddable constituency of *S.P.* differed from that of *E.H.* very much as that of the *Lock Hospital Collection* differed from that of the *Foundery Collection*.

Songs of Praise was therefore, and has remained, the most advanced of all hymn books in respect of music. It contains a number of highly experimental hymn tunes, several choral songs, a number of unison songs, and withal very little concession to tradition. Impatient of the vocabulary of classical evangelical Christianity, its editors were equally impatient of the Victorian idiom in music.

Some of the results of this were extremely beautiful. Gustav Holst contributed tunes in the severe contrapuntal style of his secular music one or two of which are as hard and chaste as any sculptor could wish —CHILSWELL (498), for example, and HILL CREST (86). In one, MONK STREET, he allows the harmony to disappear altogether at one point (534). Vaughan Williams contributes several new tunes, ranging from the boisterous humour of MARATHON (302), the gaunt purposefulness of GUILDFORD (316), the marching modality of KING'S WESTON (392)[2] to the shimmering mystery of MANTEGNA (126). John Ireland's LOVE UNKNOWN (127), Martin Shaw's OXENBRIDGE (104) and BROMLEY COMMON (187), and Gordon Slater's FOUNTAINS ABBEY (579) and BILSDALE (361) show a cool grace that is the finest quality of this new style. Farjeon's NEED (569), Ireland's CHELSEA (164), and Geoffrey Shaw's PRAISE (624, *E.H.* 535) range farther and are more vulnerable. But there is an admirable, almost insolent boldness in Patrick Hadley's PEMBROKE (311), an experiment, at that time of day and in that company, in chromaticism.

Many of the new tunes make less demands on the singer—Hylton Stewart's ROCHESTER (595), for example, Martin Shaw's MARCHING (678, *E.H.* 503) and Slater's ST BOTOLPH (527, *E.H.* 419). Some make experiments in directions off the main track of the *S.P.* style, as does Darke's magnificent CORNHILL (41, *E.H.* 46).

---

[1] For Geoffrey Shaw's style see *S.P.* 326 and 588 and *E.H.* 535.
[2] *E.H.* 368.

Some have all the warmth of the late Victorians plus a modern purposefulness, like Geoffrey Shaw's DYMCHURCH (93), and FREEDOM (322), Armstrong Gibbs's CROSSINGS (661) and John Law's MONTESANO (491, *E.H.* 122).

But when all is said, and when account has been taken of the tonal experiments that are to be found in this book, it is in rhythm that it makes its most palpable hits. The story can entirely be told in two comparisons. Place side by side, first Holst's BROOK END (348) and Monk's VIGILATE (*A.M.* 269/308); The Victorian keeps his eight-bar pattern by elongating his antepenultimate note. Holst, with no show of impatience, lets the words mould the tune into a new and intriguing rhythmical shape. Secondly, compare the subtle and complex rhythmic architecture of W. H. Harris's ALBERTA with C. H. Purday's SANDON for the same hymn (both at *A.M.*(*R*) 298); the older composer settles down into an Anglican-chant rhythm for his long lines and a long sigh on the short ones. Harris's tune is, again, moulded by the words. This new speech-rhythm sometimes results in an impatient effect, but at its best it is the foundation of a later, modest style to be found in several modern books. It is the shrewdest blow dealt by the followers of that great rhythmist, Vaughan Williams, against the defences of Victorian style.

Folk song is extended in *S.P.* On the whole, it is employed less tactfully than in *E.H.*; but some of the new Irish songs, with their voluptuous and expansive melodies, provide beautiful music for occasional use (SLANE, 565, ST SECHNALL, 268; FANAD HEAD, 294; DANIEL, 376[1]: but WICKLOW, 182,[2] we think a tactless one).

The story is brought to a neat close by noting the effect that *S.P.* had on the 1933 musical revision of *E.H.* In that revision *E.H.* included no new hymns, but imported 118 new tunes, ninety-six of them from *S.P.* Thirty of these are set to the hymns to which *S.P.* set them, but many of the others are harnessed to office-hymns and other material with which they consort ill. The latest *E.H.* remains the richest accessible source of hymn tunes—781 tunes (including plainsong) for 656 hymns,[3] only thirty of which appear more than once. But it is musically top-heavy in consequence, and in practice its users tend to treat the 1933 edition (by reference to the greatly expanded appendix of sub-standard tunes) as though no change had been made in the 1906 edition. *Songs of Praise* is breezy, zestful, youthful and fresh in its approach. Here and there its atmosphere is perhaps a little

---

[1] *E.H.* 246.
[2] *E.H.* 157 (see also *E.H.* 356, passed on from *S.P.*)
[3] Compare the latest *A & M* with 616 tunes for 631 hymns.

draughty and lacking in creature-comfort. But its effect on books other than its parent *E.H.* has been very largely for good.[1]

Other books of the English Hymnal Period

Reference ought to be briefly made to a few contemporaries of the two editions of *E.H.* In the Church of England there are the *New Office Hymn Book* (1907), a musically boring collection, the *Oxford Hymn Book* (1908), our frequent references to which may be some measure of its abounding historical interest, the Second Supplement of *A & M*, which came into our last chapter, and some interesting school books including *The Church and School Hymn Book* (1926), in words and music a most exciting collection, and the *English School Hymn Book* (1938). All these are in their various ways worth consulting.

Nonconformity offers the *Congregational Hymnary* (*c.* 1916) and the *Baptist Church Hymnal* (1936), both either ignorant or shame-lessly reactionary, though the second, because of its date, was unable to miss LOBE DEN HERREN and DOWN AMPNEY; the revised *Church Hymnary* (1927), a fine collection somewhat overweighted by the part-Celtic idiom of its editor, David Evans (1874–1948), and otherwise remarkable rather for its selection of old material than for its new contributions; and the *Methodist Hymn Book* (1933), a vast collection combining unspeakable vulgarity here with remarkable austerity, experiment, and beauty there. The compositions of G. F. Brockless (ORAN NA PRASAICH, 127, FRITWELL, 789, GRAINGER, 489, TEMPLE FORTUNE, 861) have a piquant Celtic flavour; those of Alfred Beer (1874–) affect a rotund public school style in the language of Victoria's days; F. L. Wiseman (1858–1943) has a good tune in five-four time (GOD OF MY LIFE, 429), and T. C. Gregory (1901–) the most daring experiment ever set down on paper in hymnody, NEARER MY GOD TO THEE (468), a tune experimenting in the whole-tone scale. School books from nonconformity include *School Worship* (1926), edited for the Congregational Union by Dr Thalben Ball and containing some happy tunes in various styles, some of them by the composer. WARWICK (*C.P.* 591) is perhaps the best, but the tunes of C. B. Jutson (1870–1930) are to be commended. The Methodists have their *Methodist School Hymn Books* of 1914 and 1950, the second edition being remarkable for its new excursions into folk-song and for some of its refreshing modern hymns.

---

[1] See also *E.H.* 482, 531 and 615 for other tunes taken in from *S.P.*

Nonconformity has not essayed either the critical clean-sweep of *E.H.* or the breathless reformation of *S.P.* But all through their books[1] the influence of the revival can be seen. None of us can now claim to be free of some debt to the great work of Vaughan Williams.

---

[1] If *Congregational Praise* (1951) be allowed to replace the *Congregational Hymnary* for that denomination.

20

PUBLIC SCHOOL HYMNODY

THE English public school as we now know it is largely the product of Thomas Arnold (1795–1842); its religion is largely a product of the Oxford Movement. Its hymnody has in recent generations developed a style of its own to which we may conveniently devote a short chapter at this point.

Of Dr Arnold of Rugby, G. M. Trevelyan wrote:

> His emphasis on religion and the chapel services, his monitorial system and his largely successful attempt to suppress bullying, drinking, profligacy and the worst indiscipline of the old 'bear-garden' type of public school, set an example that proved infectious. The old establishments were reformed and others were started in eager competition. The 'middling orders of society' found in the reformed public school the door of entrance for their sons into the 'governing classes'.[1]

The religious ideals of this new movement were driven home most forcibly, perhaps, by the enterprise of Nathaniel Woodard (1813–91), who founded seventeen public schools up and down the country and prescribed for them all a full diet of worship, and for their chief, Lancing College, a school chapel built on the lines of a full-sized collegiate church, physically dominating the school buildings and capable not only of providing the daily worship of the school but also hospitality for the combined festival worship of all the family of Woodard Schools.

During the past half-century public school music has come into its own. The status of Director of Music in a public school is now comparable with a similar post in one of the most exalted cathedrals. The growth of public school hymn books, and of choirs and collegiate musical activity in the schools, has naturally produced its own style of hymnody.[2]

The special form of hymn tune which we call the 'public school style' evolves slowly. At first the books naturally drew on contemporary sources and contained few compositions from within their schools. Eaton Faning, of Harrow, is one of the earliest public school composers, and his HARROW (Ex. 164) shows no difference in style

---

[1] *English Social History* (1942) p. 519.
[2] Julian, *Dictionary of Hymnology* (1892), pp. 936 ff, gives a detailed bibliography of public school hymn books. The first was *Psalms, Hymns and Anthems for use in Rugby School* (1824), containing four hymns only: this book alone Julian misses. The chief of the other schools which made series of hymn books were Harrow, Marlborough, Repton, Wellington, Clifton, Rossall, and Uppingham and Sherborne (the last two sharing a book).

from that of his contemporaries. Of the next generation, W. S. Bambridge, of Marlborough (1842–1923), has left a few tunes; SHAWFIELD (Ex. 165) is a very good example of the late Victorian idiom at its best.

It is, perhaps, with WELLS, by Basil Johnson (1861–1950), written for Rugby school before the turn of the century, that we first see the 'public school style' emerging, and we must now define that style. It is different from the 'state school' style of *Songs of Praise*, in using always the traditional vocabulary of the nineteenth century rather than the experimental vocabulary of the twentieth. It uses a broad melody, warm harmony, often a rich organ accompaniment varying through the verses, and now and then (especially in W. H. Ferguson) decisive but not difficult modulation. The atmosphere is one of amiable but grave *bonhomie;* at its best, the public school tune has great dignity. At its worst, it becomes as sentimental as a public school speech-day.

The full-blooded pomp of, say, LADYWELL and WOLVERCOTE (*C.P.* 163, 447) by W. H. Ferguson (1874–1950), of Lancing, St Edward's, Oxford, and Radley, is also the notable quality of the public school itself. The public school of post-Arnold days is a close-knit, highly-disciplined community half way between an army-barracks and a monastery. Although the coarseness and harshness of older days have now gone, life in such a community, where a large number of boys share not only their hours of study and of leisure, but also their adolescent years of high emotional stress, is bound to be emotionally highly coloured and productive of a good deal of psychological experience, religious and otherwise, that is warm even when it is not enduring.

The public-school boy is a warm-hearted creature, with warm-hearted virtues and vices, as the traditional public-school story faithfully reports. Three or four hundred of these boys singing in concert in an impressive chapel produce an impressive effect, whether the tune they are singing is capable of sustaining it or not. Composers, therefore, who have built themselves into this atmosphere write full-blooded and warm-hearted music. It will have the resolution and popular lilt of the army-song, together with the romance of youthful piety.

This is just what we have in Johnson's WELLS (Ex. 166). Its enormous compass and its warm harmony go beyond what it desirable for the ordinary congregation; but in their context they are superbly relevant.

147

E. T. Sweeting (Marlborough, 1863–1930), gives us in WOLVESEY (Ex. 167) a setting of 'Judge eternal' which has to be heard to be appreciated. Sir George Dyson, late of Winchester, has a broad unison tune in WINTON (Ex. 168) that is precisely the public school-boy's idea of 'Abide with me'. W. H. Ferguson exploited modulation boldly, but was also very effective in the more modest style (see his HOMINUM AMATOR, *E.H.* 276, and FRILFORD, *Methodist H.B.* 743); he achieves the extreme of bombast in CUDDESDON (*B.B.C.* 65) and LANCING (*B.B.C.* 230).

Ferguson's successor at Lancing, Alexander Brent Smith (1889–1950) left two characteristic tunes in manuscript to be published after his death—LANCING and COTSWOLD (*C.P.* 193, 496)—broad unison tunes with plenty of rhythm and melodic sweep. Henry Ley, late of Eton, gives us RUSHFORD (*C.P.* 512), and Sydney Watson, his successor, STONOR (*A.M.(R)* 404).

In the *Clarendon Hymn Book*, published originally for Charter-house in 1936, are some admirable examples in the modern style, especially Sir Reginald Thatcher's NORTHBROOK (252) and several tunes by the present Director, John Wilson, of which a very good one is HADLOW (Ex. 169).

In the *Public School Hymn Book*, edition of *c.* 1919, we have a delightful essay in this vein by (though not there attributed to) Kenneth Stubbs (1899–1949), of Rugby—OCKBROOK (354). Of the 'local' school hymn books in current use, the *Wellington College Hymn Book* introduces W. K. Stanton, who has recently given us many more tunes in the *B.B.C. Hymn Book* (1951). His SHERSTON[1] first printed in the Wellington book but now to be found in the *B.B.C. Hymn Book* (287) with one note altered,[2] is the boldest essay in modulation we have yet encountered. The *Worksop College Hymn Book* (1938) introduces Leonard Blake, now of Malvern, who shows himself well at home in this idiom in CLUMBER (132 in that book).

It is not to be thought, of course, that public school boys live exclusively on this kind of music, or that their Musical Directors are incapable of writing in other idioms. The versatility of Ferguson is a case in point. Stanton's quieter tunes in the *B.B.C. Hymn Book* are as effective as his noisy ones. Leonard Blake's REMISSION (*A.M.(R)* 324) is more beautiful than anything he did in the public school style. Armstrong Gibbs (never a public school teacher, but all his life a teacher) is as effective in his DANBURY (*S.P.* 81) as in LITTLE BADDOW (*S.P.* 646). Percy Buck (1871–1947), late of Chaterhouse,

---

[1] In the Wellington book this is ascribed to T. S. Williams. Presumably, the secret has now broken open with the publication of the *B.B.C.* book.
[2] Originally, phrase 6, *n.* 3 was A sharp (in D minor); the tune first appeared half a tone higher

never affected the public school style at all, but remained faithful to a refined modal idiom, well seen in RESURRECTION MORNING, (*E.H.* 136), GONFALON ROYAL (*E.H.* 141) and DRAW NIGH (*E.H.* 307); but he came near to the older style in MONT RICHARD (*E.H.* 633). H. A. Dyer (1878–1917), of Cheltenham, used the simplest effects with great success in BROMSGROVE (*B.B.C.* 235). Thomas Feilden, late of Charterhouse, strayed never far from the beaten track in his tunes in the *Clarendon Hymn Book*.

Sir Hugh Allen (1869–1946) was not a public school director, but came nearer to the spirit of this kind of music in his invention of community hymn-singing in Oxford shortly after the First World War. Out of this, of course, comes his stirring and typically abrupt tune, MIDIAN (*A.M.* (*Shortened*) 91) for 'Christian, dost thou see them'. Arthur Warrell (1879–1946), another great teacher, gives us the broad and warmhearted FARMBOROUGH (*E.H.* 509), which is in the same succession. Basil Harwood in LOWER MARLWOOD (*Public School Hymn Book* (1949) 152), Charles Wood in RANGOON (*C.P.* 338) and E. W. Naylor in FROM STRENGTH TO STRENGTH (*C.P.* 497) all come near the same tradition.[1]

The most extreme form of the public-school style is to be found in the generous contribution of C. S. Lang, late of Christ's Hospital, to the latest (1949) *Public School Hymn Book*. Unhappily, this composer allowed his music to become as mannered as that of Walford Davies, but in a different style. Many of his tunes end on the fifth of the scale,[2] many others use the device of moving the bass from the flattened sixth to the second degree and back to the dominant.[3] But his tunes, there to be found in a group, are a good example of the lengths to which it is thought permissible to go, in the context of public school worship, in care-free warmth and exuberance of expression. The danger of the style is its fatal tendency to slip over from youthful zest to youthful brutality. Here and there among public-school tunes, one seems to hear the degenerate monitor and the beaming bully; and one turns back to *Tom Brown* with new and regretful understanding.

The public-school tune, then, as a leaven in the diet of public-school worship, derives in its modern form from the broad melody of Parry[4] and the tramping bass of Vaughan Williams[5] and Holst. It is the best

---

[1] Cf. Thomas Wood's tunes at *E.H.* 271 and *S.P.* 511.
[2] Nos. 13, 179, 210, 215, 327, 384, 450, 502, 537, 546.
[3] Nos. 231, 313, 464, 500, 537.
[4] Observe the essentially 'public school' style of REPTON (*E.H.* 383), which was actually first arranged as a hymn tune in the *Repton Hymn Book* (1918). Note, also, an early example of modulation in Parry's FRESHWATER for 'Crossing the Bar' (*A.M.(S)* 694).
[5] Note how many ancient tunes in *E.H.* Dr Vaughan Williams harmonised with moving basses; examples are PSALM 3 (512), PSALM 68 (544), PSALM 86 (640) and his arrangement of ST PATRICK'S BREASTPLATE (212).

fruit of that 'orthodox' revival which preceded and was all but extinguished by the radical revival of *E.H.* There is no folk-song revival here. All is said well, though the accents be the accents of Mr Disraeli.[1]

---

[1] For much of the material in this chapter, I am indebted to a penetrating paper by L. J. Blake, in the *Bulletin* of the Hymn Society, Vol. II, No. 12, October, 1950, on 'The Public School Hymn Tune'.

21

THE HYMNODY OF THE
ROMAN CATHOLIC CHURCH

OUR apology for including the story of Roman Catholic hymnody within one brief chapter must be along the following lines: the story of the hymnody of that church is largely the story of Christian hymnody in general. The principles which have emerged from the foregoing pages apply equally to Roman Catholic as to Protestant hymnody, and the stages of the story of Protestant hymnody can be shown to have their reflections in the Roman Catholic story. It is really necessary in this chapter only to deal with two main issues, namely, the points at which Roman Catholic hymnody appears to diverge from that of the Protestant churches, and the positive contribution which Roman Catholic hymnody has made to the English treasury.

In the first place we feel entitled to make one generalisation concerning Roman Catholic hymnody. Although hymns have played different parts in the liturgies of different Protestant churches, the part they play in the Roman Catholic system of public praise is widely different from most Protestant traditions. In the central liturgy of the Mass, for example, hymns have no part at all, except for the occasional use of the Corpus Christi hymns of St Thomas Aquinas. The place of hymns in Roman Catholic praise is at Benediction and in popular evangelistic services. The Protestant tradition that stands furthest from the Roman Catholic is therefore that of the Reformed (Independent, Presbyterian, and Baptist) churches, in which hymns are an integral part of public worship.[1] The Protestant tradition nearest to that of Catholic hymnody is the mission service of the Salvation Army or the down-town parish church, where hymns are sung as popular folk-songs, more or less uncritically and indiscriminately. Hymns in Roman Catholic services are, indeed, folk-song: nowhere but in the hymnody of the evangelical revivals of the late nineteenth century do we find the folk-song element so consistently emphasised as we do in Roman Catholic hymnody.

The consequences of this are two. First, we find at all periods after the Reformation a tendency for Roman Catholic song to slip into the prevailing idiom of the day; it is only very rarely that we find Roman

---

[1] See, for example, Bernard Manning, *The Hymns of Wesley and Watts* (1942), p. 6.

Catholic hymnody making a stand against debased standards such as we frequently find in Protestant hymnody. And, secondly, as a corollary of that former consequence, we rarely find Roman Catholic hymns attempting notably high standards in words or music.

Catholic Hymnody of the Sixteenth and Seventeenth Centuries

An examination of Exx. 170–182, which should be conducted alongside an examination of Exx. 1–26 and 64–94, will show how closely the idiom of Catholic hymnody after the Reformation followed that of Lutheran hymnody; but it will show also the tendency of Catholic hymnody always to lean towards the popular folk-song style. Catholic hymnody never established a church-style. German Catholic hymnody never had a Crüger. It will also have been observed already, and the examples will call attention afresh to the fact, that the frontier between Catholic and reformed hymnody was never fully closed. We have seen how many mediæval catholic melodies were absorbed into Lutheran use—ACH GOTT VOM HIMMEL (*E.H.* 478) for only one out of many. *Piae Cantiones* (1582) was specially designed to save Catholic music from falling out of currency in Lutheran Sweden. The tune WIR DANKEN DIR (Ex. 171) is a tune (cf. *E.H.* 534) which has found currency from the earliest times of the Reformation through Western Christendom. SINGT AUFF (Ex. 181) and BEYM CREUZ MIT LIEB (Ex. 178) are only two of the many Genevan psalms that were adapted for Catholic use in the seventeenth century, and the great LASST UNS ERFREUEN (Ex. 176) tells its own tale.

But in spite of occasional deviations, the general rule is that Catholic hymnody is, above all things, creaturely and homely. WER DA WONET (Ex. 170, original of *E.H.* 35) looks like a chorale, but only because chorales often look like and indeed imitate the songs of the Minnesinger. GELOBT SEY GOTT (Ex. 172), repetitive, small-compassed, popular in every phrase, is a shade more secular in in idiom than anything contemporary in Lutheran hymnody. CHRISTUS IST ERSTANDEN (Ex. 173) is another carol of traditional sound. The *Andernach Gesangbuch*, of 1608, was not uninfluenced by Reformation austerity, and it produced some tunes in the weightier style, like ANDERNACH (*E.H.* 50) and REX GLORIOSE (*E.H.* 183); QUEM TERRA, PONTUS, AETHERA (Ex. 174), much less smooth and carol-like than most of its neighbours, reflects a slight uneasiness at the conflation of the two styles. ES WALT GUT JAGER (Ex. 175, original of *E.H.* 251) returns to the carol-style. JOSEPH, JOSEPH, JOSEPH (Ex. 177) anticipates that curious style, restless yet intimate, which entered into Lutheran song with the mystics, Scheffler and his contemporaries. The style is further exemplified in AVE JUNGFRAU (Ex. 179). Yet more freedom, more influence of the solo song, is to be found in O KIND, O LIEBES HERZELEIN (Ex. 180), and in JESU DER ZUNGEN LIEBSTER THON (Ex. 182), which has something in it of the lyricism of J. W. Franck and Freylinghausen.

But it will be seen that there is no tendency at any point to resist the settling down of the modes into tonality, or the substitution of short and regular rhythmical units for long and irregular ones. That criticism which Crüger and his school directed upon the chorale is quite absent from Catholic hymnody. There was little need for it, since hymns were, as we have said, folk songs and carols, not a vital part of the public liturgy, as Lutheran hymns were.

Tunes from Catholic sources in the seventeenth century can be referred to in *E.H.* at Nos. 115, 120, 131,[1] 164, 264, 288, 443, 578, 635 and 647. Of these only 264 and 635 are exceptions to the rule that Catholic hymn tunes are generally closely allied to carols and folk songs. These two show a style nearer to the chorale and the psalm-tune.

Later Developments in German-speaking Catholicism

Catholic hymnody continues to run parallel to that of the Protestants after 1700. The Tochter Sion tune which is well known in this country in Richardson's revision as ST BERNARD (*E.H.* 71), shows in its original form[2] the conventions which were guiding Dretzel and König in the same period. But the popular style which we found at Exx. 134–138 and 141–2 is the characteristic style of Catholic hymnody as the eighteenth century advances. Ex. 183, GROSSER GOTT (cf. *E.H. Appx.* 39), is one of the most famous German tunes in both Lutheran and Catholic books, and it has a Catholic origin. In the same style are O DU FRÖHLICHE (which we call SICILIAN MARINERS, *C.P.* 371), SCHÖNSTER HERR JESU (or ST ELIZABETH, *C.P.* 175) and the carol, STILLE NACHT (*C.P.* 714).

Johann Michael Haydn (1737–1805), brother of the more famous Franz Josef, gave his life to Catholic church music, and left a number of hymn tunes or sources for hymn tunes. Vestiges of the popular style can be seen in tunes made from his works, such as OFFERTORIUM (*A.M.* 666/176) and SALZBURG (*C.P.* 55). Both these have something of the traditional song about them, and Haydn's best

---

[1]   Correct rhythm at *A.M.(R)* 294 and *C.P.* 140.
[2]   *S.P.D.* at 537.

F 153

work was done in writing popular music, often adapted from traditional tunes, for Catholic congregations. If his OFFERTORIUM be placed alongside the Swiss Catholic tune STAFF OF FAITH (*C.P.* 518), COR JESU (Ex. 184), and SAWSTON (*Westminster Hymnal* (1940) *Appendix* 6, usually sung to 'Faith of our fathers') we see the appearance of a family which obviously has folk-song origins. Haydn's tune is a little masterpiece, but at the other end, SAWSTON is unashamedly vulgar. Another Catholic tune of great popularity from the eighteenth century is that which appears variously as PADERBORN (*A.M.* 704/226, *E.H.S.* 759) and DAILY DAILY (*E.H.* 568).

This corresponds to the easy-going melodic quality of many German and English tunes of the same period. It gives place to a voluptuously chromatic idiom in the nineteenth century which abounds in the 1912 edition of the *Westminster Hymnal* and of which the late Sir Richard Terry (1865–1938), despite the admiration he came to feel for the Genevan style, was by no means incapable. An example that has found its way into Protestant use is REQUIEM (*E.H. Appx.* 21), by Johann Schulthes, German-born organist of Brompton Oratory (1816–79).

Other nineteenth century sources for Catholic hymnody are in the works of R. L. Pearsall (1795–1856), who, living most of his adult life in Switzerland, contributed a good deal posthumously to the St Gall *Gesangbuch* (source of *E.H.* 292) and left us PEARSALL (*E.H.* 495) and GLORIA (*E.H.* 567), both unenterprising but unpretentious. His best work was done in the larger styles, especially in his famous arrangement of 'In dulci jubilo'. His tune for ADESTE FIDELES (Ex. 185) is something of a curiosity, and also a good example of his easy-going style.

About the time of the re-establishment of the Catholic hierarchy in England (1850), a number of tune-books appeared, such as *Catholic Hymns* (1849), *Easy Music for Catholic Schools* (1851) and *Crown of Jesus Music* (1864). Sufficient evidence of the style of tune thought suitable for Catholic education is to be found in TYNEMOUTH or ST CATHERINE (*C.P.* 106), STELLA (*E.H. Appx.* 54),[1] INTERCESSION (*A.M.(S)* 363), WELLS (*C.P.* 382) and TICHFIELD (*C.P.* 400), all of which come from or through these sources.

This is the style affected by the more popular tunes in the *Mirfield Mission Hymn Book*. It is the Catholic counterpart to English

---

[1] The connection, noted in *E.H.*, with an English traditional tune is very dubious.

revivalistic music; and its popularity is due to the same cause, that both English revival music and Catholic hymnody are only very loosely connected with any kind of ceremonial liturgy.[1]

Movements for Reform

We noticed in the Andernach book of 1608 a tendency towards an austerer style than that of contemporary Catholic song. This book was the work of an early Society of St Cecilia. Societies of St Cecilia, aiming at the purification of church music, came into being on a wide scale in the nineteenth century, and published an edition of Palestrina which is now judged well-meaning rather than trustworthy. But for what they were worth, the enthusiasts of the Cäcilienverein took for their guiding principles (i) that the Gregorian chant was the true music of the church; (ii) that the best harmonised music is that of Palestrina and his school, (iii) that the Viennese school of Haydn, Mozart and their contemporaries is unecclesiastical and should be abandoned, and (iv) that new music for church use should correspond in style with the tradition of the 'ages of faith'. These ideals, carried much further in the plainsong revival of Mechlin and later of Solesmes, and brought into the authoritative teaching of the Church in the *Motu Proprio* of Pope Pius X (1903) were themselves the codification of a movement that had been in fitful existence all the time, and had manifested itself in one or two important sources in the eighteenth century.

A leading figure in this movement was François de la Feillée, a priest of Chartres, who published in 1745 a work entitled *Méthode pour apprendre les règles du plain-chant et de la Psalmodie;* this reappeared in 1748 as *Nouvelle Méthode,* &c, and successive editions continued to appear, of which the fifth of 1782 and the eighth of 1808 have become celebrated. These contain collections of hymn tunes purporting to be derived from ancient plainsong, and from these two editions *E.H.*, following the example of certain anglo-catholic collections of a local kind made in the nineteenth century, included CHRISTE SANCTORUM (*E.H.* 165), REGNATOR ORBIS (465) and ANNUE CHRISTE (174)[2]. A modified form of plainsong-notation was used for these tunes, but when they are transcribed it

---

Other 'folky' Catholic tunes remaining are at *E.H.* 137, 150, 216, 229 (ii,) 399 and 529 and *Appx.* 47.

[2] Concerning this tune is may be observed that the form at *E.H.* 174 is nearer to La Feillée's than the form in eight sixes at *S.P.* 688; the tune was transcribed in eight sixes by Helmore in the *Hymnal Companion* (1852), and went from there into *A & M* and other collections. *S.P.* did with this form what *E.H.* did with VENI IMMANUEL. But, in this case, it was a solecism and perpetuated the distorted form of the tune in Helmore. The *caesura* of the words of its original setting makes it imperative that the tune be presented in the metre 5.7.5.7.D, not in eight sixes. The very squareness and solidity of the *E.H.* version is in its favour; for ANNUE CHRISTE is a seventeenth century tune.

becomes evident that their rhythmical and tonal form is entirely of the eighteenth century. They are sturdy and singable tunes in regular rhythm, rhythmical connotations foreign to plainsong being given to the neum-like characters in which the tunes are originally written.[1]

Now CHRISTE SANCTORUM is in Sapphic Metre (elevens and five). It brings us naturally to the singular collection of *Church Melodies* which is given in *E.H.* The origin of these tunes has been the subject of recent research, and it seems that they are developments from plainsong which through popular use took on the form of regular, rhythmical and tonal hymn tunes.[2] *E.H.* and the English books upon which it relies took these tunes from the Cathedral uses of Rouen, Angers, Chartres and other centres of French church music, which provide sources from the mid-seventeenth century to as late as 1868. The bulk of them are in Long Metre or Sapphic Metre; for L.M. tunes see *E.H.* 18, 38, 51, 58, 65, 123, 125, 151, 159, 176, 181 and 214;[3] and for Sapphic tunes see *E.H.* 188, 191, 208, 242, 335 and 435. Tunes from similar sources in other metres are at 33, 115 and 653.

While some of these are not far from the smooth, stepwise and flexible movement of plainsong (as UT QUEANT LAXIS, 191 and AUCTORITATE SAECULI, 176), others come nearer in their 'modern' form to the idiom of the seventeenth century tunes quoted at Ex. 170 ff (as DEUS TUORUM MILITUM, 181, and ADESTO SANCTA TRINITAS, 159), or to the expansive style of the eighteenth century (COELITES PLAUDANT, 242). Sometimes the tune is primitive and conjunct (ST VENANTIUS, 18, AETERNA CHRISTI, 151), sometimes solemnly modal (ROUEN, 18, LUCIS CREATOR, 51), sometimes it is stoutly orthodox (ISTE CONFESSOR, 188, CHRISTE FONS JUGIS, 335). The rhythmical pattern seems invariable, three-time for L.M. and four-time for Sapphic, but within this discipline there is a great variety in melodic styles.

Extending the general technique of the church melody (the technique of assimilating plainsong to more modern styles) we may say that AETERNA CHRISTI (*E.H.* 175), by Guidetti, a pupil of Palestrina, and BEATA NOBIS (*E.H.* 185) are very early examples of it; their rhythm is free but their technique post-plainsong. Very late

---

[1] See the transcription of REGNATOR ORBIS in Frere's note on the tune, *H.A.M.* at 381. For other La Feillée tunes see *E.H.* 193.

[2] The pioneer in this field of research is the Rev. C. E. Pocknee, who has provided a source-list for most of the 'church melodies' in *E.H.* (see the *Bulletin* of the Hymn Society, No. 63, pp. 96 ff, or *Companion to Congregational Praise*, p. 565). His conclusions are fully set out in his book, *The French Diocesan Hymns and their Melodies* (Faith Press, 1954).

[3] 125 and 214 are obviously variants of the same tune.

tunes like ORIEL (228) and ST MARTIN (416) seem to follow the same line, being free modern tunes in a very restrained style reminiscent of plainsong.

Whatever the details of their provenance, these tunes represent a Catholic compromise arrived at by the pressure of popular usage. The clearest clue to this found by comparing AUCTORITATE SAECULI in the versions at *E.H.* 176, where it is a measured triple-time tune, and at *H.A.M.* 492, where it is a plainsong-type tune with reversed slurs. The former is a popular transcription, the latter an expert one.

The 'Church melodies' represent the most robust hymnody the Catholic church has to offer. Musically, they are the counterpart of the English psalm-tunes for our own tradition. But the time came, in the middle of the nineteenth century, when compromise was deserted for a genuine revival of plainsong. It did not happen all at once. In hymnody we have first the books from Mechlin, in Belgium, the *Vesperale Romanum* (*E.H.* 154), the *Gradual* (*E.H.* 326) and the *Antiphonarium* (*E.H.* 2). These books revived plainsong hymn tunes but presented them in a form less violently in conflict with nineteenth century convention than their original form would have been. Compare *E.H.* 154 (ii) with *E.H.* 154 (i), or 326 with 95, and it will be seen how the intervals are smoothed, the piquancies repressed, the wild passion of classic plainsong (especially in 95) tamed. It was not until the monks of Solesmes set to work on their definitive treatises on plainsong, published in 1883 and 1891, that the opportunity was given to congregations at large, Protestant and Catholic, to savour the authentic delights of plainsong. Thereafter came quickly in this country the work of J. H. Arnold[1] (1887-1956) and E. T. Cook,[2] (1889-1955) and the collections of plainsong tunes in *E.H.* (1933) and in the *PlainsongHymn Book* (1932); both these books follow a style of accompaniment that compromises ingeniously between the pure melody of plainsong and the modern ear's inveterate and ineradicable habit of hearing melodies harmonically; the accompaniments hang long phrases between slowly-changing chords, a practice that would no doubt have surprised both the mediaeval monks and the sixteenth century polphonists who harmonised their tunes. But compromise of a kind is necessary to wean the popular ear from its tonic-dominant allegiance, and this is an effective one.

---

[1]   His principles are set out in his *Plainsong Accompaniment* (Oxford, 1936) and his application of them can be studied in all the plainsong tunes in *E.H.* superscribed 'J.H.A.'

[2]   See Cook, *The Use of Plainsong* (Nashdom, 1928) and his hymn-tune harmonisations in the *B.B.C. Hymn Book*.

Before leaving this group of sources we must refer to an interesting school in eighteenth century England from which we have a small quantity of chaste Catholic hymnody. The earliest exponent of this is the copyist J. F. Wade, to whose mediation, and perhaps to whose invention,[1] we owe ADESTE FIDELES (*E.H.* 28)[2] and ST THOMAS (*E.H.* 31). ADESTE has a pleasantly English, even faintly Methodist, touch, with its easy movement and chorus with repetitions. The other tune is a magnificent example of timeless hymnody which, except for its metre, could well be a psalm-tune.

Greater and more prolific than Wade was Samuel Webbe (1740–1816), organist of the Sardinian Embassy in London. The Embassies were, of course, the obvious bridge-heads for Catholic culture in England in the eighteenth century,[3] and Webbe made the most of his chance. His two collections, the tunes in *An Essay on the Church Plain Chant* (1782) and *A Collection of Motetts or Antiphons* (1792) have given us MELCOMBE (*E.H.* 260),[2] VENI SANCTE SPIRITUS (155), BENEVENTO (469), TANTUM ERGO or CORINTH (63) and the modern version of O FILII ET FILIAE (626 (ii)). Which of these are Webbe's own composition is not certain; but the central three mentioned above have a repeated-note motif that suggests a family likeness, and they are not found in earlier sources. If we may attribute them to Webbe we find in him a composer of cool and imperturbable music strikingly in contrast with the Viennese idiom of Michael Haydn and his contemporaries. BENEVENTO (469) is a clear failure, but all the others have popularity and grace.

Modern Developments

The first authorised Catholic hymnal in this country was the 1912 edition of the *Westminster Hymnal*, musically edited by Sir Richard Terry. In 1902 there had appeared *Arundel Hymns*, a book for local use, musically somewhat superior[5]. But both show a strong leaning to the popular idiom of 1900, about which we have said enough already. The 1912 book makes the 1889 *A & M* look remote and passionless. The revised edition of the *Westminster Hymnal* (1940), edited by Dom Gregory Murray, shows a striking advance in taste. The new compositions in it exploit English folk-song idioms to some

---

[1] See Dom John Stéphan, *Adeste Fideles*, a pamphlet published at Buckfast Abbey in 1947, which argues cogently for Wade's claim to be composer of both these tunes.

[2] In Wade's earliest MS. this appears in triple time.

[3] The Portuguese Embassy was another home of Catholic culture. It was here that ADESTE first became popular, and for this reason when it appears in Protestant books of the period (e.g. Rippon's of *c*. 1796) it is called PORTUGUESE TUNE. It is always set in the early Protestant sources to hymns in four tens anapaestic (the metre of 'Immortal, invisible'), requiring two repeats of the first six syllables of the last line.

[4] The faithful preservation of Webbe's bass in *E.H.* suggests that Webbe was no great harmonist.

[5] The source of WELWYN, *E.H.* 346, and BODMIN, *C.P.* 291.

extent, and Terry's late interest in Genevan tunes is reflected in one or two noble melodies by the Editor. The indications are that Catholic congregations are slow to follow the lead of the new book, but much is being done, especially by Father Agnellus Andrew, to educate them in musical taste. Hymn singing is increasing in Catholic churches and with it a sense of responsibility to good taste which was notably absent from earlier Catholic hymn books.

The influence which Catholic hymnody has so far exerted on Protestant hymnody has, however, been small. Hymn singing has not historically been a central activity in Catholic circles. Protestant books have been enriched by some fine tunes from Catholic musical revivalists, and disfigured by some disastrous ones from popular Catholic books. The score is, on the whole, about even.

22

WELSH HYMNODY

ONE of the subsidiary achievements of *E.H.* was the cautious introduction of a few Welsh hymn tunes to English congregations. *Songs of Praise* increased the Welsh element very considerably, and some of the new Welsh tunes came back into *E.H.* in 1933. But it may be observed that before 1900 only the barest handful of Welsh tunes was known to English congregations of any persuasion. *Hymns A & M* avoided them, the Methodists used only one or two.

There is an interesting story behind all this, which goes back to the early centuries of British culture. Historians will recall that the fifth, sixth and seventh centuries in Britain were a time of violent tension between the invading Saxons and the indigenous Britons. The Saxons in the end drove the Britons into Wales and Cornwall, if not actually into and across the Irish Sea. Religiously, this tension was heightened by the fact that the foundation of English church life and organisation substantially as we know it by Augustine, Theodore, Benedict Biscop and their successors, though frequently even now thought to be the Christianising of Britain, was to the Britons an unwarrantable incursion of foreign ecclesiastical politics into their own Christian society. All this must be read elsewhere,[1] but let it be accepted that Offa's Dyke has always represented a cultural and religious frontier over which bishops and poets alike must pass with caution.

It seems that the cultural autonomy of Wales persisted substantially through the Reformation, and that although it was the Welsh House of Tudor that compassed the English Reformation, puritanism had not in Wales the violent and picturesque effects it had in England. Welsh Puritans like John Penry and John Owen came to England to make their voices heard. Welsh Puritan music is virtually non-existent; we have only a handful of strange tunes preserved in Ravenscroft (1621) under the name 'Welch tune'. Two of these appear at Exx. 186 and 187, and another is ST DAVID (*E.H.* 166).[2] They are incredibly unvocal and wayward, and one doubts whether they can have been much sung. Archdeacon Edmund Prys's Psalter in Welsh, of 1621, includes not these but ST MARY (*E.H.* 84) and a selection of English

---

[1]   e.g. in Hugh Williams, *Christianity in Early Britain* (Clarendon Press, 1912).
[2]   Original version at *Oxford Hymn Book*, 128 (i.)

psalm-tunes for Welsh consumption including what we now call SONG 67 (*E.H.* 197) (see above, page 66).

Welsh puritanism produced neither music nor, in any marked degree, theology. It remained for Methodism to arouse Wales from religious torpor and glum silence.

The way was prepared for the Methodist invasion of Welsh culture by the Bangorian Controversy of 1717, which arose over an unusually scandalous instance of episcopal absenteeism. It was an assertion of Welsh nationalism. That Methodism which so offended the established Church of England was meat and drink to Welsh enthusiasm. Wales embraced it, not in Wesley's Arminian, but rather in Whitefield's Calvinistic form, and Welsh Methodism remains Calvinistic Methodism.

Revival proper began probably with the preaching of Griffith Jones, rector of Llandowror, in 1761. Other prophets arose in their turn, Theophilus Evans (1684–1769) of Llangamarch, and Goronwy Owen (1722–70) of Llanfairmathafarneithaf. And among Welsh singers were William Williams of Pantycelyn (1717–91), author of 'Guide me, O thou great Jehovah', and Evan Evans, Glan Geirionydd (1725–99).

It is from this revival that what we now call the Welsh hymn tune was born. A few Welsh hymn tunes of earlier date survive, such as BRAINT (*S.P.* 505). But there was so little Welsh hymn writing and tune composition before it, that the Revival may be safely said to be the origin of modern Welsh hymnody.

A selection of Welsh tunes will be found at Exx. 188 ff, and at the following numbers in *E.H.*: 56 (an unusual one), 75, 108, 143, 198, 207, 222, 237, 301, 303, 319, 324, 334, 349, 391, 397, 407, 430, 437, 439, 473, 514, 539, 551, 556, 563 and 575. Three Welsh traditional secular tunes are at 203, 268 and 423. The best contemporary source for Welsh tunes is *Emynau a Thonau* (1929), the Hymn book of the Welsh Calvinistic Methodists.

The chief and virtually inalienable quality of Welsh tunes is their intense rhetorical power. This is derived partly from their remarkable sense of melodic form and architecture, partly from their harmony, which is always inseparable from them, and partly (it must be admitted) from an external cause in the quality of the Welsh singing voice. The two musical causes are, it will be noticed, characteristics of eighteenth century music; but it is the difference between the music of English Arminian Methodism and that of Welsh Calvinistic Methodism that while the tunes of the former are easy-going, intellectually slow, superficially showy, those of the Welsh are intense, using only one device of repetition at all frequently—the elongation of the 'four' in 8.7.8.7.4.7. (as LLANILAR, 75, CAERSALEM, 397, BRYN CALFARIA, 319, CWM RHONDDA, *C.P.* 500), and depending entirely on a melodic climax for their effect. The bass in a Welsh tune of the classical type always moves firmly.

There is something concentrated and canalised about the power of early Welsh tunes. This is often produced by the use of a very economical melodic form. Traditionally, this form is simple ternary without development (FFIGYSBREN, *E.H.* 324, CRUGYBAR, *C.P.* 342, GWALIA, *S.P.* 54, LLANFAIR, *E.H.* 143). But it is only a little later that we find this form varied by melodic development, the first phrase (usually repeated) leading to a third phrase using new material and introducing the climax, and the last phrase consisting of a passage leading back from the climax to the second half of the first phrase. This powerful device is seen in CYFAMOD (Ex. 188), ELLIOT (Ex. 190) and ST DENIO (*E.H.* 407). BENWIL (Ex. 195) takes this a stage further. Another form of melodic development, using a 'subject' in various ways through the tune, binding the tune together by rondo-like repetitions is in ABERYSTWYTH (*E.H.* 87).

This kind of melodic development is most easily achieved in symmetrical metres. Where the metre is either unsymmetrical or too short to allow full play for repetition, we have the rhetoric concentrated simply in melodic shape, as in LLEF (*C.P.* 384), LLEDROD (*E.H.* 556) and MOAB (*C.P.* 483); and it is, of course, always possible for a Welsh composer to rely all the way on steady development without overt repetition, as in GLAN GEIRIONYDD (*S.P.* 592), GWYNFA (Ex. 192), CAPEL TYGWYDD (Ex. 193) and in the three great tunes of Morfydd Owen (1892–1918) of which the most characteristically Welsh is WILLIAM (Ex. 197).

Rhythmically, the Welsh tunes have their own rules, which correspond neither to the traditions of psalmody nor to those of English post-restoration music. Normally, the Welsh tune is square and solid; but the constant appearance of anapaestic metres (like ST DENIO, *E.H.* 407) produces a haunting and even hypnotic effect when the middle syllable is heavily stressed as in CRUGYBAR (*C.P.* 342). CYFAMOD (Ex. 188) takes this a step further in introducing a five-fold rhythm, which is striking but a natural development. Most of the tunes that employ this insistent rhythm relieve it at least at one point; both those we mention do this, CYFAMOD especially dramatically. In shorter metres we now and again find the rhythm bursting the bounds of the metre as in LLEDROD (*E.H.* 556) and CAPEL CYNON (Ex. 189). Insistent rhythmical figures are employed in tunes like EBENEZER (*E.H.* 108) and GWYNFA (Ex. 195) with an effect that, in tunes of less ruthless harmonic construction, would be irritating, but which in the best Welsh tunes gives them a piled-up power which never fails of its effect.

Harmony is inseparable from the rhetoric of Welsh tunes; Ex. 195 is printed in harmony to provide a good example of Welsh technique. Not the least part of this technique is the judicious and dramatic use of unison passages. Another example of the almost terrifying effect of unison in Welsh is TREWEN (*C.P.* 399), one of the most numinous of all Welsh tunes. But the close spacing of the parts, and their essentially vocal nature shows the Welsh genius for improvised and intimate part-singing. Chromaticism is abhorrent to the Welsh vocal genius; it is the nation of instrumentalists, not the nation of singers, that leans to this device; chromaticism at a deeper level, involving modulation, appears only once in all the 700-odd tunes in *Emynau à Thonau*—in Morfydd Owen's PEN UCHA (No. 559).

The tonality of Welsh tunes is, as one would expect from their origin, nearly always orthodox, with plenty of use of the melodic minor. Modality, in the rare cases where it occurs, is a survival from ancient tunes. A superficial characteristic of many Welsh tunes in major keys is an insistence on the notes of the common chord, especially in their use at the emphatic points of the tune; (see ST DENIO (*E.H.* 407), GOBAITH (*E.H.* 551), CAERSALEM (*E.H.* 397), RAMOTH (*S.P.* 464) and ELLIOT (Ex. 190)). This, again, is an indication of their eighteenth century origin: the common chord was not, before those days, regarded as part of the vocal vocabulary.

Offa's Dyke effectively insulated Welsh hymn tunes from contemporary English traditions until well on into the nineteenth century. There is, indeed, a stream of Welsh hymnody running from the early anonymous tunes right through to John Hughes's MAELOR (Ex. 198), which shows no change whatever in idiom, and in which all the tunes baffle any attempt to date them from internal evidence. But there did appear in the nineteenth century a certain anglicising tendency, which produced tunes by Welshmen less exclusively in the Welsh style. One of the earliest of this school was John Ambrose Lloyd (1815–74), in whose CROMER (*E.H.* 237) and GROESWEN (Ex. 191) very few traces of Welsh style remain. He could assume the authentic bardic robe at will, as in his EIFYONIDD (*Emynau à Thonau*, 479) but, normally, his tunes are more English than Welsh. Lloyd's idiom was almost always strong, but his ABERGELE (*Church Hymnary*, 183) is an indication of degeneracy. Caradog Roberts (1879–1935), one of the greatest of Welsh teachers, may be taken as an example of the complete desertion of the Welsh idiom by this school of composers; his GOSPER (Ex. 196) and BERWYN (*C.P.* 189) are unhappy instances of this.[1]

But it remains the exception in the Welsh genius for dramatic diction to be wholly absent from a tune by a Welshman. A good modern example of a tune almost too intense for any English words is CYMER (Ex. 194)—a little less austere, but a little more personally intimate, than the classics of the form. Joseph Parry (1841–1903) is the greatest example of the successful combination of Welsh and English cultures. His tunes are always chiefly Welsh, but they have, as we see in the musical form of ABERYSTWYTH (*E.H.* 87) and DIES IRAE (*C.P.* 583) a touch of superficial polish gained from wide culture in the larger world of music. Normally, however, the greatest Welsh tunes are the work of amateur precentors like R. H. Prichard (HYFRYDOL, 301) and J. D. Jones (GWALCHMAI, 424), and their work is always as simple and as powerful as the best Welsh preaching.

Despite the trivialities of CWM RHONDDA (*C.P.* 500), BLAENWERN, PENLAN (*C.P.* 412) and their like, and the debasement of Welsh dramatic power in many of the tunes in Welsh hymn books, Wales has, until recently, maintained a high and distinguished standard. With the new impact of English anglo-catholicism in Wales since the Disestablishment of 1912, and the dissemination of musical culture of English origin, there is a real danger, exemplified in the new *Emynau'r Eglwys* (1952) of the Church (of England) in Wales, of the damping of Welsh enthusiasm and the extinguishing of the native fire in its hymnody. Wales gave to England Walford Davies and Hubert Parry and Dr Vaughan Williams. We cannot yet be certain whether England's reciprocal gifts will be as advantageous to Wales.

---

[1] It is possible, however, to discern in Welsh hymnody traces of traffic with French culture. ARFON (*E.H.* 116) is known in France as a carol tune, to 'Un nouveau présent des Cieux' (Legeay, *Noel's Anciens*, 1875) and 'Joseph est bien marié' (Guilmant, *Noel's*, 1885). BRYNTIRON (248), by Ascan Lutteroth (1802–89) is set to No. 110 in *Chants Chrétiens* (1881). Conversely, there is much of the Welsh idiom about PICARDY (*E.H.* 318).

23

AMERICAN HYMNODY

THE story of American hymnody must be told with unbecoming brevity here because, with one or two distinguished exceptions, its composers have not yet made an extensive impact on English use. But the very recent widening of its influence, and the dramatic emancipation in the 'forties' of American hymnody from what looked like being a supine subservience to debased standards calls for some attention.

In one sense American hymnody is like that of the Welsh; it was born in the tonal orthodoxy of the eighteenth century. But there the resemblance ends. There is no 'American style' as yet in normal hymnody.

The indigenous 'American style' is, of course, the music of the negroes; the 'negro spiritual' was born of the Kentucky Revivals, of 1797–1805, consequent on the evangelisation of the negroes, and of their great sufferings in the days of slavery. They were evangelised just early enough for their sufferings to be expressed in this sublime and primitive music.[1]

Apart from this, America lacked a musical tradition. Wales in the new enthusiasm of the Methodist revival could use a music that had at least some historic roots in the Wales of Arthur and Taliesin and Teilo; America, in the beginning, had to use English music. One of the oldest native American tunes is probably HULL (Ex. 199), with its curious minor-mode variant at *E.H.* 342. Its history is obscure, and there is a case for giving it an English origin. But when it is compared with CORONATION (Ex. 200), which is quite certainly an early American tune, or with TRUMPET (Ex. 201), it shows the same melodic primitiveness, a sort of tom-tom stamp of monotonous melody, and for this reason we assign it to America. This is, of course, an American version of English Methodist music, but it is Methodism without any of its Handelian sophistication, Wesley without his Oxford degree.

It was not long before the warmth of negro music made itself felt in church hymnody. The swinging rhythm and easy-going tonality of

---

[1] The reader should consult K. S. Latourette, *History of the Expansion of Christianity* (Eyre and Spottiswoode, 1940-48), Vol. IV, for the history of early Christianity in America. He will there read the tragic causes for the absence of any indigenous music of the American Indians. See also L. Ellinwood, *The History of American Church Music* (Morehouse-Gorham Co., New York, 1953).

TOPLADY (Ex. 202) are the white man's approximation to the style of 'Swing low, sweet chariot'; but the white man has, of course, lost the pentatonic scale and the flexible rhythm of the negro's music.

American hymnody swiftly descended after this into the slough of sentimentality, and it might have presented an unrelieved picture of music-hall sloppiness and camp-fire heartiness had it not been for the work of Lowell Mason (1792–1872). Mason was the first American to attack the prevailing tendencies in church music, and to attempt to broaden the nation's musical culture generally. He founded the Boston Handel and Haydn Society, and published in 1821 that Society's *Collection of Church Music*. In 1841 he published *Carmina Sacra;* and these two books ran into many revisions which give us the sources for his hymn tunes.

By modern standards, Mason is a composer of indifferent merit. He was entirely defective in musical imagination. But when his MISSIONARY HYMN (*E.H.* 577) and OLIVET (*E.H. Appx.* 58) are set against their contemporaries, they are seen to be models of austerity and restraint. Other well known tunes of his are BOSTON (*C.P. Appx.* 5), founded in the First Tone of plainsong; DENNIS or RIPON (Methodist Hymn Book 548, arranged from Nägeli, q.v. above, page 105) and the popular arrangement from Filitz called MANNHEIM (*E.H.* 426). He is often supremely dull, but he is very rarely vulgar.

But Mason did not, of course, prevent the progress of American hymnody from bad to worse. Any current American hymn book furnishes abundant examples of the hectic and hysterical, or of the monumentally tedious music which was the daily fare of Americans in the nineteenth century. Horatio Parker's MOUNT ZION (Ex. 203) is probably one of the best hymn tunes of its age. JOHN BROWN'S BODY is perhaps the best of all. At best this music is honestly flamboyant and redolent of the buoyancy of the civilisation that created New York and Pittsburgh and Chicago; at its worst it is flabby and futile.

We put this strongly in order the better to draw attention to the revival that has taken place in the past generation, chiefly under the inspiration of Winfred Douglas (1867–1944). American popular taste has proved itself hard to rescue; but a brave effort has been made in the *Hymnal* (*1940*)[1] of the Episcopal Church. Winfred Douglas was a liturgist and musician of high standing, as well as being an Episcopal priest. His ST DUNSTAN'S (Ex. 204), published in 1918, shows a

---

[1] Note that the date (1940) is part of its title. It is the date of the authorising of the book. Its publication date is 1943.

new clean style of melody. Following his lead several composers experimented in the *Hymnal* with either a return to ancient styles or a genuine effort towards fresh ones. The limpid simplicity of MALA-BAR (Ex. 205) makes an interesting contrast with the adventurous tonality of LYNCHBURG (Ex. 206) and between them the two tunes show the wide range of expression that we find in that hymn book. It is a new thing for America. Other tunes from this book, or from other recent American books, are to be seen in the *B.B.C. Hymn Book*—BELLWOODS (27), THE KING'S MAJESTY (89), and SURSUM CORDA (202), to which may be added CONQUEST (*C.P.* 187). Free rhythm, modality, and modern harmony are all exploited in these fresh tunes, and although it it early yet to say whether they have found success in America, they amount to a very substantial revival of musical taste. The leading composers in this revival are David McK. Williams, Henry Hallstrom, Alfred M. Smith, Graham George, Anne Miller, Bates G. Burt and Leo Sowerby. In the background of the movement stands T. Tertius Noble, once organist of York Minster, but for forty years a distinguished New York musician.

Canadian hymnody does not provide material for a separate discourse; it has shared the sorrows, and in a measure participated in the resurrection of the hymnody of the U.S.A. The *Hymnary* (1930) of the United Free Church of Canada, musically edited by Dr Healey Willan, shows a high standard of critical taste rather in its selection of older treasures than in its new contributions, which are very few.[1]

---

[1] The 'Sankey' idiom originated in America, of course. It has been discussed above (p. 131 f.) . Some other American tunes will be found in *E.H.* at 573, 581, 582, 583, 593, *Appx.* 22.

24

A NOTE ON CONTEMPORARY DEVELOPMENTS

IT remains to consider the present position of English hymnody as it is reflected in some recent hymn books, and to endeavour to draw to a conclusion the work which these chapters have been designed to set forth.

It will have appeared from Chapter 20 that English hymnody in the 'thirties was in a restless condition. What we now see is a converging of the styles of the various denominations, and a cross-fertilisation between the experiments of *Songs of Praise* and the conventionality of the Public School books. All through those turbulent years there comes a steady stream of friendly, fresh, sound, but not forbidding hymnody, of which we have already noticed examples in Harris's ALBERTA and Gordon Slater's ST BOTOLPH, and as a further distinguished example of which we can refer the reader to W. S. Vale's HILLINGDON (*Mirfield Mission Hymn Book*, 4).

Two[1] recent hymn books carry the story into the present situation. The first is *Hymns Ancient and Modern* (Revised, 1950). Sir Sydney Nicholson was the leading musical assessor of this book until he died in 1947, and of its new tunes he provides the largest single contribution. He first appeared as a composer of hymn tunes in *H.A.M.* (1904), where the reader should look up his two contributions (329 and 531). In these youthful compositions his idiom is fresh but not unconventional. In the 1916 *Second Supplement* he produced CRUCIFER (745/633) and HOSANNA IN EXCELSIS (724/421), strong tunes still in an orthodox style, and TOTTERIDGE (692/310), which is one of his first experiments in that free rhythm which later becomes his normal style. Two more tunes, perhaps his two best, BOW BRICKHILL (200/215) and FENITON (717/392) are in the 'Shortened' (1939) edition, together with CHISLEHURST (147). In the 1950 edition he carries his freer style much further in LEAMING-TON (385), AETHELWOLD (143) and ST NICHOLAS (576). All through his compositions there is an open-air, friendly quality, seen at its best in AIRLIE (340/453) and TENBURY (*A.M.(R)* 627).

---

[1] It is possible that some readers may judge *Congregational Praise* (1951) worthy of addition to this list. The present author is not in a position to review it; but a good criticism of it will be found in *English Church Music*, July, 1952. Its outstanding new contributions are those of E. H. Thiman, Kenneth Finlay, Peggy Spencer-Palmer and J. P. B. Dobbs.

Here and there he misses the true congregational idiom through failure entirely to integrate the turbulent forces at work in his age, but his influence on *A & M* has been radical. Not only did he compose tunes of this style, but he found other composers, who could do the same, and encouraged this style in his pupils. The large number of new tunes in different styles, but all manifesting something of this alertness of idiom, is a real enrichment to the book. For sheer contemplative beauty we must mention Leonard Blake's REMISSION (324), for cheerful friendliness in the right context, Chadwyck-Healey's RADWELL (441), for youthful but not bumptious vigour, Jesson's BARNET (223) and Symonds's MERNLE (445), for lusty strength, Statham's ARNCLIFFE (381), for old-world courtesy, Blackall's SWANMORE (396), for grave dignity, Watson's STONOR (404). John Dykes Bower contributes three modest but penetrating tunes, AMEN COURT (237), AVE VERUM (405) and ELTON (534). The other musical editor, G. H. Knight, has VERYAN (9) and VALLEY (546), choral pieces of singular attractiveness. Copyright-barriers prevented the use in this book of the sublime DOWN AMPNEY for 'Come down, O love divine', and Sir William Harris's NORTH PETHERTON, the most graceful of all the modern experiments in rhythms, meets the challenge more bravely and successfully than anyone could have thought possible.

The trend in 1950, as here represented, is away from the clever towards the compassionate. There might well be great danger in this. It might, through inducing admiration for this catena of lovely sounds, lead us back into the Victorian trough. But the preservative of this new music, I think, is to be found in its acknowledgment of the fundamental principles, even though it repudiates some of the external characteristics, of *E.H.* Those principles are centred in reverence for all styles and in especial reverence for truly English styles. There is in the latest *A & M* a catholicity of outlook combined with an essential patriotism and love of English music which makes it, even against the background of *E.H.*, a candidate for genuine popularity and a source of valuable agents in the cause of English religion.

The other book of today, providing a strong contrast, is the *B.B.C. Hymn Book*. Here was a book unique in two external accidents: it had no predecessors, and it has the certainty that everything printed in it will be performed and heard. Its musical editors were Dr Stanton, sometime Musical Director at Wellington School, now Professor of Music at Bristol, Dr G. Thalben-Ball, organist of the Temple Church and music-adviser in chief to the B.B.C., and the Reverend Cyril Taylor, parish priest, precentor, and at the time member of the Religious Broadcasting staff.[1] Thus, in the editorial board who contribute fifty-seven tunes between them, we have the public-school tradition, the cathedral tradition, and the parish-church tradition. Evidence of these traditions stand out quite clearly in the work of these composers. Dr Stanton's tunes are normally astringent in the extreme, though here and there his idiom is kindly and graceful; they employ violent modulations and abrupt melodies; but they are always full of gusto. Dr Thalben-Ball is at all times the faithful pupil of Sir Walford Davies, and his idiom is usually caressing and comforting. Taylor is a master of the 'big popular' tune, though not irretrievably wedded to it; his tunes come nearest to holy vulgarity, and he uses the 'public school' device of broad unison melody with rich accompaniment more than the others. If we lay alongside each other Stanton's SHERSTON (287), Thalben-Ball's JESMIAN (63) and Taylor's already widely famous ABBOT'S LEIGH (176) we have good examples of their contrasting styles.

The other composers represented here for the first time have contributed a number of tunes of real distinction. Herbert Murrill (1909–52) has left us CAROLYN, which has a substantial claim to be the most pregnant utterance in the book and the finest tune written since DOWN AMPNEY; Norman Cocker, G. H. Heath Gracie, and Greville Cooke contribute tunes of hardly less distinction.

In this book we have a more experimental spirit than in A & M; there is less concession to the old guard. There are some bold and controversial experiments, less emphasis on lovely choral sounds, more on meeting the harsh challenge of the modern world and showing in hymnody not only the smile but also the muscle of Christianity.

Finally, and by way of epilogue, for our story is now fully told, let it be observed that the art of hymn tune writing is not dead, nor has the last word been said in these latest books. Our two last examples are designed to indicate this. TEILO SANT (Ex. 207) is the original version of the tune now printed at C.P. 21, a magnificent example of modern and yet traditional technique. WATFORD (Ex. 208), never published before, is an example of the work being done in relative obscurity by our local organists. Mr Gosden is a Methodist and wrote the tune for Charles Wesley's 'Jesus, the first and last'. It has complete candour, complete modesty, and an imperturbable reverence for tradition. It takes us full circle back to the Genevan tradition.

---

[1] Now Warden of the Royal School of Church Music

25

CONCLUSION

With these modern books we return to our starting point. It is now being realised afresh that hymnody is the folk-song of the church, and that the composer of hymn tunes is the composer of folk-songs. If we glance back over the chapters of our story, we find that the great tunes—the Lutheran chorales of 1524 and those of Crüger, the Genevan, English and Scottish psalms, the immortal praise of the English eighteenth century, the great tunes of the Victorian heyday— all have one quality in common. They have achieved immortality in their combination of the traditional with the new, being entirely generous in their regard for tradition and entirely modest in their contribution of what is new.

Now this is not a merely musical point. It is a spiritual, indeed, a theological one. The composer of the public praise of the church is in a position very different from the composer of a symphony for concert-performance, or the composer of classical chamber music. He is required not merely to compose for the delectation or elevation of an audience, or for the diversion, however cultivated, of musicians. He is not composing what will, humanly speaking, be *heard* at all. He is composing what will express what is in the worshippers, that they may sing not for musical effect but in order to achieve that communal discipline, that realisation of the Unity of the Body, which is the necessity, the fabric, and the monopoly of the Church. This composer, then, must be able to build himself into that Body as he composes; he must write what the people can sing to their edification, and in so writing he has to avoid both the temptations and snares that lie in the way of all communal disciplines : mass hysteria, superficial kindling of irresponsible emotion, and all other forms of dishonesty and guile—and also that other temptation to educate, to preach something other than the Gospel of Christ, to interpose a musical idol between the worshipper and the altar. That which links together that strangely assorted group of heroes in *Hebrews* xi, Rahab the harlot and Jacob the swindler among them, compendiously described as 'faith' by the author of the Epistle, is the obedience which allows them to be built into a purpose, to become part of a living tradition; it is a human sympathy and a divinely given obedience which, at some great moment or other, distinguishes their lives from those of the

171

faithless, the 'profane person as Esau' (*Hebrews* xii. 16). It is exactly thus with the composer of hymn-tunes. He has to face the whole challenge and paradox implied in the word 'tradition'. He has to accept a tradition and yet contribute to a tradition.

Perhaps this point may be illuminated from the work of two modern scholars. G. L. Prestige in the first chapter of his *Fathers and Heretics*[1] makes much of the fact that *traditio* in Latin has its basic meaning, 'handing over'. (*Tradere* commonly means in classical Latin to 'betray', indeed, it is the etymological root of the English word.) Tradition in its common meaning is an established body of knowledge or opinion, unalterable and accepted; but the *act of tradition* is the handing over of this body from one person to another in the long procession of history, and the very life of the tradition (in the familar sense) depends on the reality of the tradition (in the technical sense), the handing-over of the body of opinion from one person uniquely and irrecoverably into the keeping, for better or worse, of another *person*. Thus, the paradox is clear. In the idea of tradition there are two concepts, that of the communion of believers—the communion, indeed, of saints—and that of the solitary receiver of the tradition. There is, to put it in terms of our present study, the whole weight of Christian hymnodic tradition which to disregard is to cut oneself off from the continuing body of the church in that sphere, and to write what a congregation will never want to sing; and there is the isolated composer with his pen on the stave uttering what, if it is to live, must be a unique and irreplaceable statement related to, and implying acceptance of, that tradition. The tradition, indeed, is not simply the *corpus* of all hymn-tunes ever written; it is the communion of all singing congregations; it comprises not only of composers' statements but the habits, failings, predilections and aspirations of all the people who have accepted and used those statements in their public praise.

The other authority who should be quoted here is Daniel Jenkins, who, in his book *Tradition and the Spirit* (1951), and especially in its seventh chapter, places this same paradox starkly against our contemporary experience. Writing from the standpoint of a responsible reformed theologian, Mr. Jenkins there shows, first, that an uncritical reverence for tradition (in the familiar sense) can lead to formalism, legalism, and archaism.[2] He proceeds then to show how traditionalism can lead to a partial and ultimately partisan interpretation of the very tradition to which it looks with such respect;[3] finally, he makes

---

[1] S.P.C.K., 1940
[2] pp. 115–23.
[3] pp. 123 ff.

the positive assertion that the church, in its attitude to the traditional creeds of Christianity, must be 'constantly confessing', a statement which is summed up in the following sentence:

> Before joining our testimony to that of the Creeds we must honestly face the possibility that they may be mistaken and find assurance of their truth *for ourselves.*[1]

Having thus justified the 'confessing' church, he then shows that the very convention of 'confession', of placing the rule of faith in the conscience, experience, and life of the believer rather than in the tradition handed down from Constantinople or Toledo, may become itself a tradition and so restore all the dangers of traditionalism. But the words we have ventured to italicise in the above quotation are the important words. The acceptance of tradition without the honest attempt to prevent its robbing the receiver of the responsibility for making a personal choice and a personal commitment is the beginning of the evil. Tradition regarded as a refuge is a snare. Tradition without the *traditio* paralyses.

This, we believe, throws light on the whole of our story. We have passed under review many conventions of hymn-tune writing, but all the parts of the story have followed a common pattern. There have always been the eccentrics, the experimenters, the educators; there were Schütz and Mergner in Germany, and the adventurers of 1906–33 in England. There have been the formalists and legalists, like the Scottish Calvinists who set a virtually official seal on twelve common tunes, or the eighteenth-century Germans and nineteenth-century English who lived on capital and so became sentimental or dull. There have been the purists, perfectionists, enthusiasts, and separatists who have ignored tradition for the sake of a closed community of mysticism, like the German mystics and pietists with their florid and preposterous melodies: these were they who elevated a 'confession' into a tradition. But all the way there have been those who, accepting the tradition, have accepted it positively and kept it alive by adding their personal touch of belief and commitment to it. Hence, the anonymities, the apparent plagiarisms, the authentic quality of tunes written in Calvin's Geneva and Roosevelt's America. Hence, the uniqueness and the immortality of Dykes's NICAEA. These are the implications of the word 'traditional' which is frequently to be found in the ascriptions of hymn-tunes. Indeed, our contention is that all great hymn-tunes, even when the composer's name has been carefully preserved, are essentially traditional.

It is by the same token that we justify the inferences we have made between the quality of the hymn-music of an age and the spiritual

---

[1] p. 132.

condition of that age. The tradition of hymnody is swayed and conditioned by the demand of the congregations at large as well as by the musical abilities of composers and the critical faculties of editors. And yet, in order not to depreciate the worth of musicians, we must state the conclusion in the following fashion.

The early chorales of Luther's time reflect faithfully the enthusiasm of the Lutheran Reformation; but without Luther's own musical genius and the organising faculties of Walther they might have been merely vulgar popular songs. The Genevan psalm-tunes recall to us the essential serenity and discipline of the *Institutes* and the *Commentaries* of Calvin; but we owe it to Bourgeois that these tunes express the peace and confidence of the theology of the Promises and not the turbulence, the despotism, and the artificial rigour of Calvin's Geneva. The glory of Pietism is to be seen in the greatest tunes of Freylinghausen and Bach which express its personal fervour and childlike, intimate, candid devotion. But in the hands of lesser musicians the music of pietism shows us not so much devotion as introversion. The later German chorales express little but complacency and security, and it was upon precisely these aspects of decadent Lutheranism that the rebels of the nineteenth century in Germany were fed. The German tunes that form the epilogue to our Lutheran section are full of the spirit of return to primitive conditions of battle and persecution; they reflect no compromise either with the idiom of the complacent church of the previous century or with the idiom of secular entertainment; in a country threatened and eventually controlled by idolatrous Nazism nothing could be more natural than this; but the embattled church of Germany has not yet thrown up a new unifying musical idiom.

The psalm-tunes of England and Scotland reflect the ruggedness and simplicity of the Puritan outlook and practice; but if it were not for the editorial genius of Ravenscroft we might well be left not with the most inspired but with the most humdrum of these melodies, which would faithfully reflect that which is earthbound and repressive in puritanism: and Ravenscroft was not a Puritan but an Anglican musician. The music of the English Restoration is full of the richness and pageantry of that age at its best; but we think kindly of it only after contemplating the gracious work of Clarke and Croft; we have less good to say of the undisciplined music of Methodism. The dull psalm-tunes of Green are a perfect picture of unconvinced eighteenth-century Puritanism. The exuberant melodies of Methodism show at their best all that is generous and at their worst that is irresponsible in that mighty movement. The music of the Welsh eighteenth century expresses all the near-fanatical narrowness of purpose of Welsh Methodist-Calvinism; it would have made a less admirable showing had it not been for the native musical genius of the Celt.

In Victorian England we have in Dykes the virtues and the vices of English security, in Gauntlett the heartiness, sometimes honest, sometimes superficial, of nonconformity, in Sullivan the tragedy of the English Sunday suit. The secretive vices of Victorian England are to be seen in the Calkins and Elliotts of the age, its expansive and exhilarating virtues in the generous melodies of Parry. The activist, impatient, go-getting faith of nineteenth-century America finds its expression in American hymnody, the new responsibility and seriousness of that great country in its new hymnody. The warmth and sentiment of the public schools, the airy and functional efficiency of modern elementary and secondary education, are the very atmosphere of the work of W. H. Ferguson and Gustav Holst. The restless suspicion of tradition, and post-war confusion of Europe are adequately reflected in certain half-articulate eccentricities in *Songs of Praise*. The melodies of Roman Catholicism and Protestant revivalism have in common an easy-going quality which reflects the tendency in both to attract the convert by offering him a discipline which shall also be a release from certain intellectual doubts and responsibilities.

All this is deducible and demonstrable; but it is all *prima facie* to be expected. The hymn-singing congregation is the last arbiter of sacred folk-song, and its arbitration, always weighty and never carefully calculated, is a direct product of its faith and practice. For the consummation of Christian worship in this world neither the worshipper, with his tradition born in his bones, nor the prophet who interprets the Word of the Lord upon the present moment, can do without each other. That same community embraces both the unpractised singer and the cultivated musician. But both are bound, and the work of both is entirely made possible, by that act of faith which accepts and which builds tradition.

MUSIC
EXAMPLES

COPYRIGHT ACKNOWLEDGMENTS

The following material in the music examples is known to stand under copyright. If at any point we have infringed copyright or overlooked an owner of copyright, we apologise, and undertake to correct the matter in any future edition.

The copyright holders of the following tunes have proved untraceable:
164, HARROW: 165, SHAWFIELD: 166, WELLS: 167, WOLVESEY.

The following are reprinted by permission of their owners, to whom we express our gratitude for their help and generosity :

161, RAGLETH HILL, by Basil Harwood : from the Oxford Hymnal (Clarendon Press, 1908), by permission of the Public Trustee.

163, TREGYNON, from *A Students' Hymnal* (1923), by permission of the Oxford University Press, Ltd.

168, WINTON, by Sir George Dyson, by permission of the composer and of Edward Arnold Ltd., publishers.

169, HADLOW, by John Wilson, from the *Clarendon Hymn Book* (1936), by permission of the composer.

192, GWYNFA ; 193, CAPEL TYGWYDD ; 194, CYMER ; 195, BENWIL ; and 196, GOSPER: by permission of *Pwyllgor y Caniedydd*, c/o the Rev. E. Curig Davies, Swansea.

197, WILLIAM: by permission of Lady Haydn Jones.

198, MAELOR, by John Hughes; by permission of the composer.

204, ST. DUNSTAN'S ; 205, MALABAR; 206, HALLSTROM, by permission of the Church Pensions Fund, New York, and, in the case of 205 and 206, of their composers.

207, TEILO SANT : the copyright of the tune in this form lies with its composer, Mr. Jack Dobbs, the Malayan Teachers' College, Wolverhampton.

208, WATFORD: the copyright lies with Mr. A. T. Gosden, 53 Hagden Lane, Watford.

Abbreviations used in the music examples (where these are not self-explanatory in conjunction with the text) ;
B. I or B. II : W. Bäumker, *Das katholische deutsche Kirchenlied* . . . (Gütersloh, 1889-93, vol. i or vol. ii).

C.P.: *Congregational Praise* (Independent Press Ltd., London, 1951).

D.C. : *Deutsches Choralbuch*, Tonsatz von R. Mauersburger, 4th edition, Berlin, 1936.

E.Ps.: S.S. Wesley : *The European Psalmist* (London, 1872).

E.T.: *Emynau a Thonau*. Bangor and Caernarvon, 1929.

Frost: Frost, *English and Scottish Psalm Tunes*, 1524-1677 (London, 1953).

H. (U.S.A.): *The Hymnal* (1940), New York, 1943.

H.A.M. : *Hymns Ancient and Modern*, Historical Edition (Clowes, London, 1909).

O.H.: *The Oxford Hymnal* (Oxford, 1908).

P.C. : *Piae Cantiones*, edited by G. R. Woodward for the Plain-song and Medieval Music Society, 1910.

Peters: 371 Vierstimmige Choräle (J. S. Bach), Peters Edition.

W.H. : *Westminster Hymnal* (London, 1914 and 1940).

1

CHRISTE QUI LUX ES

Geistliche Lieder (Wittemburg), 1535

8. 8 . 8.8.

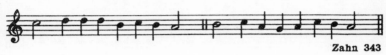

Zahn 343

Et in ter-ra pax, ho-mi-ni-bus bo-nae vo-lun - ta-tis.

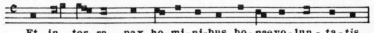

Lau-da-mus te, Be-ne - di-ci-mus te, A-do-ra-mus te,

2

ALLEIN GOTT IN DER HÖH SEI EHR

8.7. 8.7. 8.8.7.

Geistliche Lieder (Leipzig), 1539

Zahn 4457

181

3

EIN NEUES LIED

8.7.8.7.8.8.8.8.7

Encheiridion
(Erfurt), 1524

Zahn 7245

4

WIR GLAUBEN ALL AN EINEN GOTT,
SCHÖPFER

8.8.8.8.8.8.8.8.8.8.8. Iam. and Troc.

Zahn 7971

182

5
EIN' FESTE BURG

8.7.8.7.6.5.5.6.7

Geistliche Lieder, (1529), 1535

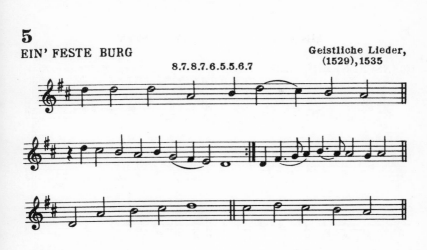

Originally written in Alto Clef, tonic F, with key signature ♭.
Here transposed up a major 6th and note-values halved.

Zahn 7377

6
ICH DANK DIR

Magdeburg Hymn Book, 1540

7.6.7.6.D

Originally printed a fourth higher. The G♯ (C♯) is original.

Zahn 5354a

7

AVE HIERARCHIA
(MENSCHENKIND, MERK EBEN)

Medieval Melody
Arr. M. Weisse, 1531

6.6.6.6.6.6.

Zahn 3294

8a

CHRISTUS WAHRER GOTTES SOHN
(CHRISTUS DER UNS SELIG MACHT)

M. Weisse, 1531

7.6.7.6.7.6.7.6. (Trochaic)

Originally written in notes of double value, the figure at the ends of the even lines
thus ▢ ♭♭ ♪ .

Zahn 6283a

184

8b

CHRISTUS, DER UNS SELIG MACHT

Harmony by
J.S.Bach

7.6.7.6. D

9
WIR LOBEN DICH

Geistliche Lieder
(Leipzig), 1551

4.4.4.4.7.   4.4.4.4.7.   4.4.4.4.7.   4.4.4.4.7

Zahn 8563

Wir loben dich	Versohnet ganz
Eimutiglich	Ein englisch Glanz
Herr Jesu Christ	Die selbig Nacht
Der du uns bist	Gross Freuden bracht
Ein kleines Kind gebören	That uns den Fried verkünden.
Dein Kindheit hat	Die Hirten all
Dit Misse that	Mit grossen Schall
Da mit wir all	Erfurchten das
Durch Adams fall	Ihn seltsam was
Verdient deins Vaters Zören.	Erledigt uns von Sünden.

10
HERZLICH THUT MICH ERFREUEN

Arr. by J. Walther in
Ein Schöner Geistlicher...
Berkreyen, 1552

7.6.7.6.7.6.7.6

Zahn 5361a

11
CHRIST DER DU BIST
DER HELLE TAG

Christliche Gesangbüchlein,
(Eisleben) 1568

8.8.8.8

Zahn 384

12
WAS MEIN GOTT WILL
DAS GSCHEH ALLZEIT

J. Magdeburg's Christliche und tröstliche
Tischgesenge, Erfurt 1572

Adapted from an air,
"Il me souffit de touts mes maulx"
Published by P. Attaignant, Paris c. 1530

8.7.8.7.4.4.7.4.4.7

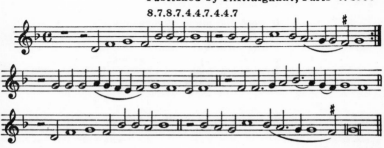

Zahn 7568

13

O WELT ICH MUSS DICH LASSEN

H. Isaak,
1450-1527

7.7.6.7.7.8.

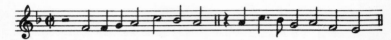

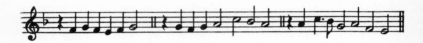

Zahn 2293a

This was composed for a secular poem. In **1539** it first appears set to sacred words;
but the sacred words are an adaptation of the same secular poem, thus:

Innsbruck, ich muss dich lassen,
Ich far dahin mein Strassen
    In Fremde Land dahin;
Mein Freud ist mir genommen,
Die ich nit weiss bekommen
    Wo ich im Elend bin.

O Welt, ich muss dich lassen,
Ich far dahin mein Strassen
    Ins ewig Vaterland;
Mein Geist will ich aufgeben,
Dazu mein Lieb und Leben
    Setzen gnädig in Gottes Hand.

The tune was used by Bach in his *St. Matthew Passion*, Nos. 16 and 46
One of these versions will be found at E.H. 278, where it is set to an English paraphrase of *Nun rühen alle Walder*, a hymn of Gerhardt with which this tune later
became associated.

14

ICH GLAUB' AN GOTT

Selnecker, 1587

8.8.8.8

Zahn 413

15

WIR CHRISTENLEUT

Gesangbuch
(Dresden), 1593

4.4.11.4.4.11

For version by J.S.Bach, see his *Christmas Oratorio* No.35 and *Songs of Syon*, No.14

Zahn 2072

16

WIE SCHÖN LEUCHTET DER MORGENSTERN

Nicolai, 1599

8.8.7.8.8.7.2.2.4.4.4.8

For versions by Bach and Mendelssohn, see S.P. 90 i and ii

Zahn 8359

17

WACHET AUF

Nicolai, 1599
harmonised by
Praetorius, 1609

8.9.8.8.9.8.6.6.4.4.4.8

The first line appears thus in Zahn (8405):

Zahn suggests that the note marked (1) should be of double length. Praetorius, it will be seen, lengthens both this and the note marked (2)

In the third phrase, Zahn has all the notes, except the last, of equal length.

In Zahn the melody appears a minor third higher.

For Bach's version, see E.H.12, but originally the words are thus distributed in the bass part in the first bar.

Wake,...... O wake, for

18

WENN MEIN STÜNDLEIN VORHANDEN IST

Praetorius, 1599

8.7.8.7.8.7.7

(Melody in Tenor)

Zahn 4484

19

"Mein Gmüth", the original of
HERZLICH THUT MICH VERLANGEN

Hassler, 1601

7.6.7.6.6.6.7.6

Zahn 5385

20

HEUT' TRIUMPHIRET GOTTES SOHN

B. Gesius, 1601

8.8.8.8.8.8

Hal - le - lu - ia, Hal - le - lu - ia.

Hal - le - lu - ia, Hal - le - lu - ia.

A version by Bach will be found at E.H. **417**
(*N.B.* The tune is composed for the metre 8.8.8. 8.8.8.)

Zahn 2585

21

O GOTT, DER DU DIE MENSCHENKIND

Vulpius, 1609

8.7.8.7.8.8.7

Compare GELOBT SEI GOTT, S.P.154

Zahn 4539

22

JESU, KREUZ, LEIDEN UND TOD

Vulpius, 1609

7.6.7.6. D (Trochaic)

Zahn 6288a

23

DIVINUM MYSTERIUM

Piae Cantiones, 1582

7.6.7.6.7.6

Di - vi-num myster-i - um..... Mo-do de-clar-a - tur

Et mens in - fi-de - li - um...... Tumens ex - e - cra - tur

Fir - ma spe cre-den - ti - um ....

Fi - des ro - bor - a - - - - - tur

Written in the alto clef an octave lower and in notes of double length (□ and ◇(♭))

PARANYMPHUS ADIENS

Piae Cantiones, 1582

7.6.7.6.7.6.7.6 (trochaic) + 8.8.8 (iambic)

Pa - - - - - - - -

[pa] - ra-nym-phus a - di - ens ....

Vir - gi - nem lae - tan - - - ter

Ver-bum summi nun-ci-ans nym-pha-le gra-tan - ter

in-quit A - ve coe-li-ca vir-go gra-vi-da - ta

Ex - tans Ma - ter De - i - ca ....

De - i - cis um - bra - - - ta

Na - to re - gi-nae of - - fe - ro

ia - cen-ti in cu - na-bu - lo

re - gen-ti cunc-ta ver - - bu - lo

ver - - - - - bu - lo.

24b

O QUAM MUNDUM (First phrase)

Piae Cantiones, 1582

O..

For the complete melody, see *Cowley Carol Book*, **29**

P.C. XLVII

25

IST GOTT FÜR MICH

Augsburg, 1609

7.6.7.6.7.6.7.6

Zahn 5394

26

VALET WILL ICH DIR GEBEN

Teschner, 1613

7.6.7.6.7.6.7.6

Zahn 5404

27

AN WASSERFLÜSSEN BABYLON

Psalmen (Strasbourg, 1526)

8.7.8.7.8.8.7.8.8.7

For version by Bach see Peters Edn. No.5 *Songs of Syon* **306**

196

Zahn 7663

28a
PSALM 1

10.10.11.11.10.10

Strasbourg,
1539

Originally a tone lower, Note-values are halved throughout Exx. 374 to 396

28b
The same, **arranged by L. Bourgeois**, 1542:

197

29
PSALM 2

10.11.10.11.11.10.11.10

Strasbourg, 1539

Originally a minor 3rd higher

30a
PSALM 129

7.6.7.6.D

Strasbourg, 1539

Originally a tone higher

30b
The same, arranged by Louis Bourgeois, 1542, for Psalm 130:

31

THE SONG OF SIMEON (Nunc Dimittis)

Strasbourg, 1539

6.6.7.6.6.7

The tune substituted in the **1547** and subsequent Genevan Psalters will be found at **E.H. 269.**

32

PSALM 15

1539

1st strain (of 5)

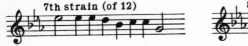

3rd strain

PSALM 36

7th strain (of 12)

8th strain

PSALM 90

5th strain (of 8)

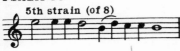

PSALM 114

4th strain (of 6)

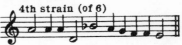

PSALM 142

3rd and 4th strains (of 5)

THE TEN COMMANDMENTS

1st strain (of 5)

33a
PSALM 6

7.7.6.7.7.6

1542

33b
The same, set to Psalm 85 in the Scottish Psalter:

8.8.6.8.8.6

1564

Old 85th

34
PSALM 23

11.11.11.11.11.11.

Geneva, 1562

(a)

Originally a fourth higher

The passage marked (a) will be found in Crüger's *Herzliebster Jesu*, Ex. 72

35
OLD 137th

D.C.M.

Anglo-Genevan Psalter, 1556

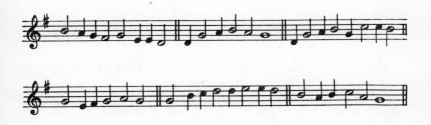

36a
IAM CHRISTUS ASTRA ASCENDERAT

Mode i

36b
JOYSSANCE VOUS DONNERAY

Attaignant,
1530

Douen i 728

36c

Strasbourg,
1542

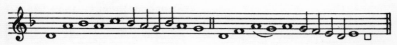

Douen i 629f
note values halved

36d
PSALM 104

Genevan Psalters,
1559 –

10.10.11.11.D

37
RAVENSCROFT'S 104th

10.10.11.11

1621

Originally 1½ tones higher with note values doubled

Note that the last line is in duple time. This ambiguity of rhythm has given rise to the following modern approximations.

Havergal 1847, and Hymns A.&M. 1861 (No.156)

Hymns A.&M. 1875 (presumably Monk) (No.167)

Yattendon Hymnal, 1899 (No.63)

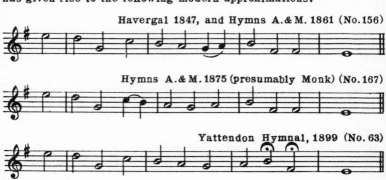

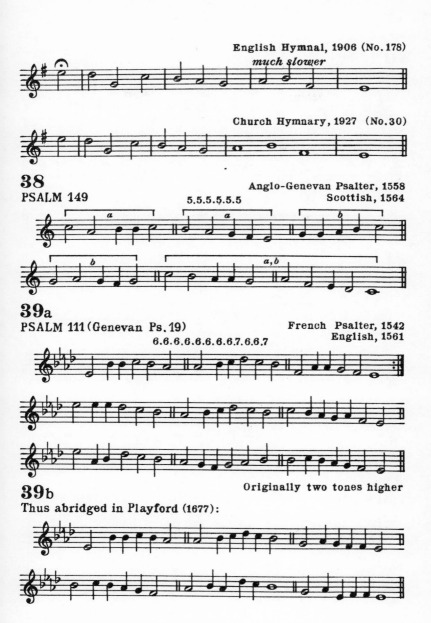

English Hymnal, 1906 (No. 178)
much slower

Church Hymnary, 1927 (No. 30)

38
PSALM 149

5.5.5.5.5.5

Anglo-Genevan Psalter, 1558
Scottish, 1564

39a
PSALM 111 (Genevan Ps. 19)

6.6.6.6.6.6.6.6.7.6.6.7

French Psalter, 1542
English, 1561

39b
Thus abridged in Playford (1677):

Originally two tones higher

203

40
MAGNIFICAT

D.C.M.

English Psalter (Day),
1562

41
NUNC DIMITTIS

D.C.M.

English Psalter (Day),
1562

* The sign of triple time

42a
PSALM 120

6.6.6.6.6.6

Scottish Psalter,
1564

42b
PSALM 143

6.6.6.6.D

Scottish Psalter, 1564

Compare Ex.171

43
PSALM 101

Geneva, 1551

The same, in the Anglo-Genevan Psalter (1561), set to Psalm 134:

From 1562 the last two lines appear thus:

From 1577 the last line appears thus:

and

It does not appear after 1595, until in 1836 W. Crotch revived it in his Psalm Tunes (1836) in the form to be found in E.H. 27

205

44
OLD COMMON TUNE

C.M.

1565

45
LOW DUTCH TUNE
(or Canterbury Tune) (or English Tune)

1565

46
THE HUMBLE SUIT
OF A SINNER

English Psalter (Day),1562
Harmonised by R.Palmer, 1621

D.C.M.

47

OLD 100th

Ps. 134 in Genevan Psalter, 1551
Harmonised by T. Ravenscroft, 1621

L.M.

This version appears in the Songs Spiritual appended to Ravenscroft's Psalter, set to No.2, *"A Psalm before Evening Prayer"*
this is Psalm 134, its original association in Geneva.

48
COLESHILL

C.M.

Barton's Psalms, 1644

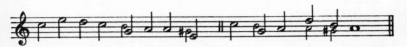

If the small notes be taken instead of the large notes at those points where they appear, you have the melody of WINDSOR (DUNDEE)

49
GLASGOW TUNE

C.M.

1615

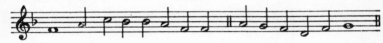

1635 No. XII

50
COUPER TUNE

C.M.

1635

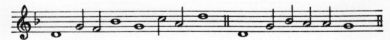

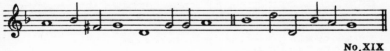

No. XIX

51
CAITHNESS TUNE

C.M.

1635

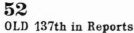

Harmony as at No. XXIX in **1635** Psalter: there written two tones higher.

52
OLD 137th in Reports

1635

* Originally Mezzo-soprano clef with 𝄡 on second line.
† Originally Tenor-clef, as tenor part.

211

Note:

The square slurs indicate the imitated phrases.

The round slurs indicate a conjectural system of fitting in the words. (1) The second line is almost certainly repeated in the alto. (2) The last note in the second stave of the alto part is difficult to fit into any scheme. It may be added to the previous phrase if the E and F before it are sung to one syllable.

The dotted slurs indicate which groups of notes are sung to single syllables if the foregoing scheme is right.

Notes in brackets are conjectural divisions of semibreves to accommodate extra syllables.

53

MISERERE MEI

C.M.

Hunnys, 1583

*Last Verse

Cf. E.H. 403

mis - e - re - re me - i.

54

"FORD"

("Almighty God, which hast me brought")

L.M.

Cantus and
treble viol
altus and
flute

Tenor and
bandora
bass and
bass viol

Cf. HAM 94

55

FIFTH MODE MELODY

T. Tallis,
c. 1561

Metre ambiguous

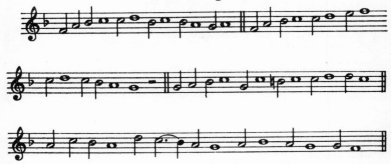

From Robert Bridges' note on this tune and the words to which it is set, (Yattendon Hymnal, 1899, notes page 26, hymn 98):

The unbar'd original is divided into syllabic sections, thus 6, 6,4,4,6 repeated; and there is some uncertainty about the metre of this tune, which is discussed in the note on the words. Tallis may have been confused by the Archbishop's literary machinations, or he may have thought that such a device as he has adopted was suitable to such words.

Bridges quotes the first verse of Matthew Parker's 42nd Psalm:

Even like (in chase) the hunted hynde
    The waterbrooks (doth glad) desire:
Even thus my soule that fainting is
    To Thee (my God) would fayne aspire.
My (very) soule did thirst to God
    To God (the fount) of lyfe and grace;
I said even thus: when shall I come
    To see (at eve) God's lively face.

By variously using the brackets the psalm may be sung to a tune in L.M., C.M., or S.M.; although here and there the grammar and syntax suffer.   Bridges sets the tune to original words which may be read at S.P. 483

In his note on the words, Bridges wrote:

The divided eight-syllable line (i.e. the third and seventh of the tune) follows Parker's custom of a mid-caesura; he generally makes these two four-syllable components rhyme, and it seems certain that Tallis must have been following such a model when he wrote this melody.

56
SIXTH MODE MELODY (for Psalm 139)

T. Tallis,
c.1561

D.C.M.

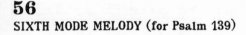

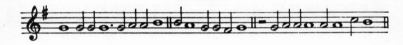

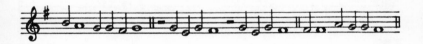

Expend, O Lord,
My plaint of worde,
  In grief that I do make,
My musing mynd
Recount most kynd,
  Geve eare for thine owne sake.

O harke my grone,
My crying mone,
  My King, my God thou art;
Let me not stray
From Thee away,
  To Thee I pray in hart.

57a
SONG 34   Gibbons, 1623

L.M.

57b
SONG 9 (Song 44)

6 × 8

Song 44 repeats the last two phrases.

57c
SONG 34 in Playford   Playford,
                                                                        1671
For Psalm civ   L.M.

57d
For Ps. XL and others   Playford,
                                                                        1677
WESTMINSTER   C.M.

Frost 362 (b and c).

58
SONG 41

6 × 8

Gibbons, 1623

Frost, 363

59
SONG 47

7 × 10

Gibbons, 1623

REFRAIN

60
GIBBONS'S "Signature"

SONG 1

SONG 22

SONGS 9,34,44

SONG 13

SONG 5

SONG 14

61

SANDYS, Psalm 7   8.4.8.4.8.8   H. Lawes, 1637

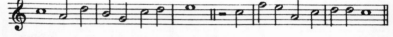

* The bass under this note is B♭. In **1676** the melody note was G and the bass note C, which alteration makes the phrase almost identical with the opening of Psalm 8 (E.H. 234)

62

PSALM 9, 1st phrase (of 4)

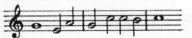

PSALM 7, 4th phrase (of 6)

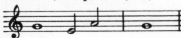

PSALM 72, 3rd phrase (of 4)

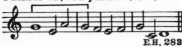

E.H. 283

PSALM 12, 3rd phrase (of 6)

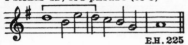

E.H. 225

PSALM 136, 1st phrase (of 6)

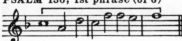

PSALM 8, 1st phrase (of 4)

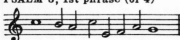

PSALM 72, 2nd phrase (of 4)

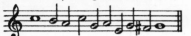

63

Lawes's final phrases:

PSALM 13

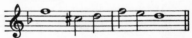

PSALM 14

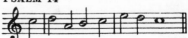

PSALM 22

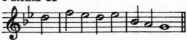

PSALM 31

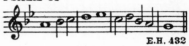

E.H. 432

PSALM 47

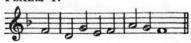

PSALM 111

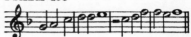

PSALM 136

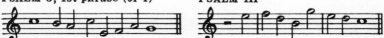

PSALM 72

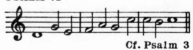

Cf. Psalm 3

64

MACHS MIT MIR, GOTT

8.6.8.6.8.8

Schein, 1628

For versions by J.S.Bach, see R.H. **138** and *St. John Passion No.40*

Zahn 2383

65

HERR GOTT, DU UNSER ZUFLUCHT BIST

(PSALM 90) 8.6.8.6.8.8

Schein, 1627

Zahn 2362

66

ALLEIN NACH DIR

12.11.12.11.10.9.5.7.7.9.7.6.7.9.7.6.7

Schein, 1627

Zahn, 8542

67a

ACH GOTT UND HERR

4.4.7.4.4.7

As Hymnodus Sacer
Leipzig, 1625

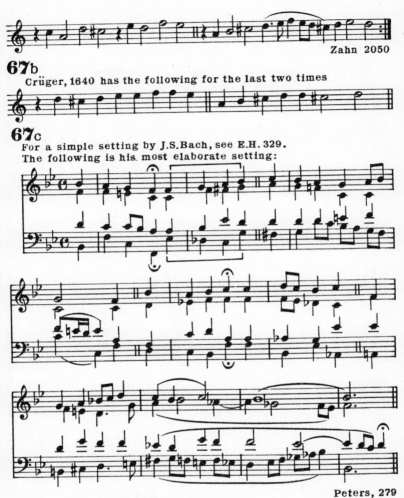

Zahn 2050

67b

Crüger, 1640 has the following for the last two times

67c

For a simple setting by J.S.Bach, see E.H. 329.
The following is his most elaborate setting:

Peters, 279

Solls ja so sein,
Dass Straf und Pein
  Auf Sünde folgen müssen,
So fahr hier fort,
Nur schone dort
  Und lass mich hier wohl büssen.

(v. 4 of "Ach Gott und Herr," Jena 1613)

221

68

PSALM 138

7.6.7.6.7.6.7.6

Schütz, 1628

Zahn 5419

69

PSALM 15

8.8.8.8

Schütz, 1628

Zahn 539

70

PSALM 84

7.6.7.6.7.7.6

Schütz, 1628

Zahn 4306

71
PSALM 45

Schütz, 1628

8.7.8.7.4.4.4.4.4.7.8.7.6

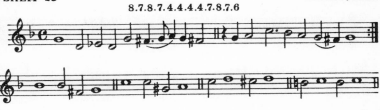

Zahn 8293

72
HERZLIEBSTER JESU

Sapphic

Crüger, 1640

Zahn 983

For settings by Bach, see *St. Matthew Passion* Nos. 3 and 55 (E.H. 70 i and ii), (and an extended setting at No. 25) *St John Passion* Nos. 7 and 27.

73
HERR, ICH HABE MISGEHANDELT

Crüger, 1649

8.7.8.7.8.8

Zahn 3695

74

AUF AUF, MEIN HERZ

7.6.7.6.6.6.6.6

Crüger, 1648

Zahn 5243

75

The same

Freylinghausen, 1705

Zahn 5245

76

LASSET UNS DEN HERREN PREISEN

8.7.8.7.8.7.7.8.7.7

Schop, 1641

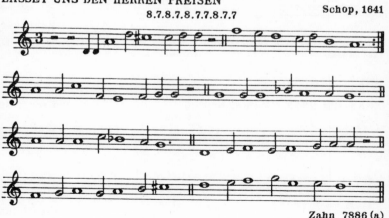

Zahn 7886 (a)

77
WACH AUF, MEIN GEIST

Schop, 1642

8.8.7.8.8.7.8.8

Zahn 5817

78
JESU MEINE FREUDE

Peter, 1655

6.6.5.6.6.5.7.8.6

Zahn 8033

79
MERKT AUF

Ebeling, 1666

7.6.7.6.7.6.7.6

This is now sung in Lutheran churches to Gerhardt's "Du meine Seele singen."
(G.Sch. Hol. 248)

Zahn 5490

80
DIES IST DER TAG
DER FRÖMLICHKEIT

Sohren, Praxis Pietatis
1668

8.7.8.7.8.8

A modern form of this tune will be found at E.H. 188 ii

Zahn 2392

81
NUN LASST UNS GEH'N

7.7.7.7 (iambic)

Praxis Pietatis
1668

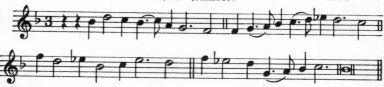

The Dresden (1694) setting of the same hymn will be found at E.H. 104   Zahn 178

82
ES IST GENUG

4.6.6.4.6.6.9.9.4

Ahle, 1668

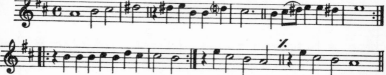

Zahn 7173

Es ist genug,
So nimm, Herr, meinem Geist
Zu Sions Geisten hin.
Lös auf das Band,
Das allgemächlich reisst
Befreie diesen Sinn.
Der sich nach seinen Gotte sehnet,
Der täglich Klagt und nächtlich thränet;
Es ist genug.

83
DIE GÜLDNE SONNE KAMMT HERAN

8.8.8.8

Weichmann,
1648

Zahn 623

84

UM DEN LIEBEN FRIEDEN
8.7.8.7.8.8.7.7

Neumark, 1657

*The accidentals here would, of course, be written ♮ in modern notation.

Zahn 6789

85

GEH AUF, MEINS HERZENS MORGENSTERN
8.7.8.7.4.4.7.4.4.7

Joseph, 1657

Dotted bars are here added for convenience in reading the rhythm of this tune.

Zahn 7612

86

DEIN EIGNE LIEBE ZWINGET MICH

Scheffler, 1657

8.8.8.8.7.8.8

Zahn 4958

87

WIE SCHNECKT ES SO LIEBLICH

Hasse, 1659

8.8.6.6.10 (anapaestic)

was mich er freu - - - - - - en

und sä - tig - en soll.

Zahn 2022

88

O ELEND, JAMMER, UNGST UND NOT!

Hasse, 1659

8.8.8.8.8.8

The accidentals in this tune are extremely erratic. In Sohr, *Musikalischer Borschmack der Jauchtzenden Seelen im Ewigen Leben* (1683), in which several of Hasse's tunes are reprinted, the notes marked (*) are sharpened.

89
O SÜNDER, DENKE WOHL

Neander, 1680

6.6.6.6.6.6.6.6

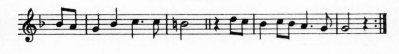

Zahn 5064

90
DAS GROSSE LICHT DER WEITEN WELT

J. W. Franck
1681

8.7.8.7.9.9

Zahn 4168

91

SEHT, WIE WECHSELN ALLE SACHEN

8.7.8.7.8.8.7.7

J.W. Franck, 1685

92

ZEUCH MEINEN GEIST, TRIFF MEINE SINNEN

Nürnberg, 1684

9.9.8.8

Zahn 788

93

JESU DEINE LIEBESFLAMME

Darmstadt, 1698

8.8.7.7.8.8.7.7

Freylinghausen (1704) alters the penultimate phrase thus:

Zahn 6880

231

94

Two settings of WAS DER GOTT THUT

J. A. Freylinghausen, 1704

4.4.11.4.4.11.4.4.11.4.4.11

65

%

6 65 54

6

6

Da capo al %

6

6

Zahn 8221

95

1708

Zahn 8222

This tune should be barred thus:

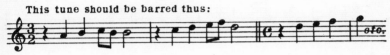

The full text of the first verse of this hymn is as follows:

> Was dein Gott thut
> Ist alles gut,
>   Da benn befiehl ihn alle deine Sachen;
> Dein Kümmernis
> Kann er gewiss;
>   Bald enden und dich wieder ruhig machen.
> Ab es gleich scheint,
> Er sei dein feiud,
>   Wenn du das Kreuzgewitter hörrest trachen;
> Bei Gottes Hut
> Sei wohlgenut;
>   Denn seine Kraft ist mächtig in den Schwachen.

It will be seen that the first setting fails to reflect the change of rhythm between the short and the long lines; the second setting repairs this defect.

96

Two settings of MORGENSTERN,
IM FINSTERN NACHT

7.7.3.3.7

J. A. Freylinghausen,
1705

Zahn 1853

97

1708

DAS IST MEINE FREUDE (Freylinghausen, 1714: Zahn 4807)   Zahn 1854
will be found, two tones lower than its original key, at E.H. 97

98

O LIEBE SEELE

9.8.9.8.5.5.4.5.5.10

J. S. Bach, 1736

Zahn 7787

99
ON THE DIVINE USE OF MUSICK

1677

L.M.

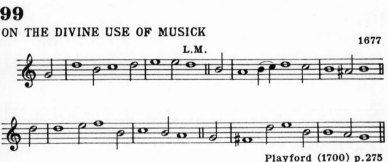

Playford (1700) p.275

We sing to Thee, whose wisdom form'd
    The curious organ of the ear;
And Thou, who gav'st us voices, Lord,
    Our grateful Song in kindness hear.

We'll joy in God, who is the Spring
    Of lawful joy and harmless mirth;
Whose boundless love is fitly call'd
    The harmony of heaven and earth.

These Praises, dearest Lord, aloud
    Our humblest sonnets shall rehearse
Which rightly tun'd are rightly stil'd
    The MUSICK of the Universe.

100
CHICHESTER

6.6.8.6.6.8

J. Bishop, 1711

For Psalm 122. Melody in Tenor

101
ECKINGTON

C.M.

James Green, 1715

Psalm 33

102
ST. DAVID'S

C.M.

as in J. & J. Green, 1715

Compare E.H. 166

Psalm 48

103
RAVENSCROFT'S 104th

10.10.11.11

as in J. & J. Green, 1715

Compare Ex. 37

Psalm 104

104

PSALM 98

D.C.M.

Chetham, 1718

Presumably an early variant of *St. Matthew*, E.H. **526**, which first appeared in 1708

105

PSALM 126

12.12.12.12.10.10

Chetham, 1718

106a

ELTHAM

L.M.

Harmonia Perfecta, set to "Had I the tongues of Greeks and Jews", Isaac Watts
Hymns I 134
Melody in the tenor

106b

The same, arranged by S.S.Wesley

1872

The European Psalmist, No.68

107

W. Knapp, 1st Ed., 1738

DORCHESTER TUNE
(later called WESTON FAVELL)

Ps. 16th v. 8.9.10.11
for Easter Day

* Melody in the tenor from this point

108

ISLINGTON TUNE

The Foundery Collection, 1742 p.26

L.M.

Bro - ther in Christ, and well - be - lov'd, to Je -

-sus and his servants dear, En - ter and shew thy - self ap -

-prov'd, en - ter, and find, en - ter and find that God is here.

The barring in the above version is, of course, erratic in phrases 2 and 4.

109

8 × 7

J. F. Lampe, 1746

Hymns on the Great Festivals, No. 10

110
BRENTWOOD

T. Tallis. as in Whitefield's
Divine Musical Miscellany,
1754

L.M.

111
CARLISLE

Lock Hospital Colln. 2nd Ed.,
1792

8.7.8.7.D

Light of those whose dreary dwelling borders on the shades of

death   Come and thy dear self re - vea - ling   dis - si -

- pate the clouds be-neath. The new heav'n and earth's cre-a -

- tor   in our deepest dark-ness rise   Scatt'ring all the

light of na - ture Pour-ing day up-on our   eyes

Rippon 95

112
RONDEAU

C.M.

Lock Hospital Collection
1769

Lock Hospital Colln., page 10. Set to "Sweet is the memory of Thy grace."
"Set by F. G[iardini]"

The tune is set to a C.M. verse by using the first line as the refrain thus:

Sweet is the memory of Thy grace,
My God, my heavenly king.
(Sweet is the memory of Thy grace).
Let age to age thy righteousness
In sounds of glory sing.
(Sweet is the memory of Thy grace).

The refrain-line is "Sweet is the memory...." throughout the hymn.

113
PASTORAL HYMN

8.8.8.8.8.8

1769

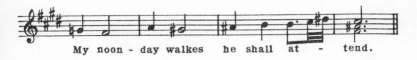

My noon - day walkes he shall at - tend.

Lock Hospital Colln. page 18. Set to "The Lord my pasture shall prepare."
Set by [Mrs.] J. B[romfield]

114
BRIGHTHELMSTONE

7.6.7.6.D

1769

Lock Hospital Colln. page 29. Set to "O Lord, how great's the favour"

The knowledge of this tune may have come through Jacobi's Collection (1722),
but the present form is, of course, English.

115
MANSFIELD

A - wake and run the heav'n - ly race and put a cheer - ful cou - rage

A - wake and run the heav'n - ly race and put a cheerful cou - rage

* $\frac{4}{6}$ means, of course, $\frac{6}{4}$

244

on .... and put

on   and   put

Lock Hospital Colln. page 60. Set to "Awake, our souls, away, our fears."
Set by C.B[urney].

116
DENMARK
L.M.+
1769

Andante maestoso

Be-fore Je - ho-vah's aw-ful throne, Ye nations bow with

sa - cred joy. Know that the Lord is God a - lone, He can cre-

- ate and He des-troy, He can cre-ate and He des-troy.

His sov-'reign pow'r with-out our aid Made us of

clay and form'd us men; And when like wand-'ring

sheep we stray'd, He brought us... to... His fold a-

- gain, He brought us ..... to... His fold a - gain.

③ (1796)

Andante affetuoso

We are his peo-ple, we........... his care, Our

souls and all our mor - tal frame. What last - ing,

last - ing hon - ours shall.... we rear, Al-

- migh - ty Ma - ker to.... Thy name? What

last - ing hon - ours shall.... we rear, Al-

- migh - ty Ma - ker to.... Thy name?

④ We'll crowd Thy gates with thank - ful songs, High as the

heav'ns our voi - ces raise; And earth, and earth with her ten

thou - sand, thou - sand tongues Shall fill thy courts with

sound - ing praise, Shall fill thy courts with sound - ing

praise, Shall fill, shall fill thy courts with sound - ing praise.

⑤ Wide,　wide as the world is Thy com - mand, Vast as e-

- ter - ni - ty, e - ter - ni - ty Thy love; Firm as a　rock Thy

Truth must stand When rol - ling years shall cease to　move, shall

cease to move, When rol - ling years shall cease to　move, When

rol - - ling years .... shall cease to　move.

Lock Hospital Colln. page 94. Verse 3 added by W. Dixon (c. 1790) as a duet for
treble and bass. The remainder is in 3 parts — treble, tenor and figured bass.
Expression marks in v. 3 are as in *Rippon* (tune 87), elsewhere they are as in
the 1769 source. The whole set by M[artin] M[adan].

117

AMESBURY (last verse)   5.5.5.6.5   1769

O that each from the Lord may re-ceive the glad Word, Well and faith-ful-ly done,........ faith-ful-ly done, en-ter in-to my joy and sit down on my throne ‰ throne, and sit down on my throne.

Lock Hospital Colln. p. 139 to last verse of C. Wesley's "Come, let us anew" (C.P. 639). Set by S[amuel] A[rnold].

118
PUTNEY HEATH

C.M+

1770

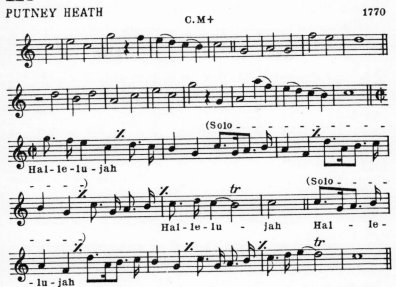

Hal - le - lu - jah

(Solo - - - - -

Hal - le - lu - jah

(Solo - - - -

- - - -

tr

- lu - jah

I. Smith, tune **12**, to Psalm **47**. Starred as Smith's own composition.

119
FOUNTAIN

C.M +

1790

I. Smith (5th Edn.) to ps. **145** iii. The phrase marked ★ is imitated in the bass.

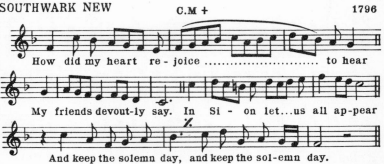

123

MANNING   L.M +   1796

When I sur - vey the... won - drous cross On

which the... Prince of glo - ry ...... died, on

which the Prince of glo-ry died; My rich-est gain I...

count but loss And pour... con - tempt.... on

all... my.... pride, And pour con - tempt, and

pour........ con - tempt..... on all my.... pride.

Rippon, 245

GLAÜBIGES HERZE   10.6.8.9.9.10   Witt, 1715

Zahn 2040

125

GOTT DES HIMMELS 8.7.8.7.7.7 Steiner, 1735

Zahn 3618

126

WOHL MIR, JESUS, MEINE FREUDE 8.7.8.7.8.8 with repeats Dretzel, 1731

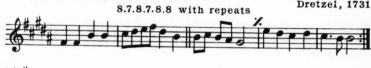

Zahn 3725

127

ACH GOTT, VERLASS MICH NICHT 6.7.6.7.6.6.6.6 Dretzel, 1731

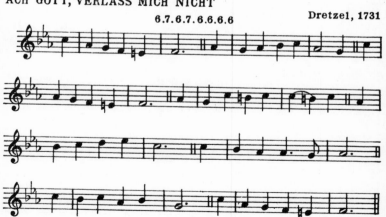

Zahn 5184

128

WAS WILLST DU DICH

11.11.10.10.5.7.11.6.8.7

König, 1738

Zahn 7845

129

THRÄNET, IHR AUGEN,
UND WEINET VON HERZEN

11.11.11.11 (dactylic)

J. B. Reimann
1747

Zahn 1511

130
UN DU ALLEIN

11.8.11.8

Doles, 1755

Zahn 881

131
SO JEMAND SPRICHT

8.7.8.7.8.8

C.P.E.Bach, 1758

Zahn 2421

132

WIE SCHNELL VERFLIESSEN MEINE TAGE

9.9.8.9.9.8

Egli, 1787

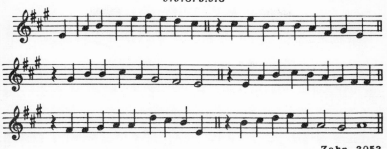

Zahn 3053

133

DER MOND IST AUFGEGANGEN

7.7.6.7.7.8

J.A.P. Schultz, 1790

Deutsches Choralbuch (c. 1936) 174

134

IHR KINDELEIN KOMMET

11.11.11.11 anapaestic

J.A.P. Schultz 1794

(D.C. 183)

255

135
WO FINDET DIE SEELE DIE HEIMAT, DIE RUH
11.11.11.11.8.11

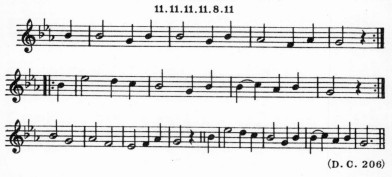

(D. C. 206)

136
SCHMAL IST DER PFAD
Knecht, 1799 (1793)

11.6.11.6

Zahn 870

137
STARK UNS, MITTLER
Knecht, 1799 (1793)

7.6.7.6.7.8.7.6.6.9.5.6.7.5

Zahn 8506

138
PREIS DEM TODESÜBERWINDER

Christmann, 1799 (1792)

8.7.8.7.7.8.7.7

Zahn 6671

139
LOBT FROH DEN HERRN

H.G.Nägeli, 1815

4.4.4.7.4

(D.C. 188)

140a

Two settings by Schicht of
WAS SOLL ICH, LIEBSTER KIND

6.7.6.7.6.6.6

Zahn 4264

140b

Zahn 4265

141

AUF, HINAUF

8.7.8.7.4.8.8.4   Tcherlitzky, 1825

Auf, hin auf zu deiner Freude   Meine Seele, Herz, und Sinn!

Weg, hin, weg mit deinem Leide Hin, zu deinem Je-su, hin.

Er   ist   dein   Schatz Jesus ist dein einzig Le-ben

Will die Welt kein Ort dir   ge-ben; bei   ihm ist Platz.

Zahn 7100

142

HARRE, MEINE SEELE

César Malan, 1827

6.4.6.5.4.5.6.5.5.4.6.4

Zahn 8427

143

MEIN HERZ UND SEEL

Kocher, 1838

11.11.10.10

Zahn 936

144

AUF AUF, WEIL DER TAG ERSCHIENEN

Filitz, 1847

8.8.7.7.8.8.8

Zahn 4921

145
MEINE HÖFFNUNG STEHT AUF GOTT

7.8.8.7.7

Layriz, 1853

Zahn 1878

146
GOTTLOB, NUN IST DIE NACHT VERSCHWUNDEN

9.9.8.9.9.8

Zahn, 1853

Zahn 3019

147
HIER IST GEDULD UND GLAUBE

7.6.7.6.D

Otto Dibelius, 1934

Music and text by the same hand

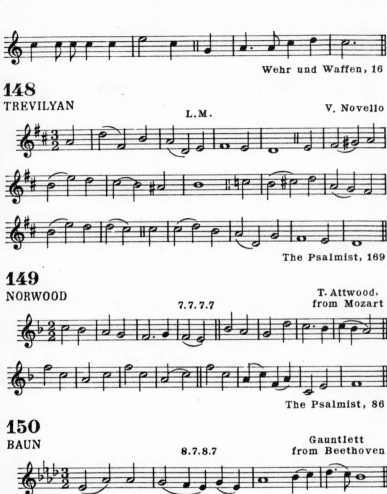

Wehr und Waffen, 16

148
TREVILYAN

V. Novello

L.M.

The Psalmist, 169

149
NORWOOD

T. Attwood,
from Mozart

7.7.7.7

The Psalmist, 86

150
BAUN

Gauntlett
from Beethoven

8.7.8.7

The Psalmist, 282

261

151
PORTLAND

7.7.7.7.7.7

T. Cooke

152
JUDGMENT

11.11.11.11 Anapaestic

Composer unnamed.
1846

Comprehensive Tune Book, 243

153

Harmony in J.B. DYKES

From STRENGTH AND STAY

A.M. 12/17

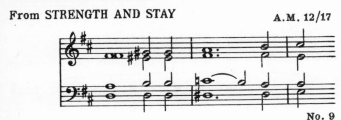

No. 9

153 contd.

From SUN OF MY SOUL

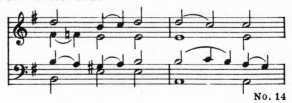

No. 14

From DERRY

A.M. 416/323

From SANCTUARY

A.M. 436/-

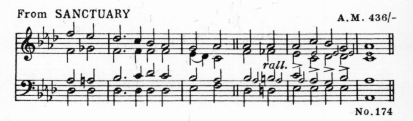

No. 174

Last phrase of THE BLESSED HOME

No. 162

Melody in DYKES (b)

(Liszt)

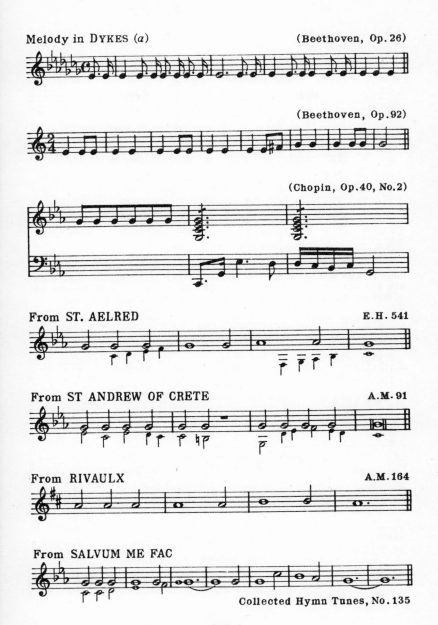

Melody in DYKES (a)   (Beethoven, Op. 26)

(Beethoven, Op. 92)

(Chopin, Op. 40, No. 2)

From ST. AELRED   E.H. 541

From ST ANDREW OF CRETE   A.M. 91

From RIVAULX   A.M. 164

From SALVUM ME FAC

Collected Hymn Tunes, No. 135

153 contd.

Beatitudo
A.M. 438/528

St. Agnes
A.M. 178/515

Dominus regit me
A.M. 197

(Liszt)

154

ORISONS: First version. The first two lines are identical in melody and harmony with the second version except (1) that they are arranged on three staves for unison singing, and (2) the rhythm of the second bar is 𝅘𝅥𝅭 𝅘𝅥𝅮𝅘𝅥𝅮 𝅗𝅥 𝅝 ‖ The tune continues thus:

E.Ps. 539

155

St. THOMAS

8.8.8.6

H. J. Gauntlett
1875

Congregational Psalmist (1886) 298 For "Just as I am".

156
ANGEL VOICES

A. Sullivan, 1872

8.5.8.5.8.4.3

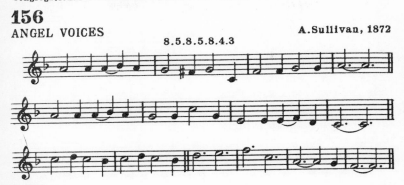

157
Style of SULLIVAN
From MOUNT ZION

Cong. Hy. 44

158
St. EDMUND

Cong. Hy. 462

Notes marked **✗** are supported by dominant seventh harmony.
Notes marked **✛** are supported by chords of the $\frac{6}{4}$ position.

158 contd.

From RESURREXIT

From BISHOPSGARTH

From St. GERTRUDE

From FALFIELD

From O GLADSOME LIGHT

From THE LOST CHORD

From THE MIKADO

159

Victorian infelicities (a) Melody

FATHERHOOD   D.C.M   J. B. Calkin, 1887

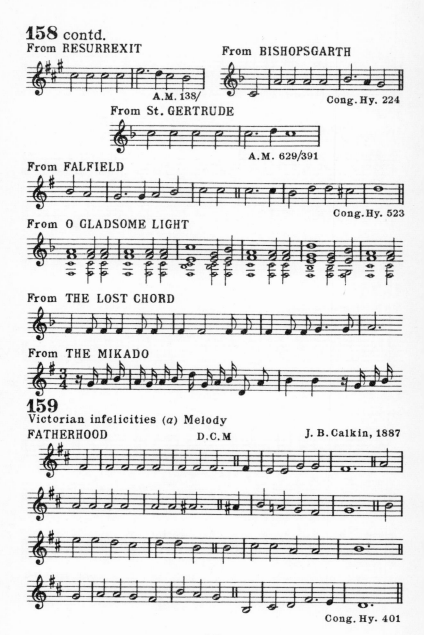

A.M. 138/

Cong. Hy. 224

A.M. 629/391

Cong. Hy. 523

Cong. Hy. 401

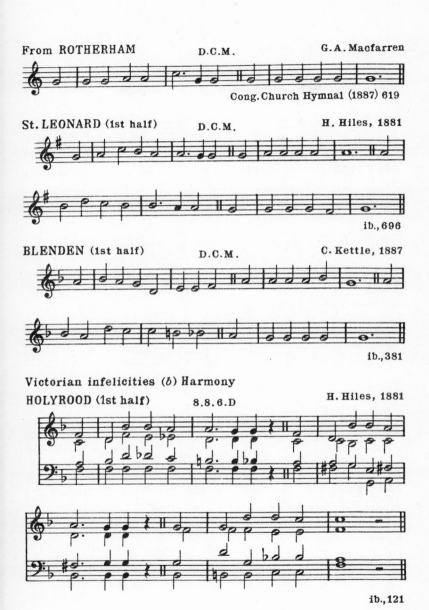

From ROTHERHAM   D.C.M.   G.A.Macfarren

Cong. Church Hymnal (1887) 619

St. LEONARD (1st half)   D.C.M.   H. Hiles, 1881

ib., 696

BLENDEN (1st half)   D.C.M.   C. Kettle, 1887

ib., 381

Victorian infelicities (b) Harmony

HOLYROOD (1st half)   8.8.6.D   H. Hiles, 1881

ib., 121

269

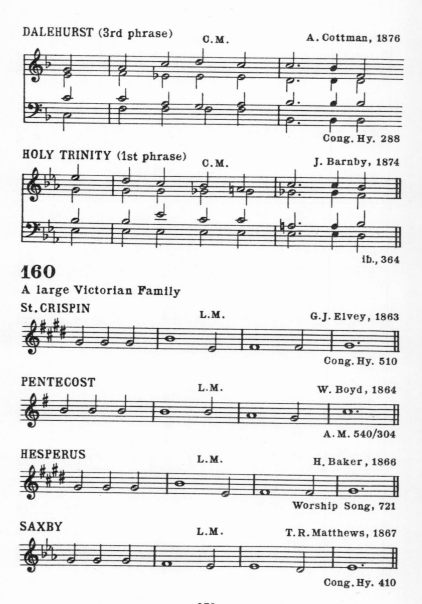

DALEHURST (3rd phrase)   C.M.   A. Cottman, 1876

Cong. Hy. 288

HOLY TRINITY (1st phrase)   C.M.   J. Barnby, 1874

ib., 364

160
A large Victorian Family

St. CRISPIN   L.M.   G. J. Elvey, 1863

Cong. Hy. 510

PENTECOST   L.M.   W. Boyd, 1864

A.M. 540/304

HESPERUS   L.M.   H. Baker, 1866

Worship Song, 721

SAXBY   L.M.   T. R. Matthews, 1867

Cong. Hy. 410

270

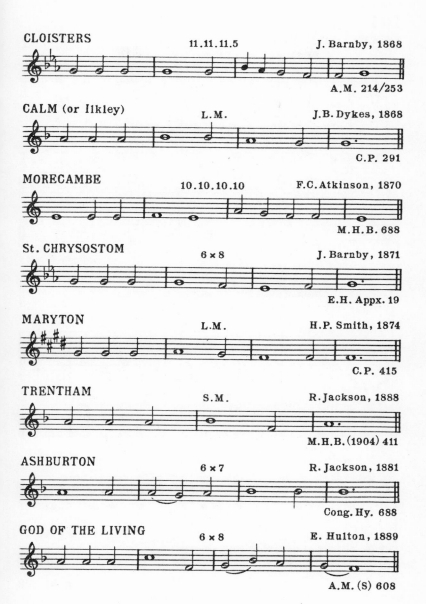

CLOISTERS   11.11.11.5   J. Barnby, 1868
A.M. 214/253

CALM (or Ilkley)   L.M.   J.B. Dykes, 1868
C.P. 291

MORECAMBE   10.10.10.10   F.C. Atkinson, 1870
M.H.B. 688

St. CHRYSOSTOM   6 × 8   J. Barnby, 1871
E.H. Appx. 19

MARYTON   L.M.   H.P. Smith, 1874
C.P. 415

TRENTHAM   S.M.   R. Jackson, 1888
M.H.B. (1904) 411

ASHBURTON   6 × 7   R. Jackson, 1881
Cong. Hy. 688

GOD OF THE LIVING   6 × 8   E. Hulton, 1889
A.M. (S) 608

161

RAGLETH HILL, Part II

C.M.

Basil Harwood, 1908

Come, Lord, when grace has made me meet

162

Style of WALFORD DAVIES (a) Melody

FIRMAMENT (Last half of tune)   1908

C.P. 30

GOD BE IN MY HEAD

C.P. 745

VISION

C.P. 170

RESURRECTION

Je-sus lives!   S.P. (1926) 280

QUINTA

Ch. Hy. (1927) 120

The   Lord   is   ris'n   in - deed!

CHRISTMAS CAROL

C.P. 718

WENGEN

A.M. 642/65

SEGENBALM

And that love may ne-ver cease,   I   will move Thee

Students' Hymnal, 83

162 contd.

ETHERINGTON

Students Hymnal, 64

Hark, the glad sound, the Sa - viour comes

SOLEMN MELODY

From the R.A.F. March

Style of WALFORD DAVIES (b) harmony
GOD BE IN BY HEAD

RESURRECTION

Al - le - lu - ia, Al - le - lu - ia.

HAMPSTEAD

May rich - er ful - ler be

A.M. 699

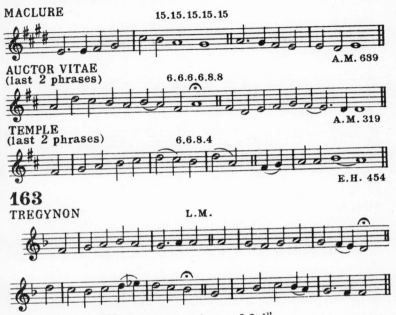

MACLURE 15.15.15.15.15

A.M. 689

AUCTOR VITAE
(last 2 phrases) 6.6.6.6.8.8

A.M. 319

TEMPLE
(last 2 phrases) 6.6.8.4

E.H. 454

163
TREGYNON L.M.

Students' Hymnal, **186** "To thine eternal arms, O God"

Note: 'Some of the tunes in this book, whose authorship is collectively marked "University of Wales," have been composed by a small community of minds. In two cases no less than five melodists took an essential part in a four line tune.' (Preface to *A Students' Hymnal*, p. xi).

The first line of TREGYNON appears as the first line of an imaginary or experimental hymn tune in Walford Davies and Harvey Grace, *Music and Worship* (1932), p. 17.

164
HARROW L.M. Eaton Faning

Cong. Hy. **223** "Lord of the brave" (J. H. Skrine)

165

SHAWFIELD

8.7.8.7.8.8

W. S. Bambridge
1842-1933

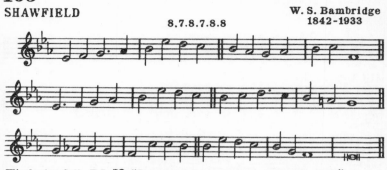

Winchester Coll. H.B. 72 "Though we long, in sin-wrought blindness."

166

WELLS

L.M.

Basil Johnson
1861-1950

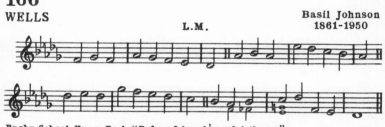

Rugby School Hymn Book "Before Jehovah's awful throne".

167

WOLVESEY

8.7.8.7.8.7

E.T. Sweeting
1863-1930

Winchester Coll. H.B. 167 "Judge eternal".

WINTON

G. Dyson, 1928

10.10.10.10

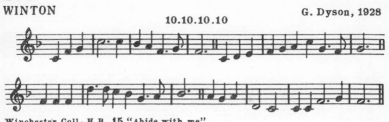

Winchester Coll. H.B. 15 "Abide with me"

169
HADLOW

John Wilson, 1936

Irregular

Clarendon H.B. 125 "God's saints are shining lights"

170
WER DA WONET

Vehe, 1537

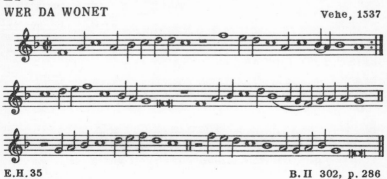

E.H. 35

B. II 302, p. 286

171
WIR DANCKEN DIR LIEBER HERRE

Leisentritt, 1567

Ky-ri-e e-lei-son.

B.I 205, p.460

172
GELOBT SEY GOTT DER VATER

7.6.7.6.7.7.7.6

München, 1586

Ky-ri-e-lei-son

B.I 302, p.600

173
CHRISTUS IST ERSTANDEN

Mainzer, 1605

Al - le - lu - ia Ge-lobt sei Gott und Ma-ri - a.

B.I 259, p.533

174
QUEM TERRA, PONTUS, AETHERA
8.8.8.8

Andernach, 1608

B. II 47b, p. 114

175
ES WALT GUT JÄGER JAGEN

Paderborn, 1616-7

E.H. 251

B.I 18, p. 260

176
LASST UNS ERFREUEN

Köln, 1623

B.I 280

177
JOSEPH, JOSEPH, JOSEPH
WIE HEIST DEIN KINDELEIN

Vogler, 1625

B.I 156, p. 408

178
BEYM CREUZ MIT LIEB UND LEYD VERWUND

Mainz,
1628

B.I 30, p.102

179
AVE JUNGFRAU

Köln, 1638

B.I 23, p. 266

180
O KIND, O LIEBES HERZELEIN

Prague, 1645

B.I 159, p.410

181
SINGT AUFF, LOBT GOTT

L.M.

Erfurt, 1666

(From Genevan Psalm 118)

B.I 28, p. 269

182
JESU DER ZUNGEN LIEBSTER THON

Nordstern, 1671

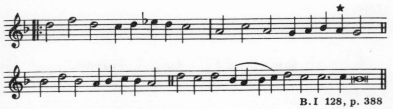

B.I 128, p. 388

*G in 1671 source, A in the Münster book of 1677

183
GROSSER GOTT

7.8.7.8.7.7

Katholisches Gesangbuch
Vienna, 1774-80

184
COR JESU

7.6.7.6.D

Traditional

W. H. (1912) 84

185
ADESTE FIDELES

R.L.de Pearsall
1795-1856

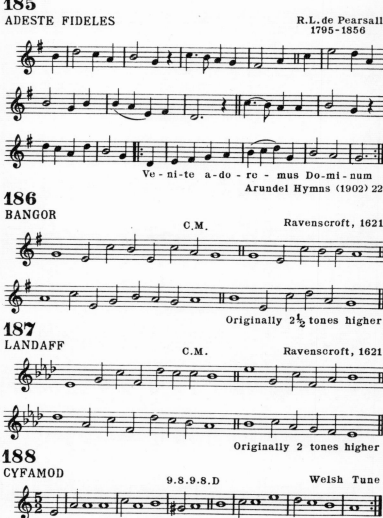

Ve - ni -te a-do - re - mus Do-mi -num

Arundel Hymns (1902) 22

186
BANGOR

C.M.

Ravenscroft, 1621

Originally 2½ tones higher

187
LANDAFF

C.M.

Ravenscroft, 1621

Originally 2 tones higher

188
CYFAMOD

9.8.9.8.D

Welsh Tune

E.T. 334

189
CAPEL CYNON

8.7.8.7 (tr.)

Hugh Jones
1749-1825

E.T. 405

190
ELLIOT

9.8.9.8.D Anapaestic

John Ellis
1760-1839

E.T. 186

191
GROESWEN

8.7.8.7.3.3.7

J. Ambrose Lloyd
1815-74

E.T. 164

283

192
GWYNFA

8.7.8.7 D

J.H. Roberts
1848-1924

E.T. 490

284

193
CAPEL TYGWYDD

6.5.6.5.6.6.6.5

David Jenkins
1848-1915

E.T. 205

194
CYMER

S.M.

Lewis Davies, b.1863

E.T. 302

195
BENWIL

9.8.9.8.D Anapaestic

Hugh Hughes
b. 1876

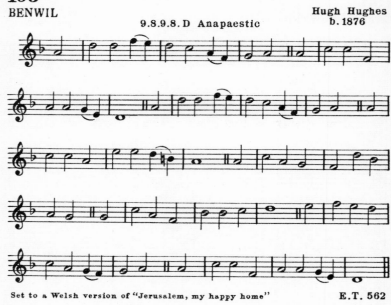

Set to a Welsh version of "Jerusalem, my happy home"   E.T. 562

196
GOSPER

6.5.6.5

Caradog Roberts
1879-1935

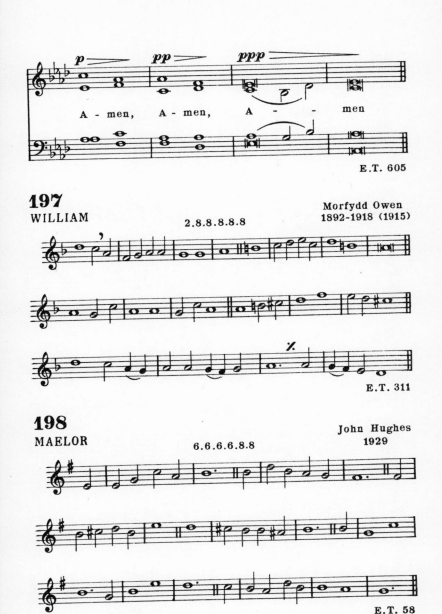

A - men,   A - men,   A -   men

E.T. 605

197
WILLIAM

2.8.8.8.8.8

Morfydd Owen
1892-1918 (1915)

E.T. 311

198
MAELOR

6.6.6.6.8.8

John Hughes
1929

E.T. 58

199

HULL ("The Indian Philosopher")

Northampton, Mass.
1798

8.8.6.D

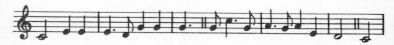

Compare C.P. 607

Cowan & Love, p. 74

200

TRUMPET

Lewis Edson, c.1782

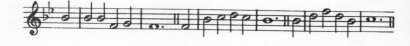

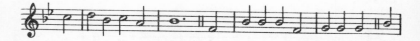

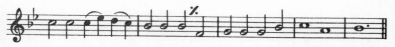

The Chorister's Companion

201

CORONATION
C.M. +
(Melody in Tenor except phrase 3)

Oliver Holden,
1793

Union Harmony, 1793

This tune is the normal one in the U.S.A. for "All hail the power of Jesus' name"; the version above is copied literally from the facsimile in the *Hymnal (1940) Companion*, p. 238. There the tune is set out on four staves. The first four alto notes in our third stave are almost certainly misprinted G for E. Nowadays it is arranged, of course, with the melody continuously in the treble.
See *The Hymnal* (U.S.A.) 355a

202
TOPLADY
7.7.7.7.7.7

Thomas Hastings,
1830
Fine

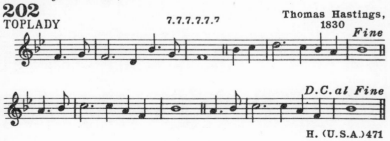

D.C. al Fine

H. (U.S.A.) 471

203
MOUNT ZION

Horatio Parker, 1886

D.C.M

204
St. DUNSTAN'S

6.5.6.5.6.6.6.5

Winfred Douglas,
1917

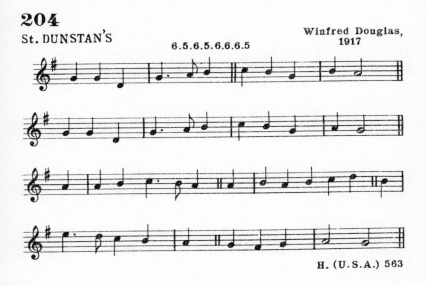

205
MALABAR

8.7.8.7 (Iambic).

D. McK. Williams,
1941

"Strengthen for service, Lord"

206

LYNCHBURG

C.M.

Henry Hallstrom,
1941

H. (U.S.A.) 526

207

TEILO SANT

8.6.8.8.6

J.P.B.Dobbs,
c. 1944

"Eternal Light! Eternal Light!" A simplified version of this tune appears at C.P.21.

208
WATFORD

6.6.6.6.6.6

A.T. Gosden

"Jesus, the first and last."

Unpublished

INDEX TO NUMBERS IN THE ENGLISH HYMNAL

This index is provided for the convenience of those who wish to use this book as a reference-book for the *English Hymnal*, to which at present no ' Companion ' exists. Where a tune is not mentioned in this list, it may be gathered that it is (a) plainsong or folk-song, with which this book does not profess to deal, or (b) within a category dealt with in the book, to which general reference can be made by looking up its composer's name in the index, or by consulting the Table of Contents for the period within which it falls.

All names of hymn tunes are printed in SMALL CAPITALS. Where the name of a tune appears in brackets, the tune is mentioned at the reference, but by number only and not by name: to assist the reader in identifying the reference, the hymn-book number of the tune (English Hymnal, unless otherwise stated) appears with its name in this index in these cases.

No first lines of hymns are indexed here. Titles of hymn books are indexed only where there is a primary reference to the books in the text. ' Ex. 55 ' means ' example number 55 ', not ' page 55 '.